THE
LIFE AND LETTERS
OF
EDWARD EVERETT HALE

VOLUME TWO

THE
LIFE AND LETTERS
OF
EDWARD EVERETT HALE

BY
EDWARD E. HALE, Jr.

VOLUME TWO

With Illustrations

BOSTON
LITTLE, BROWN, AND COMPANY
1917

813
H161X
vol.2

TYPOGRAPHY BY THE PLIMPTON PRESS, NORWOOD, MASS., U.S.A.
PRINTED BY S. J. PARKHILL & CO., BOSTON, MASS., U.S.A.

CONTENTS

VOLUME TWO

ILLUSTRATIONS

VOLUME TWO

THE LIFE AND LETTERS OF
EDWARD EVERETT HALE

VOLUME TWO

∴

CHAPTER EIGHTEEN

THE NEW CIVILIZATION

1865–1870

MY father, at the close of the War, was forty-three years old, and had advanced well along most of the lines of work which he followed in his later life. He was a leading clergyman, well known as an interesting preacher as well as a sympathetic adviser in the spiritual life; a leader and organizer in and out of his especial denomination, full of ideas for the public service; a man of letters who had gained the public ear, and who was able to use his ability to interest people for the furtherance of great ideas as well as for the entertainment of the moment. In these directions especially did his work develop during the remainder of his life, and in these capacities did he become best known to his fellow-citizens as a public man.

During the War my father had been led more and more into public activities, not only outside his own parish but outside Boston or Massachusetts. I do not know when the idea that he famil-

iarly thought of in later years as "the larger life"
first came to be an effective factor in his thinking
and acting, but he certainly now enjoyed this
branching out beyond the confines and limits of
the average ministerial round of duty. He had
left Worcester, for one reason, because a Boston
parish offered him more of an opportunity for the
kind of work he thought he could do. Now, after
ten years or so at work in the larger opportunity,
he found himself continually called and tempted
into efforts which before he had hardly thought of.[1]

He did not, however, for these other activities,
neglect the especial work to which he had been
called. He had his morning and afternoon Sunday service, and although he sometimes spoke
lightly of his work as a sermon-writer, and on some
occasions read old sermons or spoke extempore,
yet the regular record in his daybooks for these
years shows that he was continually adding to that
stock of sermons which was becoming the admiration of his colleagues. He had also a good deal
of parish work: he was very conscientious about
marriages, christenings, and funerals, and could
always be recalled from anything that did not
make it absolutely impossible by a death in the
parish. He could not make many parish calls:
he often spoke of his regret at not seeing more of
his parishioners, but his daybooks record as a rule
between one and two hundred parish calls a year.
There is mention among his engagements of parish

[1] The Emigrant Aid Society is the only one of his Worcester activities
that I recall which can be said to have had anything of a national scope.

parties and other such occasions, in which he could meet his people. He had a study at the church and was there almost every day, and generally some afternoon or evening in the week had a class of young women or young men to read and study matters of religion, history, or literature through the winter. Besides these distinctly parochial occupations, he had others by virtue of his position as minister and member of the Unitarian denomination. He had his connection with the Christian Unity, almost as important to his mind as the church itself, with the Benevolent Fraternity of Churches, with the American Unitarian Association, with the Christian Register Association, each of which called for a good deal of energy and interest if not of the day-to-day sort needed by the parish itself.

Besides these connections, he had others which called for less exertion, like the Board of Overseers of Harvard College to which he was elected about this time, the Boston Library of which he was a Trustee as he was shortly afterward of the Fellowes Athenæum in Roxbury, the Massachusetts Historical Society in which he was a member of the Library Committee, the American Antiquarian Society in which he was still a member of the Council, the lately formed Examiner Club with which he dined and talked monthly, and other less formal organizations. He also found time for preaching at the theaters or out of town, for lectures either in Boston or in towns round about, for studying German with the German Club, not to mention such matters as "bowling with the children", "billiards at Mrs. Hemenway's," or getting flowers at Brookline.

These things, with his literature, for he published a number of stories and articles during these years, not to speak of the books in which he collected them, would seem to have provided interest and occupation enough for anyone.   In his case, however, it is clear that they formed the background at the moment for other interests and occupations which he deemed of greater, or at least of more especial, importance.   As he had said in writing to his brother Charles, the War had forced upon him a series of interests which he had felt that he could not decline, — the Sanitary Commission, the Freedman's Aid, the Soldier's Memorial, the Emigrant Aid, all of which called on his attention and energy.   With the close of the war these activities continued, with something of a change in immediate object.   The idea of Reconstruction was in everybody's mind, chiefly in its political bearing.   But he himself thought the reconstruction of the country to be really "much more in the hands of these agencies, if they be bravely and broadly administered, than it is in the hands of the Government itself."   In fact, the idea of Reconstruction took a larger form in his mind than the political or even the social reconstruction of the South only; it embraced a general advance, along the whole line, of the American people.   He did not himself so commonly think of it as reconstruction or call it so.   He called his vision of America by no less name than the New Civilization. I do not know just how this phrase arose. My father may have invented it, or it may have been current at the time. He had used it in an article in the *Atlantic*, June, 1864, on "How to use Victory." Before the end of the War, he was writing to Charles, then Consul General of the United States in Egypt: —

TO CHARLES

"MEDFORD, MASS: *Jan* 31, 1865. I have been to New York, — on what I call familiarly the work of the New Civilization. We have got very well convinced that with the end of the war the time will come for us not only to colonize the South, but to convert the Southern cities by an infusion of all Christian life and charity in a way they have known nothing of. In place of the Sanitary for the body, we shall have to see that body, mind, and spirit are properly cared for, and this must be done, if it is done at all, by distinct and avowed religious influence. Not, of course, by preaching of sermons, or by arguing much with religionists. I hope that is not the idea of your missionary friends in Egypt. But by a distinct religious supervision of all that needs to be done, — whether in the way of free schools, of hospitals, of books, or of any of the other organisms of social order, as well as in the way of pulpits and churches.

"This conviction gives rise, 1st, to a new missionary zeal, and 2nd, to the organization of the Liberal Church of America, which has always been satisfied heretofore to work without organization, in the separate and atomic conditions of a pure independency or congregationalism. In the first matter we held an especial missionary convention in December, of which I wrote you, and voted to raise 100,000 dollars for the year's service of the Unitarian Association in place of less than 10,000 its income last year. This thing we are steadily doing. We marked out the country and divided it, Boston for 30,000, New York and Brooklyn for 20,000, and so on: — and our returns begin to be highly gratifying. But at the same time we press the necessity for such organization of our churches that there may be some central body competent at least to advise the rest, and to lay out between East, West, South, Pacific coast, and the respective colleges, such missionary or other work as we may have in hand.

"You, who have heard all your life of Autumnal Conventions, may not know that the Unitarian Churches of America never met in convention. A pure independency or congregationalism has always governed them or parted them. There has never, I mean, been any choice of delegates with any power, even verbal, to represent them in any central or national body. Our meeting of New York was a committee meeting preliminary to a bona fide National Convention of our churches. We shall make a great effort to get a commanding and intelligent lay representation here, and we shall lay out and try to carry through essential work, and to the churches represented, and to our different associations we shall make recommenda-

tions as the old Continental Congress did, hoping
to give them much of the force of laws. We shall
get rid, we hope, of discussing the origin of evil
and other philosophical subjects, which have been
the bane and ruin of our conventions. We think
we shall assert a national position and establish
an amount of work in the new states and the Southern states respectable enough to show that we
really are the marrow of the New Civilization.
We expect also to re-establish Antioch College,
under our own men, and to lure into the ministry
by this means and by the attraction of its greater
activities, men enough to run our enlarged machinery.

"Everything at New York was thoroughly encouraging. The laymen, men of the first mark
too, were more in heart than the ministers, and
the mere presence of ten men, all there were on
the committee, from Chicago, Boston, Philadel-
phia, Brooklyn and New York was in itself thoroughly inspiriting.

"You have guessed that in this movement I
am the New England captain. Bellows is the prime
mover and it is a great thing to have the prestige
and practical skill which he brings from the Sanitary[1] enlisted in it. I stayed at his house while
I was at New York and was more than ever amazed,
not by his brilliancy but his working power.

"Adieu

"Le suite en prochain numero. All well.

"EDWARD."

[1] Doctor Henry W. Bellows was President of the Sanitary Commission
during the War.

We get here the spirit which dominated his larger
work and plans of work for many years. Here
was a great chance, not only for the South, but for
East and West as well. The Unitarian denomination was the right wing, or advance, of liberal
thought; if what it thought of itself was well-
founded and true, it ought, if not to be the acknowl-
edged leader of the country, at least to be ready to
point the way and show where progress tended.

In my father's mind the particular steps which
were of importance were:

1. The closer organization of the Unitarian denomination, which was begun by a Convention in
New York in the spring of 1865.

2. The organization of educational opportunities, including especially Antioch College, Humboldt College, and the Meadville Theological School
for the extension of liberal theology and the education of men who would push the work of the liberal
church.

3. The better organization for charitable and
other such purposes of Boston itself, as was shortly
carried out by the Suffolk Conference of which he
was for many years the President.

4. The establishment of some journal or organ
for liberal thought, an idea carried into effect a
few years later by *Old and New*.

The letters of this period give a good idea of his
activities in these directions. They do not give
much notion of the detail of any one piece of work,
but they show clearly the spirit with which he went
into everything.

Nowhere does his particular power show better than in his work of these years. He was not, as he often said, a great organizer. He was far too much of an individualist by nature to be able to conceive a great plan and also to imagine all the details of its right working, and see that they were properly carried out. I doubt very much whether he would have defined his idea of coöperative work as "a uniform systematic constructive utilization" of the Christian power of the country. He would have liked to make use of that power, and, if it were made use of, it would certainly be in a constructive way. But that the thing should be uniform, even that it should be systematic, was not in his mind. Such ideas as Efficiency, Standardization, so common to-day, he hardly thought of; his notion of common work and common progress was based on something else. Even in organization as he thought of it, he does not seem to have believed himself a great captain. But he was a constant force in getting things done. Some years after this time I remember his describing the adjutant of a battalion as the man whose business it was "to get the men forward anyway" as he used to put it. His optimistic temper led him to believe that plans were possible, if every one would work with a will. As a rule in cases where he had not much knowledge of the actual circumstances, he felt sure that things would come out right. If they could not be done in one way, they could be done in another, — provided there was always someone on hand determined to see that they were done. He was always ready to be the someone on hand. So in a great work like this, having made up his mind definitely as to the importance of the thing to be done, he plunged actively into affairs to see that they went through right.

In his "Life of James Freeman Clarke" he summarizes the feelings and objects of those years. He is speaking of the "bringing about in the Unitarian Church a higher sense of its responsibilities in the matter of missionary work. Under the lead of Dr. Bellows at a special meeting of the Unitarian Association in December, 1864, in Hollis Street Church in Boston, measures were taken which led to the establishment in April, 1865, of a National Conference of Unitarian and other Christian Churches. From that time this National Conference has been the representative body of the Unitarian Church of America.

"In the preliminary arrangements for this conference, and in the formation of its constitution, Mr. Clarke was a central actor. When, on the 4th of April, 1865, the delegates to a national Unitarian convention met in the city of New York, he gave the first address ever delivered to the united body."

An extract from Doctor Clarke's sermon is reprinted in the "Life." It states that the reason for union at the moment is the desire to unite for work. The following passage is of interest:

"The church is the body of Christ. It is an organization through which the spirit of Christ can

work. If, hitherto, it has preached him in the
pulpit, rather than gone about with him to seek
and save the lost; if it has taught doctrines about
him, rather than carried him to a world lying in
wickedness; if it has rather called on men to "come
to Jesus" than taken Jesus to find and help them
where they are, the time has come, we think, for
a great change. We wish to take part in the great
and opening civilization of the new day and hour.
We wish to do something for such a Christianity
as the world has never yet seen, a Christianity
which shall fill all life with the sense of God's
presence; which shall cast both Death and Hell
into a lake of fire; which shall give us a new
heaven and a new earth, wherein dwelleth righteous-
ness."

Particular details seem unnecessary or even impossible here. The Unitarian Church had its plans
as has been noted. The Soldiers' Memorial Society,
which was a sort of successor to the Sanitary Commission, set about industrial education in the South,
chiefly, I believe, among the whites. My father
was much interested in the schools of Richmond,
Virginia and Wilmington, North Carolina. From
the first (in 1868) he was not merely interested,
but entirely identified with the negro schools at
Hampton, under the direction of General Armstrong,
and later under Mr. Frissell. For a long time Hampton was one of the interests really nearest his heart,
and he went there whenever he could. It was
doing with great success exactly what he was sure
ought to be done. The Emigrant Aid Society

was revived with a view of sending people to Florida; he once urged Charles to come back from Egypt that he might go to Florida and become Senator from that State.

TO CHARLES

"*March* 14, 1865. I am in great spirits about our own work of the New Civilization. Our New York Convention of Unitarian churches will be really an imposing body. I think it will be an energetic and harmonious one, — resolved to put the Liberal Church of America before the country as the motive power of the re-establishment of social order in the states newly freed. Bellows and I are the two people who hold the working oar here. It brings an immense amount of correspondence and conversation, and what you know I like least of all, attendance on boards for both of us. I do not like to leave busy important meetings of our clergy to the tender mercies of some blundering brother or of the apathy of some of our sadduceeish or skeptical ministers. You see we are handicapped by men like —— and —— , who in their fears of the ghost of Theo. Parker choose to say that our day is over, that the sooner we die the better. But the universal determination of the laymen of the body carries the ministers along. In eighteen churches, many of them small ones, we have raised 46,000 dollars of our new missionary fund. Bellows led off in Boston and I here.

"Of which you will hear enough more,
                    "Ever yours, EDWARD."

TO MRS. HALE

"NEW YORK, *April* 5, 1865. I have nothing but
Clarke's sermon [1] to write about, nothing but that
and dinner having happened since I wrote. It was
really a magnificent success. That beautiful church
was jammed full of people standing in every corner
where there were no seats. The music was solemn
and admirably expressive. Bellows opened the service, William Channing offered prayer, and then
came Clarke. The mere trio, considering all things
in a few years' history is striking. I forget if I
told you of the text: 'Then Paul and Barnabas
waxed bold and said, Since then ye consider your-
selves unworthy of eternal life we turn from you and
go to the Gentiles.' The sermon was on the change
of base they then made, abandoning the existing
church because it had made secondary things more
important than the essential thing, and of course
had made the essential thing secondary.

"But what is the essential thing? Then he worked
up the story of Martha and Mary, and said that
the church was mighty apt to be eager about many
things, one only being needful, which is to sit at
the feet of Jesus, — discipleship, — not having attained. Starting on these two points he went on to
show the necessity of carrying the knowledge of
Christ to those who had him not, rather than crying 'Come to Jesus'; urging all along how much of
good there is outside the old church which it is our
business to get hold of.

[1] See *ante* p. 10.

"Then he addressed the difficulties which people made about the convention, perfectly familiarly — as his way is — reserving his invective for indifferent people whom he characterized very fairly.

"The sermon ended with a parallel between the achievement of the Country which has secured Union and Freedom, and the duty of the church which is to secure Union and Freedom, a point you see perfectly well taken, — and, just now, capable of great effect, which he certainly used it for. When he described the entry of black troops into Richmond no rustle satisfied the congregation, but they fairly clapped as in Chrysostom's days."

TO MRS. HALE

"New York, *April* 7, 1865. I leave here for your mother's at 2:30 today and shall be at home, God willing, to dinner tomorrow. I hope I shall find you as well as I left you, and the children better.

"When one of the Massachusetts delegates returned from the convention which made the constitution of the United States, being asked to give some explanation of that instrument, he said it was made much as Mr. Adams wanted it. I should find it impossible to state our views of yesterday so briefly as to say, that by overwhelming majorities and unmistakable 'sense of the meeting' the Christian National Conference organized itself 'much as I wanted it.' I take no credit to myself for this result, nor disown any. For after assenting as you know, in countless schemes, where I had and had

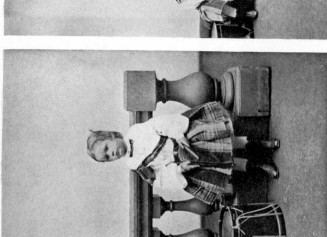

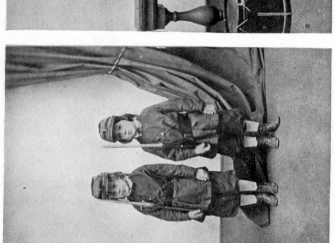

ARTHUR AND CHARLIE   EDWARD   DR. HALE AND THE THREE BOYS

Dr. Hale and his three elder sons. *From photographs taken about the time of the Civil War*

not suggested and yielded, pared and pruned, I saw this brought in by a committee half of whom did not know the others' faces, carefully read and discussed, not dissented to in substance by anybody, and voted against only by the merest fraction of the extreme left wing.

"As to fundamentals, I have always held that the Unitarian Body, when it came into the world, crystallized from the mists and fogs and aspirations and ether of the Unitarian Spirit, would have to articulate first, last, and always that it was at work 'in the name of our Lord Jesus Christ.' If it was not, it had no place among Christian bodies and if it had not that, why it would live so little while that there was no need of having it born at all. Per contra I have always said that to attempt any refinement on this in the way of definition or historical statement, was more than Paul did, who had vastly better chances for success than we, more than Christ did, who had vastly better right than we, more than the church ever succeeded in, and also would be of no sort of use in the line of Christian work which is given us to do. It would reduce us to one of the Orthodox sects, picking for our field of influence among the handful of people who are satisfied with intellectual statements, and competent to them.

"But though I have found many people to assent to my proposal that this formula of Paul's was in word and spirit, all and enough, I have found nobody willing to say so. And although I meant myself to move it in convention, if the convention came to a deadlock, as being in itself the *deus ex superis* who should solve the entanglement, I did not at the last have any hope that, before such entanglement, anything so simple would be proposed by anyone.

"You may imagine my pleasure, therefore, when a committee of twelve appointed by no packing whatever, brought in as a preamble to a constitution this identical panacea. It went over every whisper of opposition by the most majestic momentum of the assembly.

"Here I must stop. Likely I shall see you before you see this."

The following letter shows something of the fortunes of Antioch College. It had been hoped through the summer that Governor Andrew would accept the Presidency, but after a good deal of consideration he had declined the position.

TO JOHN A. ANDREW

"*Oct.* 10, 1865. I am sorry to have to acknowledge the receipt of your letter of Saturday.

"I suppose I must regard it as final, and as I have, through these three months, tried to refrain from annoying you with solicitation or argument, I do not now attempt to remove the consideration to which you allude.

"It only remains for me, as a matter personal between ourselves, to show you that I have met what I supposed was my duty, in providing for your wishes.

"The arrangements have been definitely made

which contemplated and prepared for the settlement on your wife and children of such a sum as should relieve you from anxiety for them; the intention of the gentlemen interested was to ask your acceptance of this testimony of the gratitude of Massachusetts for your distinguished services at this close of your official term. Some of them had an impression, which I did not share, that there was an impropriety in the proposal while you were yet in office.

"In the endowment of the college we were greatly encouraged. I said in a speech in Providence on the subject on Sunday night, that I supposed we should have to ask for only fifty thousand dollars in addition to gifts already determined upon. We expected five professorships, from five distinct sources known to us, and had to solicit in smaller sums only the closing fifty thousand.

"I must ask you now that the matter comes untimely to its end, to make in such form as may be most agreeable to you, some statement which shall show the public that you have seriously entertained our invitation. The journals which claim to be the keepers of your conscience and honor are fond of accusing me and my colleagues of playing the part of sharpers all through the transaction. To myself this is a matter of great indifference. I would certainly trust my reputation against Mr. Slack's in any collision. But I find some of my colleagues are more sensitive, and on their account I make a request which I am hoping you will be glad to comply with.

"Wishing you all success, in whatever line of duty may open before you,
            "I have the honor to be
                "For the Committee of the Trustees,
                        "EDWARD E. HALE."

TO CHARLES

"*July* 22, 1866. But it answers your second question as to my coming out at once to you. If I can go to Egypt at all, and there are a thousand chances to one against it, it can only be after October 9th. I am very largely responsible for and to our second national Unitarian Convention which will be held on that date at Syracuse. There are not five men in the country who regard this as having any such importance as to make any man change his plans for it; far less renounce a voyage to Europe. But I am one of the five. If the various wings of our body, and our various localities can be made once more to pull in harness together, we can come out of that convention an important National body, destined to a very large influence as a Church and as individuals in the reconstruction and new civilization of this country. Schools at the South, emigration, order out of chaos generally, require that some such assertion of place and dignity shall be made by people with whom religion is a reality, and neither a creed nor a ritual merely. Once through that test I shall resign my trust as secretary of this conference. I am resigning many similar trusts, not with a view to Europe especially, but to freedom and rest. After the 9th of October, then, I may think of this but not before."

TO SAMUEL G. MAY

"*Sept.* 13, 1866. I have yours of the 9th, and have had full conference with Lowe and letters from Dr. Bellows on yours of the 30th.

"1. Let it be settled that the service of Tuesday evening shall be at your church. You say 7:30. The call says 8 P.M., I do not know why. The two will amount to the same thing.

"2. To the Committee on the spot we leave the arrangement for Conference and prayer meetings, highly approving of the plan of having them. I should think they might be held from 8:30 to 9:30 every morning. To the same committee we leave the plans for the Lord's Supper. I would only suggest that this service is better near the close than near the beginning, unless indeed it were possible, as we have in election week here, at the very beginning.

"But so far as the Council and sub-committee are concerned this is purely a business meeting, to devise and carry out plans of general influence through the country. I think we cannot do enough in the two journals to make people understand that the Convention comes together, not for the edification of its own members, so much as for the improvement of the aggressive effort of the churches on the whole land.

"3. Retaining Wednesday evening, as you proposed, for a general missionary meeting, at which there shall be speaking by the best men we can assign, we accede wholly to your plan of a similar

meeting Thursday. This may be an adjournment of
the other, or it may take some other general topic.
I know nothing better than one you suggest —
"What is Religion?" What do we want "to propa-
gate"? I shall invite all the gentlemen you name
to be prepared to speak at one or other of these
evening meetings.

"4. I will thank you to engage at the hotel which
is most suitable for head-quarters, the rooms with
a private parlor for the gentlemen of the Council.
We will early announce that this has been done (in
conversation I mean) and that hotel will naturally
be that which delegates first resort to. I have a
good deal of faith in the working power and elec-
tricity induced by the meeting of men in the parlors
and halls of a hotel on such an occasion. As for
the question you suggest how your invitations can
be best given, I can only propose that you should
see that the committee ask all the clergy at least
from the country parishes at once. I think a note
sent to each one of these gentlemen would be a
great help in filling the convention. One hundred
and fifty invitations would cover the whole number
outside of Boston, Roxbury, Cambridge, New York,
etc., etc. I post you by today's mail ten copies of
the Convention's register which may be convenient
for this purpose, and if you will send me word to
that effect, I will give notice that it is hoped that
all the clergy will be entertained at private houses.
At New York the register says there were one hundred and ninety clergymen present. But I doubt
if there were so many in the person.

"5. Governor Andrew will, as we suppose, call the Conference to order, as its president and sit as such through the first day, perhaps till the new officers are chosen. I will see that he is especially invited to speak.

"I do not at this moment think of any other details, but we shall have frequent occasion to discuss them as the time goes on. I look forward with great pleasure to a Sunday in Syracuse. I wish I might make a chance to visit some friends in Aurora, but I do not see how that is to come about.

"Do you remember —— to whom, a bright boy you used to lend books when you were in Scituate, and he at Dr. Otis's? He is doing a clerk's work for me now, being quite adrift in the world. I wish anybody in Syracuse wanted him as a book keeper, for there are reasons why he had better leave Boston. Believe me, my dear friend,

"Always yrs,
"E. E. HALE."

TO WILLIAM B. WEEDEN

"*Sept.* 18, 1866. I must write to you by this boat, I fear (or better hope) if I am to write to you again before you take to the water. And therefore I must write on this wasteful and disgraceful paper. I have been here making a speech in behalf of the schools for poor white trash in Richmond and the other Southern cities. It seems as if the Lord had opened a way for us to upset the F. F. V. and so I hope all the gentry of the South, by the elevation of the mud-sills. We have got five hundred Oregon smashers and Sydney bull dogs of the Richmond canaille at our free schools, and the present enterprise is undertaken in the hope of making the five hundred five thousand. As we get the children, we convert the parents, establish a democratic self-sufficiency among the rabble and, when the Southern heart is next fired and the mob of Richmond is called upon, we mean that it shall not be our windows that are broken.

"You will say that Hale is quitting his metier in speaking in such a matter, and that I had better stick to my mutton. No, the New Civilization is my metier, get it in where I can. I wish I could hold my beloved A. U. A. up to this work of disentangling the Southern web, but they are still ecclesiastical and believe in tracts and black morocco sermon-cases. Tant pis. But for a' that we will make them do all we can, and make Antioch do its much more, get in our free schools in Richmond, Wilmington, and Charleston, and be ready for a new Antioch in Florida and Georgia."

TO WILLIAM B. WEEDEN

"*Dec.* 20, 1866. I spoke my piece at Worcester and we had a bit of a skirmish after it. A man named Richardson got up and said he was for crushing the South and trampling it out, and the sooner we give up civil talk, or for that matter Christian, the better. Governor Devens and I then pitched into him, and this gave a lovely little breeze to our meeting. The truth being, as Bellows very well said to me, that the North does not care very vitally

about the South just now. It has found that with
the West it can run the machine very well, and
thinks little and cares less what becomes of the
Southern states. I do not think I should find it
very hard to drop into the same delusion, though
on the whole it is a delusion, and to say that our
business was to train the seven or eight northern
states. Keep their people, and make them masters,
as Attica over Boeotia or England over Ireland. Old
Ezra Stiles in 1755 wrote a wonderful tract, in which
he proved that in 1855 the population of New England would be 5 or 6,000,000 people all land owners,
all educated, and all Congregational Christians, that
this homogeneous population would be a greater
power than the England of his own day was, etc.,
etc., etc.

"Only two things missed his prescience.

"1. That the people of New England would go
to better soils and milder climates.

"2. That the people of better soils, milder climate, and *worse government* would come to New
England, and upset his homogeneity of race."

TO SAMUEL G. MAY

"*Dec.* 26, 1866. I had a thousand things of which
to write to you after that charming visit after the
Convention. But I came home to arrears of writing, then to my mother's painful illness, ending with
her death. At the same time one of my own children was critically ill. I have not yet got back to
the place I was in in life when I went to Syracuse.
You know that I never shall. When a man's father

and mother are dead, he is no longer of the rising generation. He is a hundred years older.

"We watched with great interest the launch of your Local Conference. I am more than satisfied with the starting of ours here. For the want of just such an institution, we have I think, lost three or four Unitarian churches here in the last ten years. We have lost more than their worth, in the want of mutual acquaintance, mutual confidence. Men did not know who were Unitarians. At our first meetings there was constant surprise to see that such a one or such a one was there.

"Then there are fifty philanthropic necessities in a town like this which no organization but the church can attend to.

"I had a pleasant glimpse of President White when he was here. I hope we may see him soon again."

TO CHARLES

"*May* 7, 1867. I sent to Jacksonville last week the man who is to publish an Emigrant Aid loyal paper there. Marshall our agent is getting up the first colony under a special charge. If you can spare a hundred dollars, I wish you would put it into Emig. Aid preferred stock. Because as I have intimated, I think there is a chance for doing there what Edward Livingstone did in Louisiana if any day you want to. There is no individual liability, and you will probably get your money back anyway. Forbes and Brimmer are the two men most interested, I advising and bringing in the old traditions of the Company."

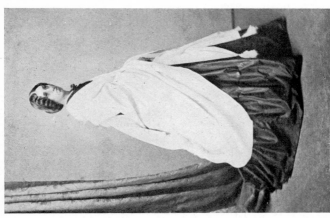

CHARLES HALE   LUCRETIA P. HALE   NATHAN HALE, JR.

From photographs taken about the time of the Civil War

TO CHARLES

"*June* 16, 1868.   I give up my annual expedition
to Antioch which would naturally take place next
week. We are well pleased with our year's success
there. The spirit and character of the men em-
ployed and the women, have been such as to lift
the school wholly above the level of a mere secta-
rian academy, and we are now quite independent of
the intrigues of the Christian sect or any others. We
have in the last year increased our endowment near
$10,000, we have increased the income from scholars,
the real test of success, $1700; and with this real
prosperity have been able to collect, almost without
solicitation, about five thousand dollars for the running expenses of the institution.   I call it *school* because I think that is beginning to be the respectable
name.   In truth, the age of the scholars averages
more than that of those at Cambridge. The professors are young and have their reputations to
make, eager to see the institution succeed so that
they do twice as much work as the men at Cambridge seem to me to do. Off there by themselves,
there is indeed no temptation to them to do
otherwise.

"I am equally well pleased with the year's results
of my other two a-vocations, Richmond and Florida.
Of Florida I spoke in my last. Last Tuesday we
had the annual meeting of the S. M. S. as we call
the Soldiers' Memorial Society which runs the Richmond schools. The result of the year, fairly stated,
is that we have forced into the new Virginia con-

stitution ample provision for free schools for both races. More than this, we have now made to us a proposition from the Common Council of Richmond, to carry on our schools as city affairs, if we will extend for the present some assistance. Exactly the same proposal was made to us in Wilmington by a board of local trustees. All this is an evidence that the thing can be worked out on the real democratic basis. It is true that the Common Council is one made by Gov. Schofield, then the head of the Bureau. But we believe that we have such a hold on the unwashed whites, unwashed until we washed them, that so soon as the people of Richmond choose their own Councils there will be chosen one acting in the same spirit as this board acts in. If three years ago when the war ended, we could at the North have done what we were entreated to do by all men of loyalty and intelligence in the Southern cities, established some six or eight really well-endowed and supported newspapers at the effective centres, the real work of reconstruction would now be very largely advanced. But that was the thing that people could not be hauled up to do. Newspapers cost a great deal of money, and no one sees their influence at any fixed time.

"I told you in my last how well pleased I was with the results in Florida. These three — Antioch, Richmond and Florida, have been my pet outside enterprises of the year."

CHAPTER NINETEEN

CHURCH WORK IN BOSTON

1865–1870

THESE larger interests occupied much of my father's time, but not to the exclusion of interests nearer home. Indeed, though he always liked to help somebody off at the very ends of the earth, he was also most careful about not neglecting the people of his own town. In the few years after the War he had thought out more carefully and had settled much more definitely in his own mind the theoretical position at the bottom of his practical activity. He believed that the especial duty of the Christian ministry in any town was not merely to proclaim the Gospel, but to help and urge people to take that way of life. Faith was fundamental but to be faith it needed works. Every church must be a radiating center of Christian charity, which was no more and no less than Christian love in an efficacious form. But though the church was a radiating center it was not to content itself with giving its warmth and light to those only who came within its doors. It must go out and find the people who needed it, must find people in their homes. For the home was the center of life. Considering tenement life in Boston he said, "Where a considerable part of the people live in such homes our best devised charities, either for moral culture or physical relief, work at terrible odds. Your City Missions, your Ministry at Large, your Industrial Aid Society, or your Overseers of the Poor are all working against a steady dead weight which, as we all know, presses down and holds down the man who is in an unhealthy or unhappy home."

In other words my father was one of the pioneers in the modern movement for social work. He perceived the immense importance of regenerating the life of the poor in our cities. His relation to other pioneers may be seen by a note or two concerning their work. It was as late as 1890 that Jacob Riis published "How the Other Half Lives"; in 1886 Charles Booth began the inquiry which resulted in his book on "East London." It was in 1889 that Hull House was founded, in 1887 the University Settlement in New York (first the Neighbourhood Guild), in 1884 Toynbee Hall in London. It was in 1878 that the Salvation Army was organized, although General Booth and Catherine Booth had begun their work years before. In the sixties these matters, now so familiar, were only just coming to public notice: it was as late as 1869 that Dickens took his walks in East London (protected by the police), of which he gives account in "The Uncommercial Traveller."

From such bare dates one can get an idea of the growing interest, not in charity but in social work. There has always been charity in the Christian Church; people have always wanted to give money or other things to help the poor; the essence of this movement is to give oneself. There were, of course, many workers and thinkers before those just named, but two were especially interesting to my father. In 1872 Charles L. Brace published "The Dangerous Classes of New York", after twenty years' work among them. Charles Brace had received the education of a clergyman at the Yale Divinity School and the General Theological Seminary, but had felt the need of knowing a little more than he did of the actual life of men and women. He got some of this knowledge in this country and abroad, and about 1852 settled in New York City. He organized the Children's Aid Society in 1853 of which he became the Secretary; in 1853 he founded the Newsboys' Lodging House.[1] As the years went on he gained more and more knowledge of that element in the city which is now glibly called the Underworld or the Other Half or some other name of the sort. He got to know poverty at home. My father knew him well, respected him highly, and learned much from him. I do not think he could ever have done just the work that Charles Brace did so finely. That, however, is a very minor matter; he did not do such work, but he eagerly took up the ideas which were fundamental therein and expanded and developed them into all sorts of forms by which they could be made to reach the hearts and minds of people. The other name omitted in our list is that of F. D. Maurice. Although Maurice came particularly into public notice as a theologian, or at least on account of his theological views, — his views

[1] It was about this time that my father came to know him; see I, p. 239.

of the atonement,—he was really a more important
influence in a different direction, namely in the application of Christianity to modern life, — that is to
say in the pointing out the possibility of trying on
a large scale under the conditions of the modern
world an experiment which Our Lord showed in a
small scale in the simple condition of the ancient
world. The influence of Maurice may be seen in
Charles Kingsley and in Thomas Hughes. One
will perhaps remember Tom Brown's work with
Grey in London, and Grey's delightful remark that
"Going out of one's own class and trying to care
for and help the poor, braces the mind more than
anything else." Maurice himself, I believe, never
tried to put his ideas into the form of actual fact,
except in the direction of education. But my father
felt his influence very early: In writing to Nathan,
March 2, 1855, he states, "I have been reading with
a good deal of satisfaction a book . . . by Maurice,
the man who started *inter alia* The Working Man's
College in London." When he went abroad this
was one of the places he wanted to see; he took
pains to visit it and take out a member's ticket.

He was therefore at that time a man ahead of the
common thought of his day. He believed that the
Christian everywhere must be in touch with life
and be ready to help out in its difficulties. Any
Christian minister, therefore, must be in close touch
with life and must give his chief attention to the
difficulties of life, for which the teachings of Jesus
Christ were a true panacea, something that would
cure every evil and without which nothing could

be cured; and any Christian church must be in close touch with life and especially with the life directly about it. Such doubtless was the old way when there was no division in the Christian church; each church, it may be imagined, cared for the poor, the miserable, the unhappy, right around its walls. Nowadays, in the multiplicity of organizations, people no longer go as a matter of course to the church nearest them; they go to all sorts of places, according to the accidents of sect, fashion, convenience, or various other things. And a given church, therefore, may have nothing to do with the people who live on either side of it. This condition my father did not make any effort to correct; he doubtless wished that all Christians could be one, but he felt that failing that unity, one ought to do at least what he could.

His own church, however, was, as far as he could make it, a neighborhood church, not because all the people who lived near it went to it, nor because all who went to it lived near it, but because it was a place where anybody in the neighborhood could come when he needed anything that the Church could or ought to give. His congregation stood by him here; they believed in him and wanted only to know his plans that they might help carry them out.

The practical way in which he worked this matter out was, like most of his plans, a very simple one. It is described in a letter written rather before this time, and showing the plans which he began to put into form almost as soon as he got settled in Boston.

TO C. F. BARNARD

"*May* 6, 1857. What we have attempted in this parish and what we shall attempt amount to this.

"1. I try as far as possible to get a record made of the names of every family whom anybody is assisting with parish or sewing society means. There is no great difficulty in keeping this up with the help of the different young people concerned.

"2. I am constantly impressing the theory that our especial business is with our own 'neighborhood,' which I define as the belt of Boston stretching from bay to bay, between Dover St. on the South and the railroads in the North.[1] This division does not yet amount to much, but I hope it will. As the Spring opens, I am trying to get from Provident Association visitors, Howard Benevolent visitors, etc. lists of all the people they have had to do with in this section, I propose to make the same enquiries at the Dispensary and of the Overseers of the Poor, and if I can, to find out what is the present amount and nature of poverty in this particular section.

"3. We had about two hundred and fifty dollars at the discretion of our Board of Charities for these people. We adopted this rule, that none of it should be *given* away, that it should all appear to be wages, unless in singularly exceptional cases. To carry this out we started our employment scheme, which

---

[1] This was the "neighborhood" of the old church at the corner of Washington and Castle Streets. When the church removed to Union Park Street the "neighborhood" became different.

expanded at once in one direction, which I did not foresee, thus: —

"I consider that the whole business of charity with us, excepting the care of chronic sickness, is the carrying into winter of work which would otherwise be done in summer, and the carrying to places which want work people, work people who are not wanted where they are. I proposed, therefore, that we should give out in winter the making of coarse clothing such as would be wanted in the spring, undertake to sell it in the spring and get back part or the whole of our means. But there not only appeared one set of poor women who wanted to do the sewing, but another set of poor women who wanted to buy the clothes. Without meaning to we had underbid the slop-shops, and on a very small scale, we turned over our money as fast as we could make our pantaloons.

"A little success like this, however, ought not to keep out of sight the general fact that people whose business it is to make clothing will carry on that business better in the long run than we shall. We have no business nor need to be keeping up a sewing establishment (unless for exceptional cases) in spring or in summer. Our business then is to be at work to transfer these sewing women and their families into the country, or to the best, where there is a never ending demand for them.

"This, I believe, is to be done by individual correspondence with regard to individual cases, and in that way I believe it can be done to an indefinite extent.

"4. We had a parish sewing school kept by about a dozen ladies and embracing ninety-five children. We did not restrict these to the 'neighborhood,' but most of them belonged to it. We didn't like to have this stop at the simple work which the girls were taught, and we told the oldest and most competent, therefore, that we would arrange that they should go on and learn a trade. Most of them were such children, however, that there proved to be but three competent for this.

"5. I am hoping that the way may open for a little arrangement for a Paris *crèche* next autumn. I really dream of this, however, more because I have the women who need something to do, than because I have seen the necessity of it for children.

"Now as to combination of the Southern churches.[1]

"1. In all these special plans of ours we should be mightily helped forward, if we could gain that right to cling to our own 'neighborhood' poor which we should gain if we might transfer to Hollis St., Indiana St., and the Suffolk chapel, people who fall into our hands, but are not of our 'neighborhood.' We should gain even more if the Ladies' Societies of these churches would turn over to us any of our stragglers who come to them, because we should then have an *esprit de corps* compelling us to attend to these cases.

"2. The whole employment business, if it should recommend itself to the other societies, is a great deal better carried on at a joint establishment than at four separate ones. It seems to me important,

---

[1] The churches in the southern part of Boston.

however, that the main stress of this be expended on the five winter months. As soon as spring opens we want to begin the drift outward from Boston of all the people who have been killing themselves with sewing through the winter.

"3. Whatever can be done in the way of absorbing our half-employed women by the country towns which need their labor, is a great deal better done if, at such a central office the different applications received can be compared and answered. Such an office might advertise its wants in the newspapers. But as I have said I think its best work will be done through the private correspondence of individuals."

This conception of the neighborhood as the immediate field of the duty of the Christian Church he was able to put in some definite form, or help to do so, in the activities that found a center in the formation of the Suffolk Conference in 1866. As has often been said, the Unitarian denomination, being congregational in character, has no formal and general organization or hierarchy which can interfere with the independence of each individual church. The councils and conventions spoken of in the last chapter were efforts on a large scale to provide a national organization, which should unite the churches and societies of the Unitarian denomination in ways impossible to the American Unitarian Association, the Unitarian Sunday School Society, and other institutions of a general denominational character. At the same time it seemed as though there should be some more definite organization of the churches in Boston. The Boston Association of Ministers was in those days a society of clergy-men who met regularly with one or another of their number and considered matters of interest, but not in any official way. The Benevolent Fraternity of Churches had been organized in 1834 especially to provide for a ministry at large in Boston to preach the Gospel to the many people who are not attached to any especial church. It seemed advisable for the Unitarian Churches of Boston to join in some formal way, and in 1866 the Suffolk Conference was formed. Suffolk is the county of old Boston; the city now extends into Norfolk and Middlesex. Of this conference my father became President, a position which he held for twenty-five years. Through his influence there was arranged in 1866 a distribution of the responsibility for the administration of charity among the different Unitarian churches of Boston, based on the neighborhood principle that had for ten years been a directing agency in his management of the charitable work of the South Congregational Church. Some time afterward the principle of locality was adopted in the establishment of the Associated Charities, which relieved the Churches from some of their especial duties in their own districts, but not of all of them.

These matters he held to be "the first work of Christian reform", the "special duty of the Christian ministry." His book on "Sybaris and Other Homes", published in 1869, he dedicated to the Suffolk Union for Christian Work, saying, "At the meeting which formed that Society the provision for better homes in cities was publicly declared to be the first work of Christian reform. At every meeting since some person has enforced the same necessity." And in the preface he continues the subject, saying: "I have perhaps a right to explain the earnestness with which I try to enforce the necessity of better homes for laboring men by stating a single circumstance in my own history. For nearly twenty-five years I have been constantly engaged in the Christian ministry. About half that time was spent in Worcester, Massachusetts; about half of it in Boston. When I went to Worcester it was a town of about 8,000 people; when I left it, it had three times that number. Boston is a crowded town of a quarter million inhabitants. It is impossible for me not to notice in every hour of my life the contrast between the homes of the working people in these two places. . . . To watch over and improve the charities of any town is the special duty of the Christian ministry in it, — to feed its hungry and clothe its naked, to open the eyes of its blind and the ears of its deaf, to make its lame walk, to cleanse its lepers, and to preach good tidings to its poor. Will the reader imagine to himself the position of the man engaged in that duty, when he finds his sick in such tenements as they must live in in our present system?"

He spoke of the same thing in an Anniversary Sermon which he preached January 9, 1870; He called it "People and Minister."

"You know I accept, through and through, the full Protestant statement, that all Christian men and women are priests ordained, and kings consecrated, so far as they are Christian men and women. All are in the ministry of God, of Christ, and of humanity. The minister, so called, has no rights in his function but those he shares with and derives from the people acting in this sacred ministry. . . .

"Let us remember that Christ has left to us, minister and people, to the united church, the completion of the work which he indicated and began. He has not left it to the Pope or the Patriarch; nor to any little pope or little patriarch. He has left it to the church universal. And there still remains a great deal of it to do. There remains ten million times as much to do as has yet been done. Every child who dies where death was not a necessity; every man or woman who grows up in ignorance or folly; worse yet every child, man, or woman who grows up under the weight of evil rather than under the blessedness of God, is one more witness that Christ's work is only begun and not completed.

"This work of Christ's may be detailed in a thousand ways. With us the church throws a great deal of it on the civil government; as we make the city and state attend to the large hospitals, the quarantines, the drainage, and the schools. . . . None the less has the church, as church — namely the whole congregation of men, women, and children — an immense duty yet to perform. In a city like ours this duty classifies itself familiarly under the heads of Hospitality, Education, Charity, and Worship."

What is said under the first three heads is said

otherwise in one or another letter printed in this chapter. But what is said of worship is really most important of all.

"Hospitality, education, charity, in the life of a church are all subordinate to worship. What is called in our time 'Social Science' is a well meant and generally superficial effort to carry on education and popular improvement without personal consecration and surrender of the life to God. You might as well carry on a kaleidoscope without light; or the organ yonder without air; or a steam-engine without steam. When I came to this church fourteen years ago, I found it a highly organized and earnestly faithful body, somewhat singular, perhaps in its organization among Unitarian Churches, because my predecessor, the present Bishop of Central New York, had been a man of singular power for organization. We have tried to retain such organization ever since, not injured, if not improved; and so the reputation remains with us, in some little circles, of being a parish of successful methods of church-life. And it happens to me, therefore, as your minister, that one or other of the young men who are studying for the ministry comes to me every few months, and asks me, 'What is your method about this, and what is your method about that in the South Congregational Church?' To whom I always say something like this: 'My dear friend, it makes no difference what our methods are; you cannot copy the method of one church in another. The effort to do that is the ruin of the Roman Church, and of other churches which need not be named. It is the letter that killeth, but only the spirit giveth life. Go to your new parish; consecrate yourself to its service and to God's service; teach, work, and pray, in the hope and in the determination that that people shall consecrate themselves to God's service and to man's service. There is the fountain of the whole; and unless that fountain flows, you are not to look for green turf, or spring flowers, or summer fruitage in your garden. If that fountain flows, and while it flows, there is no turf so green, no flower so fresh, no fruit so rich, but that you may expect it in it. But do not trouble yourself,' I say, 'about the methods of their culture. Such questions of method are only questions for Scribes and Pharisees. Encourage the true spirit, and the method will take care of itself.' . . .

"What we are to seek for, what we are to pray for, is, that divine self-surrender which shall make us eager to find out and work out the right methods for the help of our fellow-men."

There was an element in the Unitarian body, as in every other, that could not really sympathize with his ideas. A good while afterward (1895) he wrote a sort of diary in which he put down things that interested him; he wrote as follows about an early Unitarian minister — "He was, as I believe, a thoroughly good man. But that type of man hardly knew what *Religion* meant as I understand the word. He did the decorous things and did them conscientiously and well. But as for doing anything to bring in the Kingdom of God, he had no idea that it was his business, nor had any of that set, I should say, except Ware, Jr., Tuckerman, possibly Palfrey, though he did not know what you meant by the Holy Spirit, and certainly Gannett."

Henry Ware, Jr., had been one of the chapel preachers at Cambridge while he was at college, and J. G. Palfrey had had a good deal of influence over his theological reading while he was preparing for the ministry. Joseph Tuckerman was the practical founder of the Benevolent Fraternity and the Ministry at Large. Doctor Gannett was well known and greatly loved: his disposition is indicated by what is told of him in the traditional story of what the different Unitarian ministers said when they got to heaven. Some said one thing, some another; Doctor Gannett at once leaned over the railing and looked down into the other place and asked, "Can nothing be done for those poor people down there?"

Some such opinion my father had even at this time, I believe, of the previous generation of Unitarian clergymen. Of a number of the clergymen of his own time he had a very similar opinion. He wrote to William B. Weeden, an earnest layman and a very intimate friend, on June 4, 1868:

"But, frankly, the average clergy drive me to despair: I have to forget their existence when I want to be hopeful. It is not that they are narrow. If I wanted to name twenty men who I think understand the tremendous questions of our time, — whether spirit is a mode of matter or whether, on the other hand, there is spirit which rules matter, I should name five clergymen for one scientist or physician. It is, — that knowing what they know and reading what they read, they have no more conception that their knowledge or thought can serve this generation, or of the way in which they can serve it, than they have of serving the people in the planet Herschel. It is this that makes the pure clerical meeting deadly as the bottom of a well. Truth enough there, I suppose, if that were all."

Some such view he had through life about those who were more apt to think than to do (if we can make the distinction), and preferred theology to charity. It would be a mistake, however, to think that he himself had no theology, no definite system of knowledge about God. He was very definite about it, though probably he would never have called his knowledge a system. He simply knew about God as a child knows about his father, — that is to say abundantly for practical purposes. He was always conscious that he was himself a child of God, and that everyone else was. With such consciousness he felt that he must be about his Father's business. Just how he got this extraordinary sense of God, this sense of the present revelation of God, cannot be said. He certainly did not pick it up from some "inference" or other. He did not develop it from any principles or ideas. I should not say that he always had it. But have it he did at this time of his life, and he had had it in growing strength for a long while. One can form some estimate of his thought of formal theology and practical work from an old letter which shows how eagerly in earlier days he read Maurice and Kingsley.

TO FREDERIC GREENLEAF

"New York, *Jan.* 18, 1852. I have given up a take-tea at the Bellows's to which I was engaged from the severity of the storm. Sitting here at the hotel fire I have been reading Maurice's sermons on the Old Testament, a book I bought yesterday. You will not wonder why when I tell you that the author is a friend of Yeast Kingsley. He is one of the clergy of the English church, who horrifies the old-fashioned wings, both low and high, by caring little for them or their theologies, — but setting the old machinery of the church to work for some vital purposes, as if it were a new dissenting chapel, — instead of letting it mull on in its old self-approved sleepy fashion. Well, Maurice has tried his strength on the Old Testament. A knotty matter. For in truth, the last fifty years have labored much more to show what it is not than what it is. What it is not, we have found therefore, and have preached on the whole quite often enough, I suppose, — not I think too often. It is not a gospel. It is not full of illustrations for nineteenth century life. It is not one thing, but thirty-four things. Nor was it written for one purpose, but God only knows how many. That is what it is *not*. But what *is* the essence in it which keeps it alive for 2000 or 3000 years, what that furnishes from it illustrations as apt in parts

as they are inapt as wholes, — what that makes it
the reservoir of the world's sacred poetry and the
grammar and dictionary of its language of prayer?
Nay, of these Jews, — what is the hidden principle
which keeps them as separate now, as they were
in Lot's time or Pharaoh's; and of their history,
what is the essence which has a life for all the world?

"These are not Maurice's questions, but mine.
Questions for which my answers would be much
more vague than those I could give to the first set
of negative questions. Questions which our old
enemy, the *The Church*, has generally ignored most
completely. So that it was specially refreshing
to find that Maurice had got hold and meant to do
something or die. Beginning with saying that he
would read like a man reading a book, and not like
a bigot confirming or finding proof for a system.
Nor have I on the whole been disappointed. You
shall see the book some day, — to find it fresh, not
notional, — foggy in language sometimes, but clear
in thought, with its eyes open where there is anything hard, — instead of shut, the usual habit of
books of criticism. You know how excited we
were with Kingsley's sermons. I shall send tomorrow for a volume of twenty-five village sermons
of his, of which I find the title page."

CHAPTER TWENTY

LITERATURE

1865–1870

IT was in 1868 that my father published what he rather considered his first book.[1] "The Rosary", "Margaret Percival in America", "Kanzas and Nebraska", "Ninety Days Worth of Europe", "The Gospel Year", — these fell rather into the background when he thought of making a collection of stories. The others were full of his own life and character — indeed to one interested in his personality they offer far more than some of his stories — but there is something in creative fiction which gave a character to "If, Yes, and Perhaps" that the others lacked.

He must have thought of the name of the book himself; it sounds like him. He first thought of "Four Possibilities and Six Exaggerations", but Mr. Fields, he said, did not like it.[2] It was finally published as "If, Yes, and Perhaps" with the sub-title, "Four Possibilities and Six Exaggerations, with some Bits of Fact." It was made up of "The South American Editor", "My Double", "The Children of the Public", "The Man without a

[1] He speaks of "The Ingham Papers" (1869) as "my second book."

[2] To W. B. Weeden. Undated. "Fields does not like my title to my collection of stories and essays, 'Four Possibilities and Six Exaggerations.' I do like it. How does it strike you?"

Country", and a number of stories which have not so far been mentioned. Of these "The Last of the Florida" and "The Skeleton in the Closet" were extravaganzas on themes of the moment. "The Last Voyage of the *Resolute*" was an account he had written at the time that the English Arctic exploration ship had been brought to the United States, refitted by the Government, and sent to England as a present to the Queen. "A Piece of Possible History" told of a meeting between Homer and David which he had written some time before. "The Old and the New, Face to Face" was the story of a meeting between Paul and Nero. "The Dot and Line Alphabet" was a suggestion to apply the Morse Code to various possibilities in life, which he had printed in the *Atlantic* some ten years before. "Christmas Waits in Boston" had been written for the Christmas number of the *Advertiser* in 1867.

With some exceptions — the paper on the *Resolute* and one or two others — these stories or sketches were practically all of the same kind, — a kind which was always attractive to my father perhaps for the way in which it mingled what used at that time to be called romance and reality. His mind ran more or less on the "romance of real life", as the phrase of the day was,[1] but instead

[1] The phrase is at least as old as Scott. One finds it in my father's papers early, — in his "Omnium Gatherum" about 1840. There it is applied to historical figures whose real acts had more romance than fiction. In 1853 he wrote to Mrs. Phillips, "As I grow older people write novels to suit my bent. The age grows older too. Long since I found more romance in life than in print, and accordingly novels give up the effort to reproduce romance and devote themselves to wisdom."

of trying to penetrate the smooth hard shell of actuality to see what "romance" might be beneath, he preferred, in his stories at least, to set up some imaginative fancy and show by his handling what it would have been had it been a fact. His next book was meant seriously to show some of the possibilities of life.

Among the means and opportunities for work which he found opening to him at the end of the Civil War was a much greater chance to get the ear of the public by writing. We have seen that he had always had a chance to publish. The *Advertiser*, while his father and his brothers Nathan and Charles were editors, would print whatever he wrote. By this time, after his father's death and his brother Charles' absence, the control of the paper had passed out of the family. But Charles F. Dunbar, the editor at this time, still relied on him and welcomed his contributions. A daily paper, however, was not sufficient for his ideas; he wanted to write stories and essays as well as editorials and letters. Probably he had always felt that this was one of the ways in which he could really do something, but it was only recently that he had actually tested his abilities. "The Story of a Salamander", "Paul before Nero", "A Piece of Possible History", "Margaret Percival in America", — these had been imaginative and ingenious pieces of work, but they had not made a real impression on people's minds. "My Double" had shown those interested in literature that he had exceptional powers, but even this story was not widely known. It was "The Man without a Country" which made his name familiar to the general reading public of the country. While the war lasted his hands were too full for much of anything but the regular and exceptional round of everyday duty, but when the war was over he began to find chances for work in this field which were always a relief and delight to him. He wrote to his mother, August 29, 1866:

"I have had no chance to tell you of a flattering offer I had from Fields Monday, — to furnish for the *Atlantic* six or eight sketches of any length or subject I choose, for which he will pay me one hundred and fifty dollars apiece. This is three times what he has ever paid me before. I declined furnishing so many, but have undertaken four or five before December 1867. The first of these, "How Mr. Frye would have preached it," I have had on the stocks for a year or two. The second "My week in Sybaris," for a longer time."

The first of these sketches (to use his own expression) was published in the *Atlantic* for February, 1867. It must have been rather a favorite with my father: as he says, he had it on the stocks for a year or two, and he picked it out [1] ten years afterward when he was making one of the collections he liked to make with a view of reaching a wider public. The story is an illustration of something that he not only believed in, but believed to be of the first

[1] In 1876 with "The Man Without a Country" in The Lakeside Library, one of the first of the cheap folio libraries, which for several years were so very popular.

importance, namely that an actual story will convey an idea better than abstract expression. In this case some people had heard a sermon on "The Way of the Trangressor is Hard" and were talking about it; Mr. Frye said he would have preached it differently. When they asked him how he would have preached it, he answered by telling about himself, how he had been a transgressor and how he had found his way hard. At the end the writer says, "But last Sunday, at a church I was at in Boothia Felix the man led us through three quarters of what my grandfather's spelling-book would have called 'trisyllables in *ality*, *elity*, and *ility*,' and 'polysyllables in *ation*, *etion*, *ition*, and *otion*.' It was three dreary quarters of abstract expression. When the fourth quarter began, he said, 'History is full of illustrations of our doctrine, but I will not weary you by their repetition.' 'Old Cove,' I answered, 'I wish you would. If you would just take that lesson from Mr. Frye!'"

This lesson from a popular and successful sermon-writer, a man whose discourses from the pulpit were immensely interesting both to his hearers and his colleagues, is of more importance from a biographical standpoint than from any other. It shows that since "The Man without a Country" (written for a practical purpose) had been so successful, my father had been considering the general idea of fiction as a means of expression. An idea like that of "Mr. Frye" is not very likely to come into a man's mind out of a clear sky and to vanish when it has found expression; it is far more likely to be the crystallization of a good deal of diffused thought. At least, so one would guess from general experience, and when we remember that the idea comes after a preëminently successful experiment and before a number of other applications, it seems as if the guess were pretty near the fact.

The literary question in my father's mind at this time was clearly to find means of expression for the things of importance which he had in mind. One cannot say how far the fact of expression shows the measure of importance. But it is worth noting that, while he wrote no stories just at present about Education in the South and West, or about the organization of Liberal Christianity, or the statement of Liberal Theology, he did write a good deal on the question of the position of the poor in large cities. This second article, which he speaks of in his letter to his mother, was the first of his publications about Sybaris. He says he has had "My Week in Sybaris" in mind for quite a while. It is hard to give a good guess as to how long; in the article itself, he says since his schooldays.

This sketch, "My Week in Sybaris", published in the *Atlantic* for July, 1867, and finally made part of a series published in 1869 called "Sybaris and Other Homes", was preserved as the account by Frederic Ingham (this time Reverend) of his visit to Sybaris. It begins with an amusing defense of the ancient Sybaris and the Sybarites. "It is a great while since I first took an interest in Sybaris", says the story at the beginning, namely when the Reverend Frederic Ingham was a boy and went to the Boston Latin School and was a pupil of Mr. Dillaway. Perhaps my father really first became interested in Sybaris in those far-away years; it is certain that he retained that interest for many years more. In later years Sybaris was one of the commmonplaces of his daily talk, the type of intelligent comfort. For the Sybarites, he would maintain, had always been maligned on the ground of a few anecdotes, which in this work he ran over in a few pages, and showed how perversely the world had taken them in the wrong sense. He found nothing to despise in the old Sybaris, and he found much to admire in the laws of the newer Sybaris. "Do you not see that there is one spirit in the whole? Here was a nation which believed that the highest work of a nation was to train its people. It did not believe in fight, like Milon or Heenan or the old Spartans: it did not believe in legislation, like Massachusetts and New York; it did not believe in commerce, like Carthage and England. It believed in men and women. It respected men and women. It educated men and women. It gave their rights to men and women. And so the Spartans called them effeminate. And the Greek reader made fun of them. But perhaps the people who lived there were indifferent to the opinions of the Spartans and of the Greek reader. Herodotus lived there till he died; wrote his history there, among other things. Lysias, the orator, took part in the administration. It is not from them, you may be sure, that you get the anecdotes which ridicule the old city of Sybaris."

Of course it was natural enough that Frederic
Ingham should have gone there. The reader of
1869 perhaps remembered that between the months
of March and April, 1859, Garibaldi made in the
fishing haven of Porte Cavallo a long pause, "which
was not at the time understood by the journals
or by their military critics, and which, indeed,
to this hour has never been publicly explained. I
suppose," the story goes on, "I know as much about
it as any man now living. But I am not writing
Garibaldi's memoirs, nor indeed, my own, excepting so far as they relate to Sybaris; and it is strictly
nobody's business to inquire as to that detention,
unless it interest the ex-king of Naples, who may
write to me, if he chooses, addressing Frederic
Ingham, Esq., Waterville, N. H." Frederic Ingham had been on Garibaldi's staff. "Nor is it
anybody's business how long I had been on Garibaldi's staff. From the number of his staff officers
who have since visited me in America, very much
in want of a pair of pantaloons, or a ticket to New
York, or something with which they might buy a
glass of whiskey, I should think that his staff alone
must have made up a much more considerable
army than Naples, or even Sybaris, ever brought
into the field." But however it had been with
such people, Frederic Ingham had been there, and
once received "orders, wholly secret and unex-
pected to take a boat at once, pass the straits,
and cross the Bay of Tarentum, to communicate
at Gallipoli with — no matter whom." He went
with a couple of Italian fishermen in a lugger and

of course on the way they very naturally lost their tiller and were blown off to a place they had not thought of, namely Sybaris, where Colonel Ingham had excellent opportunity to study the development of the wonderful abode of modern common-sense luxury. The first intimation was a "horse car" drawn by four mules which came dashing around the corner. The Colonel wished to ride, but as the seats were full, the car would not stop for him. Not content with mules, when they got to the city, the car was transferred to a cable.

This horse-railroad system grew out of their political theory. "'Our peculiarity in everything is,' said his friend and guide, 'that we respect — I have sometimes thought we almost worshipped — the rights, even the notions or whims, of the individual citizen. With us the first object of the state, as an organization, is to care for the individual citizen, be he man, woman, or child. We consider the state to be made for the better and higher training of men, much as your divines say that the Church is. Instead of our lumping our citizens, therefore, and treating Jenny Lind and Tom Heenan to the same dose of public schooling, — instead of saying that what is sauce for the goose is sauce for the gander, — we try to see that each individual is protected in the enjoyment, not of what the majority likes, but of what he chooses, so long as his choice injures no other man.'"

The way in which this had come about was very natural. In the old days Sybaris had been built of one-story houses. But at one time a man built a five-story house and at once filled it with tenants. Almost as quickly he was accused of "taking away from a citizen what he could not restore."

"Of course, it was easy enough to show that the tenants went willingly; he showed dumb-waiters, and I know not what infernal contrivances of convenience within. But he could not show that the tenants had north windows, because they did not. The government, on their side, showed that men were made to breathe fresh air, and that he could not ventilate his houses as if they were open on all sides: they showed that women were not made to climb up and down ladders, and to live on stages at the tops of them; and he tried in vain to persuade the jury that this climbing was good for little children. He had lured these citizens into places dangerous for health, growth, strength, and comfort. And so he was compelled to erect a statue typical of strength, and a small hospital for infants, as his penalty. That spirited Hercules, which stands in front of the market, was a part of his fine.

"Of course, after a decision like this, concentration of inhabitants was out of the question. Every pulpit in Sybaris blazed with sermons on the text, 'Every man shall sit under his vine and under his fig-tree.' Everybody saw that a house without its own garden was an abomination, and easy communication with the suburbs was a necessity.

"It was, indeed, easy enough to show, as the city engineer did, that the power wasted in lifting

people up, and, for that matter, down stairs, in a
five-story house, in one day, would carry all those
people I do not know how many miles on a level
railroad track in less time. What you call horse-
railroads, therefore, became a necessity.

"I said they made a great row with us.

"'Yes,' said he, 'I saw they did. With us the
government owns and repairs the track, as you do
the track of any common road. We never have
any difficulty.'"

So it was that they used small one-family houses,
— such as they managed to have at Naguadavick,
and such as they really had at Vineland. It may
be remarked that such is the gift of the author that
it is not possible to tell by internal evidence which
of the four — Sybaris, Naguadavick, Vineland,
Boston — are fact and which fiction. Readers of
the *Atlantic* doubtless knew that Boston was a real
place, though possibly they knew no more about
it than Laura in the story, of the particular Boston
described, the Boston "where people live sixteen
families in one house, with their swill-barrels in
their entries and their water draining on the floors,"
a Boston where "the chances for life are not as
good as they are at Emily's house, where each child
has a bath before she goes to bed and a room of its
own to sleep in." Laura asked why it was that she
who had lived in Boston all her life knew nothing
of such places.

"'Why is it,' said her husband, 'that I know noth-
thing about them, — that I take all I tell you from
the printed report of some poor fellow who is try-

ing to thorn up me and the other governors of this country to do something about it? It is simply the old story; as somebody said in London, "When the nice people of Belgravia and the rest of the West End shall be making their answers at the day of judgment, they will have some reason to say, 'When *saw* we thee sick or in prison, and did not minister to thee?' — even after it has been explained to them that seeing one of the least of his brethren is seeing the Lord. For in Belgravia they do not see St. Giles, and as for visiting the prisoners, they would find it hard to get a permit; and as to feeding the hungry, they are afraid to give them potatoes lest they should turn them into beer."' "

"Sybaris and Other Homes" was published as a book in 1869. One cannot tell just what effect it may have had. But it was itself the effect of a very serious feeling. Sybaris was, of course, but a whimsical fancy like "My Double" and Phil Nolan. But like them it was the literary form given to something that meant a great deal. He felt that people ought to live as comfortably as they could. He was very simple in his tastes, and as we know, liked nothing better than real roughing it. But he always appreciated intelligent luxury, — if the word *luxury* be properly applied to those forms of comfort which make the minor and unimportant things of life go smoothly and comfortably, so that people may be able to give their mind to the more serious and important things. He used to call his house at Matunuck the New Sybaris. Things were not luxurious there, — they were, indeed, of the plainest and sim-

plest. But though we ate mostly (in those early days)
bluefish and huckleberries from the sea and the hills,
and got about on the pond in an old ship's yawl and
on the country roads with an old farm-horse, — yet
for him those things constituted intelligent luxury,
because they gave what he liked and needed in the
material life, with very little trouble to himself or
anybody else, and so left him free to do the things
that made life worth living, which just then consisted in bathing and tramping, talking and reading,
namely communion in about the simplest form with
nature and with fellow man.

"Sybaris and Other Homes", could we but see
it as the writer saw it, would appear to us one of
his most characteristic works. He mentions its
importance in writing to Charles.

TO CHARLES

"*Jan.* 20, 1869. Dan Haskell sent me a few days
ago the civil notice of I. Y. & P. which you cut from
the *Saturday Review.* But I like to have you cut out
such things, which I very seldom see. As it happens,
I am today putting up to send to Fields the copy of
the 'Ingham Papers,' which is the title we give to
this year's volume. I withhold for yet a third
volume the Sybaris papers and the Naguadavick,
— to which I propose to add a serious and direct
article on our own tenement houses. For if we ever
mean to save ourselves from the evils of New York
and other such life it is time for us to begin."

It is not now so well remembered as many another
thing really less significant. In its own day however

it had a better fortune than some of his other work. Some of the press notices were pleasantly appreciative not only of Sybaris but of everything else that he wrote; one that he preserved, however, mingles its approval with reprehension. Its faultfinding is based upon so fundamental a misunderstanding of my father's attitude that it is worth noting, not to be refuted (some of it may be better founded than we suspect at present) but to show some of the things about my father's work at this time that might not otherwise be noticed.

"Mr. Hale has made a very considerable reputation simply on the basis of literary eccentricity. His story of 'The Man without a Country' published in the *Atlantic Monthly* some time since gave him a widely extended popularity because it was so ingeniously constructed that it had every appearance of truth. It deceived even the most cautious reader, and there were few who did not sorrow over the wretched fate of that naval officer who was forever banished from his native land, and yet found the ties of country so strong that he could never call any other land his own. The story made a great popular success, and when it was discovered that the hero was a myth, the lamentations over his suffering turned to admiration at the skillful manner in which the writer had provoked the reader's tears. But there is always danger in repeating an eccentricity of this kind, however successful the original one may have been."

Except from some such definite statement of competent judges of the time itself, one hardly

imagines that "The Man without a Country" and
other such tales by my father and other writers of
his day were of especial interest because people
really believed that they were statements of fact.
The writer goes on to speak of "The Goldbug" as
a "clever literary trap to catch the credulous," and
says that such things can be done only once. "People
will read and admire the first time because they are
uncertain whether the narrative is true or not.
When they have the fact, then there is no more
mystery; and the second narrative has as little zest
as a glass of soda-water carried across the street."

Such a view would be hardly thought of (I suppose) by a reviewer to-day. It is worth noting here
because to a slight degree my father seems to have
had it himself. That is, he really did have a certain
interest, not very serious, about presenting the thing
so that people would be taken in by it. He says one
or two things of the sort in writing to Charles, to
whom he was most likely to express himself with
the absolute frankness that is so hard to get except
with people very near one's heart. But that the
idea of such deception was really an important one,
— that he could really have thought, for instance,
that people would believe even for a moment that
there actually was a Frederic Ingham, that he
actually had been in the service of Garibaldi, that
he actually had spent a week in Sybaris, — is about
as improbable as it is that he thought people would
believe that the horsecars of Sybaris carried no
more passengers when they were full, or that they
prosecuted people there who built houses of more

than one story. The really important thing was
that people should get the idea and be impressed
by it. That was what he wanted; if a bit of a hoax
helped this object or even a bit of doubt as to
whether the thing might not be so, so much the
better. Even if the mystification were nothing
more than the long recognized literary artifices of
a supposed author and so on, — why all that was
part of the amusement of the man of letters.[1]

This same review mentions another story of the
time, namely "The Brick Moon", and says that
what had been entertaining and skilful had become
tedious and threadbare. One cannot say whether
the reader of the present day will find "The Brick
Moon" more interesting than "A Visit to Sybaris"
or less. It is certainly, however, as interesting so
far as my father's life is concerned. Sociological
studies in the form of fiction were not the only prod-
ucts of these years. His fanciful imagination was
continually suggesting ideas which could be dealt
with in the common-sense realism which he liked
so well. One of the most outrageous of these fancies
and one which, like Sybaris, was based on a real so-

[1] It might be said that just these years saw, especially in short-story writing,
a passing away of one sort of realism and a coming in of another. From the
standpoint just presented, such stories as "The Gold Bug ", "The Diamond
Lens ", "The Man Without a Country ", "Marjorie Daw ", not to mention
hundreds of others, were technically well done; they use all the devices of
literary realism of their day. It was quite another kind of realism that Mr.
Howells had in mind in the stories and sketches that he began about this time
to publish in the *Atlantic*, and that Mr. James had rather more vaguely. The
earlier realism made its great successes when it took an impossible idea and made
it seem not only possible, but probable or even plausible. The later realism
tried to get at the truth of life and present it so exactly that it would be not only
plausible but undeniable.

ciological conviction, was that of the "Brick Moon."
The "Brick Moon" was, of course, from the papers
of Captain Frederic Ingham. It is written of Jules
Verne that "he cleverly exaggerated the possibilities of science, and gave verisimilitude to narra-
tives of wild adventure." Something of the sort did
Frederic Ingham. Before the ingenious Frenchman
had published his "From the Earth to the Moon,"
Frederic Ingham, looking for a means of determining one's longitude as simple as the determining of
latitude by Polaris, hit on the expedient of a Brick
Moon. The plan was this: "If from the surface of
the earth, by a gigantic pea-shooter, you could
shoot a pea upward from Greenwich, aimed northward as well as upward; if you drove it so fast
and far that when its power of ascent was exhausted,
and it began to fall, it should clear the earth, and
pass outside the North Pole, if you had given it
sufficient power to get it half round the earth without touching, that pea would clear the earth forever.
It would continue to rotate above the North Pole,
above the Feejee Island place, above the South
Pole and Greenwich, forever, with the impulse with
which it had first cleared our atmosphere and attraction. If only we could see that pea as it revolved in
that convenient orbit, then we could measure the
longitude from that, as soon as we knew how high
the orbit was, as well as if it were the ring of Saturn.
  "'But a pea is so small!'
  "'Yes,' said Q., 'but we must make a large pea.'
Then we fell to work on plans for making the pea
very large and very light. Large, — that it might

be seen far away by storm-tossed navigators: light,
— that it might be the easier blown four thousand
and odd miles into the air; lest it should fall on
the heads of the Greenlanders or the Patagonians;
lest they should be injured, and the world lose its
new moon. But, of course, all this lath-and-plaster
had to be given up. For the motion through the
air would set fire to this moon just as it does to other
aërolites, and all your lath-and-plaster would gather
into a few white drops, which no Rosse telescope
even could discern. 'No,' said Q. bravely, 'at the
least it must be very substantial. It must stand
fire well, very well. Iron will not answer. It must
be brick; we must have a Brick Moon.'"

They made a large Brick Moon and some of them
got inside it; by some mistake it was shot off into
the heavens; it did just as they had hoped it would,
revolved around the earth; by extraordinary ingenuity Frederic Ingham, left on earth, got into communication with them; and they finally were able
to do something in sending not only messages but
a sort of parcel post, by the same means by which
the moon itself had been sent. So they learned of
the wonderful life on the Brick Moon, a life in common of course, for there were thirty-seven of them,
and the moon was only two hundred feet in diameter;
they lived inside.

Society is the right thing, one must admit, and
intelligent society is the very best thing going.
But society as it exists has often some drawbacks,
as is seen in the story "His Level Best." This story
is not precisely like the others in plan, a natural

working out of a palpably absurd idea. It is rather more the absurd working out of a very natural idea. It is not one of the adventures of Colonel Frederic Ingham; it is told by Colonel Ingham about John Boothby who, with his wife Gertrude, tried to do as society seemed to think they ought to do. Curiously enough, they ended in a poorhouse rather than, as one would imagine, a sanatarium, or a home for feeble-minded. John and Gertrude were really trying to do the wrong thing; no one could get along by abjuring one's individuality and doing whatever seemed, at any day or hour, the thing that people ought to do. One must be oneself.

Discussion of his literary plans is not very frequent in my father's letters, but here is mention of one or two things.

TO CHARLES

"*Aug.* 8, 1869. I am now writing while I preside over the manufacture of a kite by Arthur. I do not think you took much to kite building. I was rather famous for it, the scientific, sedentary, and solitary character of the amusement comporting with my taste. For some reason Arthur's kites have not yet succeeded well. Our increasing intercourse with Japan and China introduces a good many new patterns among the boys.

"Parallel with this taste you will say is my story of the Brick Moon of which the first part will be in the *Atlantic* for October. It is the success and failure of our great enterprise of sending up from township No. 9 a Brick Moon to assist in fixing the longitude. The story has spun out into three numbers and will need another for its completion. For the *Almanac* for this year, as I believe I have said, I have finished "The Modern Sinbad," the adventures of an English merchant from Soho Square who with his wife and children came to this country and did thirty-one states in thirty days. The idea is good, but the execution is crowded and tame, though it requires oceans of work. I am writing very steadily in my vacation. I get two hours at my work every morning, with very little interruption. I am now to undertake No. 6 of my Young Folks Series. This is How to go into Society, and then I shall finish the new volume "Sybaris and Other Homes" with two papers, one a chapter on tenement houses in Boston and the other a sketch of Vineland in New Jersey, which is the most promising experiment, I think, for the emigration [sic] of that class of townspeople from where a few generations have squeezed into the Norman & Saxon passion for adventure, and power for the creation of homes.[1] When these two papers are off the dockets, I shall attack my Lowell lectures, of which I may not have written you."

It need not be said that my father was a realist. It is obvious that the admirer of Defoe and the author of "The Man without a Country" was some sort of realist. But it does not get one far along to know so much, for there are and have been many kinds of realists. My father was one who under-

---

[1] He may have been looking at Arthur's kite when he wrote this sentence; there is perhaps something left out.

stood that the century or the half-century in which
he lived was a time of protest against Untruth.
Carlyle showed the imbecility of forms and vestures,
Stanley and Arnold built up a realistic school in
history, Renan and Seeley presented the life of
Christ with a vivid reality, — such are some of the
indications of realism which he mentions himself
in one place or another, when he thinks of those
who had worked in lines near his own. "Ruskin
attacked conventionality in art", he also says;
"the Crystal Palace and Kensington made men
study a real morning-glory before they even modeled
the handle to a poker, . . . Drury Lane would not
mount 'Hamlet' without a correct painting of the
castle of Elsinore." [1]   His general position was that
of a religious leader who directed men along the
ways of a religion of fact rather than one of form.
To do that one had to know what the fact of religion
was, and this was the great thing in life with him,
— the great fact of religion. It was one of the necessities of that great fact that it was unavoidable in
life as well as in religion, and therefore it would
have been idle and worse than idle to have presented Life in any other way than as a joint effort
of man to follow out the plans of God. So he is
realistic in his matter in that he generally presents
something of that kind, — something that comes
from true coöperation or else from false coöperation
— sometimes one, sometimes another. All sorts of
devices he uses to do this, from fantastic and whimsical inventions like that of a Brick Moon or a Double

[1] "May to June," p. 110.

to pretty definite plans like the polity of Sybaris echoed in Naguadavick, Vineland, the possible Boston, or the Ten Times One Clubs which so shortly sprung forth, blossomed, and bore fruit in so many ways.

In form also he was consistent. His favorite way of writing a story was to write it as if somebody were telling it. Sometimes he has to search for expedients, as when he explains at some length how Mr. Frye came to tell How he would have Preached It. Sometimes he experimented: when he gathered a number of stories in "Christmas at Narragansett," he said to himself, "People don't really sit and *tell* each other long stories. That's a convention." So he has his people *read* their stories and devotes his ingenuity to thinking out ways in which it would be natural for people to read stories to each other. But whether his general plan was meant to imitate life or not, his general way of expressing himself was an almost colloquial style, — a style colloquial in that it reproduced the tone, the mental attitude of one man talking to another, not that it tried to imitate the accidents of conversation. He became used to this mode of expression in course of time: his early sermons are a little more definitely rhetorical than his later sermons. Presumably his constant sermon-writing was an influence on his other writing, and influenced by it.

A word or two may be said of the mechanics of style, partly because this was a matter which he thought a good deal about at this time and wrote about in his papers in "How to Do it." In that

interesting and characteristic series of directions on
the practice of life is a paper on "How to Write."
To turn this into a theory of style we must connect
it with two previous papers on "How to Talk."
When we have done so, we get at the following
twelve directions, of which the first six have to do
with the substance and the last six with the style.

How to Talk

Tell the truth
Do not talk about your own affairs
Confess ignorance
Talk to the person who is talking to you
Never underrate your interlocutor
Be short.

How to Write

Know what you want to say
Say it
Use your own language (the language you are
   accustomed to use in daily life)
Leave out all the fine passages
A short word (other things being equal) is better
   than a long one
The fewer words the better.

In these dozen rules, meant for young people, he
naturally need not have put the principles which
were his own guides. But a little looking over his
work makes one think that he followed most of these
rules himself and I believe that a careful study would
confirm the impression. In a general way we get
the idea of the realist, intent on rendering the truth,
impatient of "flowers of rhetoric" or rhapsodies of

sentimentality.   In a particular way we have the general conversational tone, the use of the English element in the language rather than the Latin,[1] and the use of short sentences.   If one studies his writing closely one will see that these three principles prevail.   There is apt to be a conversational tone.   The use of words of English origin is marked, sometimes very marked.   There is a considerable number of short and very short sentences in his writing, and the average length of the sentence is quite short.   The whole thing is but a part of the great consistency in his life and thought.   He wanted truth and he was therefore true himself and to himself, otherwise what is called sincere.   His writing aimed at truth in style as well as in substance.

[1] In "How to Do it," p. 87, in speaking of the use of an English word instead of Latin, when there is one quite as good, he advises his reader "to translate in some thoroughly bad author, his Latin words into English"; he says: "To younger writers, or to those who know only English, this may seem too hard a task.   It will be doing much the same thing if they will try translating from long words to short ones."

CHAPTER TWENTY-ONE

FAMILY LIFE

1865-1870

BESIDE all these different interests and occupations of these years there was the personal and family life, the life from day to day, the life that filled all the spare moments, that gave character to all the rest, and really was the most important of all. For, though my father was a very active man in public and semi-public occupations, yet he had also time and energy for all sorts of other interests, and was very much of a person entirely aside from those things whereby he was or came to be most widely known. He had personally certain characteristics which did not come obviously to public notice. With all his care and solicitude for the public good, the "common weal" as he often thought of it, he was at bottom a thorough individualist, as New Englanders are apt to be. As a clergyman he preached to his people his own personal sense and understanding of the Gospel and the life with God, and could never have understood the assent to a creed which he did not believe, because it was the historic statement of the church to which he belonged. He was a member of the most independent of church bodies,[1] and although, as has been seen, he was very

---

[1] Notice the letter to Charles in 1867 (Vol. II, p. 6,) in which he says: "You may not know that the Unitarian churches of America never met in convention. A pure independency or congregationalism has always governed them or parted them."

active, at this time, in promoting the national organization of the Unitarian church, yet the organization was of such a nature as could not destroy the
fundamental independency of the body. Although
he believed in organized work, and was himself an
organizer, and was often thought of as such, yet he
had a great impatience of actual organizations and
always had had since his schooldays.[1]   His conception of an organization was not of a perfected
machine in which every member did exactly what
was laid out for him, but rather of a body of co-
workers whose devotion was all to one common
object, who had enough faith and hope to keep
them at their individual best, and enough charity
to believe that everybody else was doing his best
as well.

He had, it is true, been drawn into organized
work, but this (except in so far as every citizen
belongs to the State and every man to the life in
common) was rather by accident. About this time
(December 27, 1866) he wrote to William B. Weeden,
with whom he was very intimate: "In our little
circle of my own profession I have the reputation
for being a good organizer and having a good executive gift. In fact, I have this so little that Hiram

[1] Beside the natural shyness or impatience which a man of great ability is
apt to feel with people of ordinary or very little ability, he had a deep-seated
hatred of monotony, which made him intolerant of routine and desirous of doing
things in his own way. These may not have been the only or the essential
reasons for his distrust of boards and committees. He himself sometimes suggested other ones, as, that he preferred to take responsibility rather than have
it divided up, or that boards and committees were more apt to discuss and
debate than to act. Of course many things went to make up what was a strong
feeling.

Withington, who knew me perfectly well, said to me in 1847, that I was so opposed to all organization that I should some day leave the solar system in disgust at it. . . . But it has so happened to me as to Bellows, to find that the set of men who are trusted with the Christian ministry have got into an introspective habit, and are not able to attend to any detail of the external business of the profession. Failing others, he and I have both done a good deal of work which ordinary clerks in wholesale houses would have done as well. But I have never deceived myself more than he himself into thinking that we were made for this, or into wanting to do it, or into thinking that I did it more than tolerably well."

This individualism showed itself most plainly in his character as an outdoor man. The true individualist is the Robinson Crusoe, or, failing a desert island, the frontiersman, the pioneer. My father always wanted to live outdoors as much as he could. About this time (April 19, 1864), he wrote to my mother: "That I am made for an open-air life, and especially for this Bohemian life, I am more than ever satisfied. I remember, one Sunday, when I was a Senior in college, taking my constitutional, I thought all that over, wished I might be sick enough to have to give up so-called professional study and become instead an engineer or a farmer. In those days we did not think of the army. Well, I have no regrets for a life in which I have made more friends and enjoyed more opportunities than almost ten men could expect, but as you know the instinct of the savage is in me still." When younger he had been a mountaineer, fond of the really difficult feats of climbing open to the New Englander of his day.[1] In later years when he had not the time to walk much he found chief athletic pleasure in swimming. It was long before the present passion for athletics and outdoor life, and even the younger men of his day had ideals very different from those predominant now. My father played football at college, but it was in the extempore fashion in which one might lose a coat-tail or get one's trousers torn. Rowing had not come in at that time. Baseball was practically unheard of, except as a game for boys, and of course tennis and golf were still in the future. In those days if one were an outdoor man at all, it was because one loved the great world of out-of-doors, and was bound to get there somehow.

My father was strongly attached to the mountains and other forms of wild nature; to the end of his life he remembered with deep pleasure his days on Mt. Katahdin or Mt. Washington, his experience in Howes' Cave or at Trenton Falls. Even in the midst of the cares and worries of the Civil War the great relief was to escape from the city and walk for a week in the mountains. But he also loved the simpler and more particular forms of nature; he was immensely fond of flowers. Among his

---

[1] He wrote to Charles, August 2, 1868, "Thus I, if I only entertain a circle with an account of losing my way on Mt. Jefferson, with crawling head downward in Schoharie, or with swimming Wissataquic for a lodging, might represent myself as a thorough Kit Carson by as simple an expedient as the omission of all allusion to twenty-five years of peaceful life on which these high lights are embroidered."

EDWARD EVERETT HALE'S CLASS CLUB

Standing, from left: George F. Lyman, Alexander C. Washburn, George Hayward, R. C. Greenough
Sitting, from left: Edward Everett Hale, Samuel Eliot, Francis B. Hayes, C. William Loring, Samuel E. Guild

earliest journals are his lists of the wild flowers as
he found them each year: his happiest recollection
of Katahdin was that he had collected on the sum-
mit specimens which were cited in Gray's "Botany";
in earlier days he was apt to find suggestions or illustrations which helped him in his preaching.   In
college he had a garden among those at Divinity
Hall; at Worcester a garden was one of his great
pleasures; and when he settled down at 39 Highland
Street a garden and a greenhouse were among the
earliest plans to be put into execution. One ought
really to spend more time on these things, to give
some idea of the different garden books with their
careful notes about this or that experiment, of the
plans of the garden at Worcester, with its drafts of
harmonious and contrasting arrangements, of the
lists of roses and so on.   Wherever he tells us anything about the ideal life, we find that the people
had gardens.   It seems impossible that a man with
his hands so full of business could have had the time
to give to such an exacting mistress as a garden, and
I suppose as a fact that he did not do much about it
after he left Worcester.   His first house in Boston
was in a city block, where he could have no garden
at all.   At 39 Highland Street it was my mother
who cared for the garden, when the matter was
obviously impossible for him.   But he always wanted
to do something about it.   Even at Matunuck, where
the house was on the top of a windswept hill, he
planted flowers and trees.

He was also very fond of sketching. There must
have been some family adaptability in this direc-

tion, for his brother Nathan drew and painted easily
and pleasantly, and his sister Susan was for a good
many years a landscape painter by profession. My
father himself at this time painted as well as either
of them, and one distinguishes his sketches from
Nathan's or from Susan's early work, not because
they are not so good, but because they have a different quality. He was always taking a lesson or
two in drawing or painting, although his other occupations were apt to make the efforts rather desultory.
His abilities were certainly not such as to be of
interest to the general public, but they added immensely to his own pleasure in outdoor life.

One need not say any more just now about his
intellectual life as an individual. A passage omitted
from the letter to Mr. Weeden just quoted may
come in here. "Naturally," he writes, "I am a
studious person, fond of acquisition of facts, and
of placing them in relation, passionate for geography, therefore, and history. I have a reasonable
metaphysical power, and can dance what Voltaire
calls the minuet in that business as well as any
man." He had, indeed, always been a student; we
have seen his boyish aspirations to universal knowledge. The necessities of life and of time had curbed
these ambitions so that he no longer paid attention
to the chemistry and astronomy of earlier days. So
far as scholarship was concerned he had settled
down into the position of a historian. And although
all forms and phases of historical knowledge were
interesting to him, from the history of the ancient
Egyptians to the report of the Arctic adventures of

the *Resolute*, and from Paul before Nero to Marco
Polo in Cathay, yet he had by this time really fixed
his mind on two historical topics, one the history
of Boston, New England, the American Colonies,
and the other the history of the Pacific Ocean and
its shores. On the first of these he had exceptional
opportunities for especial knowledge, on the second
he had exceptional interest.

Beside his interest in history he had the general
delight in literature as literature that characterizes
men like Macaulay and Lamb. He read all kinds
of things so far as time and chance allowed him.
It is true that so far as original work was concerned
he (afterwards at least) made rather a point of his
disregard of literature for its own sake, and wanted
always to have some practical object in view. But
certainly in his reading he often had no care for any
practical object save that of amusement. He always read novels immensely; among my earliest
recollections of his reading (shortly after this time)
are "Amadis of Gaul" which he had in many paper-
covered numbers of the Bibliothèque Bleue, and the
novels of Anthony Trollope, which he loved to read
aloud in the summer evenings. He used also, now
or a little later, to read aloud the vaudevilles of
Scribe, generally translating the French as he went
along. He used, too, now and then, to go to the
theater, where, beside the more serious things, he
enjoyed about this time Mrs. John Wood and other
lighter performers. One finds in his letters, just
as one finds in his stories, the idea that literature
has other purposes than mere entertainment, but

though he recognized the other purposes and often
thought of them as being of chief importance, yet
the "mere entertainment" was important too, and
whatever spiritual stimulant or practical suggestion
he himself got from fiction, the thing that he obviously got was entertainment.

With all these strongly individualistic traits he
was deeply devoted to his family. His mother died
in 1866, and he wrote to William B. Weeden twenty
years afterward: "I felt a hundred years older
after my mother died. Till then there was some
one who thought of me as a boy, and measured me
by a boy's standard, not to say with a mother's
infinite tolerance and love. Since then I have had
to wobble on as one of the present generation,
wholly conscious myself that I am as much a boy
as I ever was." He had written something of the
sort at the time to the Reverend Samuel G. May
(December 26, 1866). "I have not yet got back to
the place I was in in life when I went to Syracuse.
You know that I never shall. When a man's father
and mother are dead, he is no longer of the rising
generation. He is a hundred years older."

He had indeed for fifteen or twenty years considered himself the mainstay of the family, father
and mother, brothers and sisters (now reduced to
four), and such he was through life. It was not
that he assumed any direction or guidance over
them, but he was always at hand, the responsible
person, the one who would see that things went on.
His father's powers failed and he died; so did
Nathan and so did Charles. He cared for them all

in life and in death, and for his mother and his sisters. His sister Susan survived him and died in the house of which he had given her the control.[1] This spirit had dominated his early life and had not been weakened in later years by his own marriage and his own family. At the close of the War he had one daughter, Ellen, and three sons; in the years immediately following four sons were born, so that during these years he had all the responsibilities and pleasures of a large and growing family. When, in 1869, he settled at 39 Highland Street, in the house in which forty years afterward he died, he had one girl and six boys. At the close of the War, however, he was still living at 67 Worcester Street, in the house he had bought not long after coming to Boston. The summers he commonly spent in or near Milton, with occasional excursions with one or another of the family to the White Mountains or some other place where life was a little nearer nature. These arrangements, however, were never entirely satisfactory, and he was constantly thinking of some place where he could have not only a larger house, but one in which the family could live comfortably in summer as well as in winter. In 1869 he found such a place in Roxbury, at that time just annexed to Boston, and full of fine and attractive old places. The house at 39 Highland Street was much farther from the church than that at 67 Worcester Street, but it was large

---

[1] The house at Matunuck was built for my father by William B. Weeden in 1873, but some time before my father's death the control of it was turned over to Susan.

and roomy and stood in good sized grounds in a half-countrified locality, and was yet near enough by steam or horsecars to get to church or to the center of Boston with what at that time seemed very little trouble.

The following letters give a few notes of various interests and occupations.

TO CHARLES

"*July* 18, 1865. I have made a holiday week of it with a vengeance in following up the Cambridge festival.[1] I have thought them a great success. In the first place the weather, according to Frank Capen's prophecy of it, was splendid. Then, of course, these two hundred and fifty heroes who came back from the army to be present, were not only at Friday's fête, but were about all the time. The attendance Wednesday was immense, Friday magnificent. The great pavilion covered the space between Holden, Harvard, and Hollis. The President's table was the length of Holden, back to it. On the side of Hollis were the College arms, and tablets with the names of the dead; from Harvard sloped down a terrace crowded with ladies who had had a collation meanwhile in the hall, then the tables were set somewhat as within [a plan is annexed] in the square. Observe that the Liberty Tree of our old dancing days was in the pavilion, which extended indeed, I think, to the picket fence. The speaking was capitally good. We actually stayed till the sun went down so far that it was

[1] Commencement at Harvard was this year a very especial occasion.

dusk in the pavilion. The ridgepole of the pavilion (not a pole but a cable) ran from the middle of Hollis to somewhere opposite. There were tall blue masts to support it."

During these years, as always, he went about the country a good deal, to New York to conference or council meeting, to visit the schools at Antioch or Meadville, and elsewhere. The year after the War he made a visit to Washington, whence he wrote a number of interesting letters.

TO MRS. HALE

"*Apr.* 8, 1866. Into town with Newell at one. Cars to Susy's, dinner on table, and so at a quarter to three to the Baltimore cars. These were over-crowded with soldiers and I began to fancy Johnson had ordered a Coup d'État. But nothing of the sort has happened yet. On the other hand, our friends who are well pleased at the condition of things, tell little things which seem to show that Johnson and Seward are hedging. On Friday night Johnson went to Gen. Grant's reception. No President has gone to a party given by a citizen since the republic has been a republic, I am told. This is conciliatory, Grant being reckoned on our side. More marked, when there the President presented Thad Stevens to Mrs. Grant. There is a scene for a historical picture, — The Era of Good Feeling."

TO MRS. HALE

"*April* 11, 1866. You ask what the new President is. It is as much a mystery here as it is anywhere,

— perhaps as much a question to himself as to anyone. This is certain, I think, that he is a morbid
excitable man; just now he is possessed with a
mania about assassination. He seldom appears in
public, — yet on the other hand, receives everybody
and talks on public affairs with an almost mad
facility with everyone, always taking the opinion
of his interlocutor and expressing it as his own. The
best accounts I have heard agree that he is not
drunk when people see him. I have heard it ques-
tioned whether he did not drink at night, — this in
the mere desire to account for this almost wild un-
easiness which everyone notices. The Republicans
are universally very sick of him. Literally I have
met with no one who expressed confidence in him.
But, on the other hand, they all say that he snubs
the Secesh Democrats. My own judgment is that
he and Mr. Seward are quite satisfied with the feeling of the pulse of the country, and that there will
be, for some time, no more collision between him
and the Congress. I shall not see him probably."

TO MRS. HALE

"*April* 11, 1866. I have been, — have staid at
the Capitol two hours, — have returned and have
lunched. I am going to write Go. Allen's articles,
and go to dine at Charlotte's [1] at half past five. I
am glad Foster asked me to make the prayer opening the session of the Senate and am glad to make
it. You have a feeling that it is not your fault at
least, if that day they do not let the Holy Spirit

---

[1] Mrs. Henry A. Wise, the daughter of Edward Everett.

guide them. But how much power they have to hinder was well enough illustrated when half an hour after I was done, McDougall was in set speech extolling drunkenness as a condition of inspiration, quoting from Plato's Symposium to show it was, and challenging the other side to name poet or statesman who had not extolled the use of wine. With the duty of Chaplain for the day comes admission to the floor of the Senate. I sat there through the little debate on the sale of liquor in the Capitol, in which McDougall made this speech, another in Mr. Foster's room, wrote a letter for the *Register*, which you will see on Saturday, if Upham, the printer, concludes to let it go in."

TO MRS. HALE

"*April* 13, 1866. Wise is a very remarkable man. I first began to appreciate him when he was in Boston on occasion of Uncle Edward's funeral. I see him more now and understand him better. I can tell you better than I can write to you of his position and duties in this Department. How little, for instance, when we heard that he went to Japan did we understand the importance of our having a direct importation of nitre from Japan, for which in fact we were dependent on the English market. That was what he went for. When afterwards, the war began Jeff. and the rest stole most of our gunpowder, and we were, in a larger way, in the position Washington was in at Cambridge. The adventures of this bureau in supplying nitre, as he has just sketched them to me, savor really of Monte Cristo."

MEMORANDUM OF CONVERSATION WITH MR. SEWARD,
APRIL 18, 1866.[1]

"I sent in my card to Mr. Seward, and when I was shewn in, I said I wanted to thank him for his kind answers to the inquiry I had made regarding my brother a few weeks ago. He replied very sharply, 'Yes, Mr. Hale, I am true to my friends, which is more than you are to me.'

"I said, 'You have no right to say that, Mr. Seward.'

"'No man is a true friend of mine who assails the President.'

"'And where have I assailed the President' — said I.

"'You have an interest, I think, in the *Daily Advertiser* which assails him constantly.'

"This was just what I expected. I said that on the other hand I had not the slightest interest in the *Daily Advertiser* — nor had my brother — that he was obliged to sell all his interest in it when he went to Egypt — and that neither of us had the interest of a dollar in it, or any control over it. This I put very distinctly because I thought it important by way of making every tub stand on its own bottom.

"'Oh!' he said at once, and from this moment became cheerful and pleasant. 'Then I take it all back. I take it all back. I did not understand that; we have been very unfortunate in that way. There is the Albany *Evening Journal*. I felt some

[1] This was written out with care for Charles in Egypt.

of that. My son had a large interest in that. He and I are here today only because he had. And yet today — I see they have got too much for them, and they are attacking the President too. Now I do not care how much people abuse me. In all my public life, for near fifty years now I have felt sure I was right as long as I was abused. But I always make this bargain when people want any favors for presses, — I always say, let them abuse me as much as they like—I rather like it. But I don't want them to abuse the President. There is one of your papers in Boston. I do not know if it was the *Advertiser*, but Wilson or some one came to me to ask something for it, — and I said the only condition I make is that they shall not abuse the President, they may abuse me as much as they like.'

"I said that he must see that people had rather preferred the other course, that the journals which abuse the President most did not abuse him.

"'Yes,' he said, 'I do see it and I do not like it,' — and then repeated, with rather unnecessary repetitions, his comments that when he was right he liked to be abused, and so forth.

"He went on to say that from our foreign ministers, without exception, from Mr. Adams and all they had received intimations that the President's Policy was the right policy before these gentlemen could have received any account of the discussions here: 'and how absurd it is that people here will not see it. We have finished the war. Everybody is glad we have finished it. Why should we pretend to be at war longer? We have broken the military

power of the Southern States. We have abolished
Slavery, which is the only thing that could bind them
together. Why should we want to fight them still?'

"I had rather unfortunately said I was a clergyman, by way of explaining that I was not and had
not been editor of the *Advertiser*. This led him
into rather a train of Scripture — in what followed
in the conversation.

"'I have a guard around my house,' he said.
'These people here tried to kill me. But if I died,
and when I do — when I stand at the account — I
have this to say — that not one drop of the blood
that has been shed from the beginning in this war
is on my head — there is not a drop which could
have been spared by my forgiveness and wish to
forgive which has not been spared.'

"I said every one gave him credit for that.

"'Well, Mr. Hale, go to Scripture for direction in
this matter. Religion is politics. It always is.
Go to Scripture and the only direction you get is
for Charity — Charity to these people. Charity
never did do any harm and it never can do any.'

"All this was delivered with immense animation
— not to say rage. He really confessed that the
country had not seconded the President, but he
said it ought to. Indeed he took pretty steep ground
here. He said — 'I am only the President's officer.
I am his finger, if you please, his little finger. As
such I sustain and must sustain him. I wish the
country would not spare me — if it means to attack
him,' — or something to this import.

"I was determined not to enter into any argument with him, while he regarded me as in some sort your brother or representative. Besides, I was much more interested in knowing what he thought or pretended to think than in having him know what I thought. I think I have repeated everything salient which passed in the political part of the conversation. I then rose to take leave, thanking him again for his attention to my request regarding you."

TO WILLIAM B. WEEDEN

"MILTON; *July* 15, 1866. It is the first vacation Sunday, a delicious elastic air, wind east I think, sky clear, a day right out of Heaven. The row following breakfast, well-nigh inevitable, I believe, where there are four boys, subsides, and I consecrate to you the beginning of vacation. Nelly is painting flags on Edward's stamp book for him, Arthur and Charley putting soldiers into transports. The soldiers are no longer named Rebel and Union, but Austrian and Italian. Such is fame, oh, victor of seven fights! [1]

"Well, whatever else happens I mean to be sure that my children shall be glad to have Sunday come round.

"It was charming to see your handwriting, and to know that you had boldly pushed so far. Your letter was written at Genoa on the 19th; our poor Italian friends were beaten at Custozza on the 24th, — battle neither lost nor won, says the King. That they were beaten is my only evidence that you were not in charge of a field battery.

[1] Mr. Weeden had commanded a battery in the War.

"For one I am reading the history in advance, a hundred years in advance, by reading the two last volumes of Carlyle's 'Frederic.' I am disappointed in Frederic. I am not spooney about greatness, and can recognize it with any reasonable limitations. But Frederic's force of will which is, I suppose, essential to human greatness, a quality akin let us hope to the steadiness of God himself, seems to show only in a sort of waywardness or even petty obstinacy, effective sometimes, and as often ruinous. He wins some great battles, but he loses as many, which makes his generals afraid to disobey him, though they know obedience is ruin. There is nothing in the six volumes equal to the mutual confidence which Grant and Sherman have in each other, and they are by no means great men of the first type.

"No! History and posterity are not altogether fools. A hundred years have gone by and the world has agreed to accept Frederic as a great campaigner, whose campaigns may still be worth study by military men. For the rest the world has agreed to forget him. And all my friend Carlyle's abuse of the world for forgetting him will not mend that matter while he confesses that the king worshipped himself, and made his officers so afraid of him that he did not get their best out of them. Napoleon did get the best out of his. But all this by the way. I set out to say that the very geography of the Benedik-Prusso struggle of this hour is the old story of 1759–1760. Jung Butzlan, Skalitz, and all this are on those same old maps of the 'Friedrich.'

"I doubt if I have any news. I did not get to

Antioch, and the Trustees in a savage fit of economy, razeed the staff pretty badly. We chose Brigham president, but he will not take it. I think we shall try Fred. Knapp of the Sanitary now. They promise us two hundred pupils which will help out our income.

"I hear that dear Thomas T. Stowe is preaching for your people today. The wisest, kindest, loveliest of mankind, lives utterly in the seventh heaven now, and is so far unfitted for communion with earth, but excellent for an occasional lark-song heard from the Empyrean above, which makes us wonder why we do not get up at daybreak and go out into the Present Heaven every morning. Tonight I am going to Cambridge to hear Furness. Will you go? If it is cool enough we will walk, — not more than nine miles across country if so many. Then Thursday Hedge is going to address the Alumni and lay out flat all present colleges by showing the Possible University. Wednesday we Alumni choose our own 'Overseers' at Cambridge. Your friend is a candidate but will be beaten. As the overseers have nothing to do this matters little. Emily joins in love. Write at once."

TO CHARLES

"*Oct.* 15, 1867. With a hatful of other cares, and every day over-crowded, I must needs entertain myself with calling on Newman Hall, the great non-conformist London preacher, a sort of Beecher in his place and way, with some executive traits in the management of local charities and so on which interest me in addition. He was undoubtedly a vigor-

ous ally of ours with the London workingmen through
the War. A quick, intense, perhaps rather superficial man, but an earnestly religious man, master
of a platform and of an audience, and a man whom
I am glad to have seen and to know. I took him
yesterday to Cambridge and we did the lions there,
including Lowell and Longfellow to whom he had
letters. He draws very prettily and took a sketch of
Longfellow's house. The best thing we saw in the
college was Cook's splendid spectroscope, in which
he showed us the lines across the spectrum of sunlight
by which, you know, they affect to analyse all com-
bustible matter. . . . The visits to Longfellow and
Lowell were very satisfactory. It was very pretty
to see the accustomed and well-trained Longfellow
parry compliments. He told us some curious things
about his translation of Dante, and read the Fran-
cesca passage aloud, in a way that quite reminded
me of college times."

NEW YORK, *Nov.* 19, 1867

"DEAR FAMILY,

"I lost my chance to write last Thursday in dis-
charging or accepting a very pleasant invitation
which has a fair place in family history. For thirty-
odd years the Directors of the Worcester Railroad
have made in the autumn an annual trip of inspec-
tion of the road. And last Thursday was appointed
for the last of these excursions, the road now lapsing
into its new organization. Mr. Twitchell urged me
to be present, offering indeed to fix the day for my
convenience. I could not go at 7–30 in the morning
when the party started, but at 1–15 I and Mr.

Denny and Gov. Claflin took train for Framingham, and met the others at Capt. Clark's tavern there, famous in the early surveys of the road and there we all dined together. It was in unpremeditated but thoroughly good taste, that the dinner was not got by any Smith or such, but was the regular country tavern best repast, served exactly as it might have been the day before the road began to run, with perhaps the exception of four-pronged forks for those of two. The house, indeed, as it happens, is very little altered, and I think the dining-room has not changed since those early days.

"Well, here we ate our roast turkey and cranberries and sweet potatoes, things impossible to you in the first pachalic of Turkey, and here our 'quash pie also, equally impossible to you in the land of pomegranates and here with the indefatigable Twitchell of course we had speeches;—T. calling on me first. I was particularly glad to speak. I could have cried a little were it well, but I did not. But I told my unpremeditated story and made my unpremeditated toast. The toast Father gave at Albany when the Western Railroad was done was "Albany and Boston, the head of the alphabet of American cities." I repeated the *mot*, and gave the new Albany and Boston Railroad, the head of the alphabet of American Railroads. Gov. Washburn, Mr. Denny, Mr. Brigham, Gov. Claflin, Waldo Lincoln, Peter Homer, Nat'l Hammond, and indeed all the rest followed. It was very pleasant indeed to see the thorough frankness and spontaneousness with which they agreed in giving father his due. I was particularly glad I went, only sorry that I had not made Nathan go. It seemed as Emily said, to be doing exactly what Father would have been glad to have me."

The following letter gives an idea of one great family institution, hardly more than mentioned so far. Abel Fullum had been a family retainer for a long time, and was for many years afterward. He was a fine old New England character. At this time he used to come to the house in the morning and black the boots and do odd jobs, and also take the children to school. For this purpose he had sleds made, — the one that I remember was so big that I can hardly think that one man could have managed to pull it. He was for a long time night watchman at Chandler's. The subjects of note-shaving, moving, funerals, and the rest, are of course allusions to his various other interests.

TO ELLEN

"*Jan.* 27, 1868. Arthur wakes us up so early that I am writing to you before it is light. I have lighted the gas today. The babies all three slept well last night and seemed to continue well through the day yesterday.

"I did not come home to tea, but stayed down town to hear Mr. Curtis lecture. A funny thing happened when it was time for the lecture to begin. Mr. Lang stopped playing the great organ, on which he had been imitating a small organ so successfully that you might have thought yourself at any common church service, — Mr. Lang, I say, stopped

playing, and the President of the Association said
that all must wait a little for the lecture, as Mr.
Curtis would not arrive in Boston till seven-thirty,
and then must come from the Eastern Railroad. I
had had no supper, and I stepped out while they
waited and went down to Mrs. Vinton's and got
some. There I met Fullum. When I got back he
had just begun, Mr. Curtis, I mean not Fullum.
Fullum is to deliver a course of Lowell Lectures
when I am Trustee. The first is to be on wheeled
horses, the second and third on sleds to take children
to school, the fourth on shaving notes, the fifth on
grave-stones and epitaphs; the sixth is to be on
night-watching, the seventh on the life of Mr.
Ward, the eighth is to be on Paddies and the management of the Fitchburg Railroad. The ninth and
tenth are on the use of books. The eleventh is on
moving, — with a closing passage on the removal
of the bodies of the dead. The twelfth is a more
general lecture on Mrs. Grundy, or what 'they say'
with some effort at an exposition of who *they* are.
It was a great event for me to go to a lecture. I do
not know when I have done so.

"Good bye darling. Much love from Papa and
Mamma."

TO WILLIAM B. WEEDEN

"*March* 17, 1868. The little fellow[1] died at seven
this morning. The doctors forewarned us of it
when they went last night, but till the last minute
I believed he was steadily gaining, and he was

[1] Charles Alexander Hale, the second son.

spared all pain. A noble boy and a precious memory.
Pray for us and love us,

"Ever yours, EDWARD."

"WATERVILLE, *Aug.* 25, 1868. It has been a day
out of heaven. I was up early, painting away on
morning shadows. The first hour of the day and
the last are most ravishing to the artist mind. After
breakfast I succeeded in getting saddle-horses for
the children to ride; an old mare who has been
sick, with a side-saddle, and a very decent horse
with an army saddle. I took Nelly first. She rides
with courage as she does everything, and will eventually ride well. The old cow led her off into a
neighbor's yard, as we started, but once under
weigh she rode a mile and a half and back with
no other accident than shaking down her bonny
hair, and losing off her net and ribbon. I dismounted
and pocketed these and she came home like another
Berenice.

"Then it was Arthur's turn. There was but one
man's saddle. So I put Arthur on my horse and
myself mounted the side-saddle astride. The beast
was pretty hard, and the thump, thump, thump
without stirrups pretty hard practice for our hottest
day; — but Arthur was in heaven and I well satisfied. We came home and Nelly went off to fish.
Susy was a little upset by something she ate yesterday and I kept her on the bed today. So after the
riding I resorted to her room to paint, when just
as my washings began Mr. and Mrs. Hy. Foote

were announced. I came down and did the hospitable, had Madam put to bed and started Foote and his brother for the Cascades, and returned to my picture. At quarter past one I brought down Susy's portfolios to amuse Mrs. Foote with and took her in to dinner. The rest of our party, save Matty Brooks, were away on various expeditions. Susy did not come down. Nelly was late from fishing: so we mustered in small numbers.

"Edward will be pleased to know that Harry Kidder came home early from fishing reporting a bear! He was well up toward the Swasey place, where a bear and her cub came out within a dozen feet of him on the water side, he in the middle of the brook. He skedaddled and so did she, he says. Did I tell you that a deer was seen yesterday?

"After dinner I lost my nap entertaining Mrs. Foote and her returning husband. But at 4 they left and Matty B. and Kidder and I and the boys went up to Elephant Rock again. I have finished my picture for Scudder there quite successfully. We hated to come home."

TO LUCRETIA

"*Sept.* 3, 1869. We had our overseers meeting yesterday, not of the poor but of the college. It is a very interesting pow-wow. You can hardly imagine another occasion where Chas. F. Adams, Mr. Emerson, Dick Dana, and Dr. Walker, for instance get together in the same room. Stepping down a grade in years and distinction, it is pleasant to meet Parkman, the historian, Harry Lee, Gen.

Lyman, and Sam Eliot together, and wonder what chance made them sit side by side for three hours. It is always an interested as well as an interesting meeting. Our new president does not mean to have the college die of inaction, and will not mind if it gets into hot water. Dick Dana scented from far the danger that the women who pay $150.00 a year to hear philosophical lectures may get some sort of degrees. I am sure they will deserve it if they live through them. Mr. Emerson made a little speech, preeminently practical as he always is. I made one in Eliot's defence, which was handsome in me."

TO MRS. HALE

"GREAT BREWSTER, *Aug.* 16, 1870. So far as we three are concerned we think we have our wooden bowl very thoroughly. The climate is delicious. Our rooms are thoroughly neat, airy and quite large for so few as we are, — we are, of course left entirely to our own company, there being but two other residents on the island, of whom one, Mrs. Hooper spent most of yesterday at Boston, — and the fare good and abundant. As far as this last detail goes, it is the regular old staff provant of the Yankee tavern, a bill of fare which I should be sorry if my children never made acquaintance with. Very good bread and butter, mutton chops, boiled ham, particularly good potatoes, good coffee and respectable tea with oceans of the best milk, and huckleberry cakes are all that have yet made their appearance. I hope we can make Mrs. Hooper vary with fish

of which there are plenty round the island. But
Edward thus far has been the only fisherman. I
have a theory, however, that as her husband has
to spend all his nights in the Bug Light, which is a
red light on screw piles standing out of the water
as some insects appear to run upon it, he will be
able to devote himself profitably to catching fish
for our meals. Of this we shall see.

"I had no adequate conception of the beauty of
the place. Last night Nelly and I went upon the
hill about the house to see the sunset, and it was
as if the glories of Heaven opened before us. The
sun went down in majestic adornments of heavy
and lighter and glorified clouds, and the whole harbour between Boston and us was a blaze of light of
all the Apocalyptic colors. We think that in favorable light we can see the water tower [1] and probably our cupola. If therefore you are lonely you
must go up stairs and wave a handkerchief and we
will do the same to you. Silence as we know is
essential to the purest society, if therefore by the
handkerchief we be conscious of mutual presence,
all will be well. Who wants to be nudging and
squeezing all the time? We have a similar enjoyment of Susy's society if she is at Winthrop, as I
suppose, and Lucretia's if she is at Beverley, we
here, being in the key to the position.

"Mrs. Hooper reports it hot in Boston yesterday,
but I guess she was thrashing round shopping.
Nelly and I sat in the full sun all the afternoon on
the breakwater drawing and did not find it uncom-

[1] The Standpipe was not far from 39 Highland St.

fortable nor is she much burned. Edward is perfectly happy. There is a pond, wholly distinct from
the sea, where he sails his boats, and a nice fourteen
year old boy, the other inhabitant, who assists him
in his fishing. Farewell, Ever yours,

"PAPA."

CHAPTER TWENTY-TWO

"OLD AND NEW"

1869–1870

IN the fall of 1869 there came into definite form a plan which must have been vaguely thought of for years before, — the establishment of a monthly magazine. The publication of a magazine would have been a natural part of the work of the New Civilization which had taken up so much of his thought and energy during these years, and he must often have considered it, though I do not find it definitely mentioned in his letters till about this time.

It had, however, often occurred to him no doubt. His brother Nathan had published the *Boston Miscellany* in the first years after he had left college, and my father had contributed to it. Afterward Charles had published *Today*. These examples were not very encouraging, for neither paper had been a popular success. My father had himself been editor or contributor, at different times, of the *Sunday School Gazette* and of the *Examiner*, but these, he well understood, were minor matters. I suppose he always liked to think of being an editor, of influencing people by the diffusion of the best possible statement of what was being thought and done. He had had plenty of journalistic experience and had seen the conduct of a daily paper at close range. Now and always through life he had a certain feeling of opposition to journalism. When the *Advertiser* finally passed out of the family he wrote to Charles:

TO CHARLES

"*May* 9, 1865. Now the thing is over, [the sale of the *Advertiser*], I am free to say I am glad we are out of journalism. For I can say with great clearness that our father seems to me a most exceptional man, — who showed the crystal clearness of his mind and the virgin purity of his character in nothing so completely as that for fifty years he maintained both in the conduct of a daily paper. I will give you like credit for the ten years of your life, with utter frankness. And then, these exceptions made, I can say that I think the calling weakening and demoralizing in its drift for manifest reasons.

"1. The lawyers complain very bitterly, that they have to get up a subject only to forget it, that their labor is lost, as soon as their triumph or defeat takes place. How much more so the editor. And the lawyer has a competent tribunal. The editor is cursed with a tribunal which he makes himself. They really approve what he says the most when it is most like what he said to them the day before.

"2. Then the immense rapidity of work is in the end very bad. First impressions must be to a certain extent stuck to. At an average notice of twelve hours, you ought to give the opinion which is to be maintained *à l'outrance*, and of course this is bad for the opinion and for you.

"3. Absolute power is always bad for a man.

"4. The immense variety of the subjects involved

in journalism makes a wretched mental and moral dissipation. How few newspaper men can sit through an opera. Far less can they read a volume of De Tocqueville or any treatise on anything. They have to smatter and it is inevitable that their thought should be smattering.

"Father was saved from this by his railroad interest, which Theoph. Parsons and even Chandler would have called the ruin of his life as a journalist, just as you and I were always urging him to go off into side pursuits. . . ."

But as time went on this feeling changed, or rather he felt that it ought not to apply to work on a monthly magazine. He nowhere discusses the matter particularly. It is clear that in some of the directions he had in mind, magazine work was much the same as newspaper work. Rapidity of work and the necessity of writing on such a wide range of subjects would apply less to the magazine than to the newspaper. On the other hand "absolute power" (whatever he meant by it) would seem to belong to the magazine editor as well as to the newspaper editor, as well as the difficulty of having an audience or a tribunal which he makes himself. These last points are less plain than the earlier ones; perhaps they represent thoughts less definitely formulated. We get a glimpse at his ideas in a letter written about the new arrangements for the *Advertiser*.

TO CHARLES

"*Aug.* 16, 1869. There will be no public announcement nor any immediate change in the editing. Indeed he said that they had no change in view. 'What I wish,' said he, 'is that Charles Hale would turn up here with nothing to do. They would like nothing so well as to give him his old place. Your brother knows more of the conduct of a newspaper in his little finger than Waters does in his whole body, and if he chose to be at the head of this thing, he might in five years be the foremost man in this country.' You see Chandler never loses his old enthusiasm for you. And I think the horrors of his connection with W. make the recollection of other days even brighter to him. He did not propose your coming home to it, but put it simply as I do above. I look on it only as one illustration more that when you do come home there are plenty of positions of dignity and usefulness open before you. I do not, for myself, give up my old dislike for the daily press as an occupation for any man. Nay, I begin to believe that a weekly press or a monthly journal is again to be an organ of more power. Let that stand. I observe with great joy that you speak of coming home. And all I mean to say is that in the perfectly new state of all things in this country and the demand for well trained men everywhere, I have no doubt but you will suit yourself in some place; even if you are not sick of political life."

As the year went on his ideas became more definite.

TO CHARLES

"NEW YORK, *Oct.* 6, 1869. I have but a few moments to write, but I want your help in a matter of importance. I am here to confer about the establishment of a monthly journal by the funds of the Unitarian body. It will absorb the *Christian Examiner*, and the little Monthly, but will be very different from both; a *Blackwood* or an *Atlantic*, whose pervading tone will be as pure religion as we know of, instead of toryism as in *Blackwood*, or literature as in the *Atlantic*. It is quite possible that I may be the editor of this journal for a year or two, though the whole is still in embryo.

"If I am, I want as early as it can be well done, an *interesting* article by you on the Suez Canal. I do not care, for this purpose, for nicety of detail. Write as you would do a private letter to me, — telling what you think the popular intelligence of America can best understand. But if you do not want to go into detail, you need not rise from your seat to look at a document in writing. Only write the article. If it is half as edifying as your account of the Ramleh excavations I will be satisfied. Let it be twenty pages of this size, or better sixty, as you like. If I do not use it, I can easily sell it for you to some one who will.

"I rather thirst to call the monthly *Today*. But I conceive that you have the copyright of that name. Should you dislike to have me use it? If you do let me know. Even by telegraph at my expense, before December 1st. I will not air it till then. With luck I shall get your written answer before that time.

"Much love from yours always,
"Edward E. Hale."

TO WILLIAM B. WEEDEN

"Boston, *Nov.* 9, 1869.   My impetuosity is a
good deal cooled by the slow movements of the
A. U. A.   I am at last to meet their committee on
Thursday.   Lowe thinks I shall get a favorable
decision.

"I have [promised] for my first number.
    Story, Roger Williams and the Veils
    Suez Canal with Map, C. Hale
    Story for Children, E. E. H.
    Ecumenical Council, Torricelli
    Story, (I hope), Mrs. Whitney
    Religious Politics of Spain, C. E. Stowe
    Reminiscences of California, H. W. Bellows
    Some European Travel, S. Longfellow
    And for Theology, I am relying on Carroll
    Everett.

"This makes half the number.
"Criticism — very short articles makes a quarter
more.   All which quarter is to be called 'The Examiner.'   Then the Record of the Real Advance —
the 'Log Book' makes a quarter more, — under the
heads: The Universities, The Colleges, The Schools,
The Churches, The Reformers, Physics, Philosophy,
Social Science, and such other things as the best
letters we can get may squeeze into.
"I get Nathan down from Schenectady to work
up this last.   For names — How do you like The
New Crusade, The Better Times, Better Yet,
The New Crusader, The Crusader, The Crusade,

The Advance Guard, Guide Right, The Left Centre, The File Leader, Color Guard?

"And what is a good name for 'The Chronicle of Progress' with which it all closes?

"Could you possibly be in Boston at my office at Church at 11 A.M. Thursday? It would help me very much."

TO WILLIAM B. WEEDEN

"*Nov.* 14, 1869. The A. U. A. decline to be partners. But they are willing to put 8000 dollars into our hands — to be repaid 'from the first profits of the enterprise.' They are very anxious to have their imprint on the journal, which I think cannot be given them.

"Meanwhile — this is strictly confidential — Fields asks me if we would not like to buy the *North American* on favorable terms — and unite that in the team?

"I confess I am strongly tempted by the proposal. It will of course involve some further delay. It will of course tempt me to make our journal less popular. But I do not think I would yield to that temptation.

"I meet tomorrow — Shattuck, Kidder, and Kennard to draw up the terms on which they transfer to us this money. We are to appoint one Trustee, they are to appoint one, — and these a third.

"I had hoped Warren Sawyer would be theirs. But he is not well and hesitates. Arthur Lyman will do, — but not as well. For the third man I am no better off than I was, — Sawyer thinking we needed an older man than your George H. Ellis —

But I think he will grow older, — and if I can get no one else I shall still urge him.

"Houghton has come in while I am writing. He pooh-poohs the *North American* idea. I could not tell him that it had been offered to me.

"If we go on [sale] Jan. 1st as I propose to do, the name must be decided on before Friday. Unless some new name appears it will be: The Round Head, The Old and New, The Two Worlds, The Freeman, The Liberal, The American. Give your vote. The women will probably decide. If you could be with us Wednesday it would be excellent. I shall leave word for you, on the venture at the A. U. A."

TO WILLIAM B. WEEDEN

"*Nov.* 18, 1869. Disgusting that I missed you yesterday. I sat in my office from nine to quarter to four waiting a despatch from Bellows, and a summons to the Committee. At twelve I sent my own messenger to Fox for tidings, and the boy lost the note on the way and came back crying. Started him again, to be told by Fox that he had no message for me. Went myself at quarter to three, to be told you had all been hunting for me all the morning. Got no despatch from Bellows, the wires being down. Tomorrow I meet Shattuck and J. B. Thayer, my own counsel in all my little law matters. I incline to this view. Let them give us $8000 on condition that we supply them 2666 copies of the journal for the first year. In any event we should give away that number of copies and more, in the first six months. The cost for supplying them for the next six is: 6 nos. × 13 cents × 2666 copies; answer in cents (for each number costs to make 13 cents after the type is set). That is to say, we should receive $8000 clear, — at the outset, and have to pay for it $2080.00 before the year was over. I shall therefore make it my first duty to enlarge our issue of stock by the amount of $2000. For this proposal amounts to a free gift by the A. U. A. of $6000 instead of a subscription to our stock of $8000 which was what I proposed.

"I believe Waterston, who has in hand a fund of $10,000 for publication of useful reading, will like to appropriate a part of it for this purpose. So I have been told since this began.

"I must write tomorrow all the prospectuses. And I have not yet the name. I rely on finding a line from you tomorrow, — were it only to abuse me for failing you yesterday. But I do not think it was my fault. . . .

"On the very important question of trustees, — I think the A.U.A. will like to name Arthur Lyman. I shall name Alexander Williams. We can have George Ellis of the *Register* if we like for the third. But, before pressing his name, I shall have one more talk with Williams.

"Nothing has been said about shares of stock. My impression has been all along, that Bellows & Co. will hold $4000

E. E. H.	1000
W. B. W.	1000
W. Sawyer	1000
Adams Ayer	1000

I have thought that Bellows and the rest might prefer money in part, and in that event, if I can get a syllable from him, I shall go to Mrs. Hemenway or perhaps to Waterston as above. Or I should go without hesitation to Kidder. Does this meet your view? I am writing under the supposition that Kidder had, and shewed you, the formal proposal I made to the A. U. A. Always yours,

"EDWARD E. HALE.

"How do you like Both Worlds? The Theological difficulty is the greatest; — the truth being that there is but one world. How do you like Life, or True Life, The True World?"

TO WILLIAM B. WEEDEN

"*Nov.* 25, 1869. We are just pulling through the last miseries of our move from Milton. This house is not yet in order, — but is very convenient and comfortable.

"The A. U. A. under Shattuck's advice, have declined any partnership — any appointing of trustees, — and under my advice have released us from the obligation to give them 2667 copies annually. They lend us 8000 dollars. They take their interest in advertising at the same rates other people pay. This was a master stroke of mine. We are credited at wholesale prices for all we deliver, to pay the people who have paid for their Journal in advance, — and for any other copies they order. The rest we are to pay in sums of $1000 a year, when our circulation comes to average 13000 copies a month for one year. If it does not come to that in three years we

are never to pay. If we get 14000 copies circulation we are to pay $2000 a year. These papers are
in the hands of Thayer, my counsel, and Shattuck,
theirs, to be executed. If you will name any day
when you can come up next week early, I will have
Sawyer and Ayer notified, and we will appoint our
trustees. I want Sawyer, Weeden, and Williams to
be the three men. I have got at the bottom of the
Williams difficulty. He is doing all the work most
skilfully, firmly, and wisely, — and is willing to.

"But he is the agent for Harper's School-books,
— and did not want his name to appear on the
outside of any periodical which they might think
a rival. He has now had a thorough explanation
with them, and will submit to you a proposal, which
will I think satisfy you that we have in him a driving and efficient man. I do not yet know from
Bellows how much of our stock he means or wishes
to take. I expect a definite letter from him tomorrow. I do not want him to have more than
one thousand, — and propose that, — that Allen
shall have one, — Alger one, Mrs. Hemenway one,
unless she prefers to let me have the money as I
think she will, — Ayer one, Sawyer one, you one,
and I one. I also hope and believe that all these
people will permit me to buy in when I wish.

"Here is our first prospectus. I am writing them
all the time. We took your choice for the name.
I am already getting used to it. No one but myself can be made to understand that it is the great
average class of American readers that is to
be reached. Bellows will be aghast when he sees

No. 1. So will you be and every one but Emily, Grace, and E. E. H."

TO CHARLES

"*Dec.* 4, 1869. I am in the thick of the arrangement for the new review. But for the worries of my house, I believe I could have issued the first number Dec. 14, which means Jan. 1st. But I have almost determined not to begin till March 1. You can understand in such a question the pros and cons as well as I. Hurd and Houghton are to be the publishers, the Unitarian Association furnishing half the capital. I hope to give Nathan regular work in its editing. I relieve myself from a good deal of other denominational duty by taking this in hand, which is, I suppose as much in my line, as anything I can put my hand to. I enjoyed very much what I did in editing the *Examiner.*"

TO WILLIAM B. WEEDEN

"39 HIGHLAND STREET, *Dec.* 7, 1869. Many thanks for Pumpelly. Look round at once for something that you will like to do before Dec. 25. I hoped the parcel tonight was another. I will read the sermon before I go to bed. The omens look well. We had yesterday a promise of 1500 copies ordered in Chicago. A. Williams was so much pleased by the outlook that he enlarged his order to the printer from 10,000 copies to 12,000.

"Easy enough to get rid of *them.* The drag will be on No. 2 after my heavy dose of theology in No. 1."

TO WILLIAM B. WEEDEN

"*Dec.* 27, 1869. This is capital. I hope we may have many such stockholders. I hope I can tempt many men to write, — who do not write as a fencing master fences, or an elocutionist speaks.

"Whether you see it in the next number I am not so certain. We give out the last copy on the 1st. I am determined to be a day ahead of everything else. My space then must depend on the length of the articles which I have not yet seen but have promised.

"I was going to write you to ask if Burnside is in Providence, — if he liked Staunton, and if Yes, if he would not write a notice of him for me. If you think the request had better come from me telegraph me.

"I want very much to see you, but am afraid I cannot come up this week. There are so many things to decide. Our sales are still very rapid."

TO CHARLES

"*Jan.* 27, 1870. If you have kept run of me at all, you are more surprised that I am in the body at all, than that you have not heard from me. The launching of the new *Review* was I suppose the greatest enterprise I ever undertook. I should have had it through with proper time, I suppose, without much difficulty, but the trouble was to make a set of slow coaches move, all of whom wanted me to begin, and could not understand I could not begin without committing them. I received power to act in the 15th of November, 1869, at nine o'clock at night; at ten o'clock at night on the 15th of December the proof of number one passed my eye, and in twenty-four hours more 1500 copies were on their way to Chicago. I call that a miracle in literature when you remember that only two articles of the number were in existence the first of those thirty days, and that the rest was created out of the dust of the ground in that time. Meanwhile I had every single detail of the organizing the corporation of the proprietors on my hands. All this I could have done had I not at the same moment been moving into this house and fighting mechanics who would not get done; but we ended with that about New Year's. The first magazine was out Dec. 15 as above.

"I should have begun about Jan. 10 to enjoy some peace when the Lowell Lecture people came to grief. They had arranged for my course to begin March 1, but they had botched their own business and wanted me to begin Jan. 13. This I declined, but I did agree to begin Jan. 21, rather with the feeling that I would get the things out of the way. The magazine involves a good deal of correspondence and the lectures thirty pages a week. This is why I have not written."

TO CHARLES

"*Feb.* 13, 1870. Your astonishing letter of Jan. 8 arrived a few days since after an unusually long passage. I have been trying every day to answer it, but as you will see I have been crowded to the

edge of danger. I never felt anxious about my
ability to pull through my work before. But I
told Emily a month since that if I lived to
Feb. 11th I should have passed through the toughest
crisis of my life. I have lived through it and have
been perfectly well, and I begin to breathe easily.
. . . I have had a wearing correspondence (perfectly
friendly) with —— about an article he wrote for
Old and New. It was ghastly long, to say nothing
of being deadly dull. You have no idea how eager
my best friends are to choke and stifle the Journal
by their stupidities.

"Have you by the way, among your antiques,
any good device of a Phoenix — not the palmtree
but the bird. I want one for the head of my *Old
and New* notepaper. . . . Lesley is one of my very
best contributors, short and with a light pen, and
best of all with some understanding of the American
people."

TO CHARLES

"*April* 15, 1870. To my great annoyance my
last letter to Alexandria missed Wednesday's mail.
I had written it in a world or whirl of interruptions,
carried it to the post myself to make it sooner,
was arrested on the way not by a sheriff but a
woman, shook her off at the earliest as Paul the
viper, though she was not one, and arrived at the
office in time to meet the boy departing with his
New York bag. The letter was to tell what you
now know that Mr. Geo. H. Butler left New York
last Saturday. Before this reaches you you will
have taken his measure.

"If this is forwarded to you, I want you, in taking Florence as I suppose you will, on the way home, to find Dr. B. B. Appleton, my predecessor in keeping the Latin school, No. 12 Via Dei Caldie, 3^{rzo} Piano on the Pitti side of the river, at whose house is his sister in law, Miss Matty Brooks, one of our most intimate friends here. For two or three years she came into the house almost daily, at work with Miss Tallant or to see Emily and the children, and you can get more news from her about our life than from anybody in Europe, perhaps she will have some messages or commissions for friends.

"We are all very well here, though my dinner of today, I am sorry to say does not digest very well. As it is good Friday, perhaps it ought not, though it was the canonical salt fish. We are taking much comfort in Lucretia's visit. By a fatality her last letter to you went by dispatch bag instead of direct mail as I had intended.

"I have just been speeding off my May number, and we begin to talk of June. A monthly magazine makes the year very short. With June you see we have a title page and index already. Before the month is over I hope we shall see you."

TO REV. JAMES MARTINEAU

"What we wish is that you would send us a series of articles, say ten in all, which might illustrate or discuss any great division of religious or psychological science which you might choose. I am well aware of the hourly pressure upon your time. Still it seems to me that you must have in the form of sermons or lectures, manuscripts which you would be willing to use in such a series, and which we should be only too happy to accept. If you will so far recast them that they shall form together one connected whole, we shall be wholly satisfied. Nor should we insist on receiving them once a month. You might send them at your convenience with simply the understanding that they are to follow each other so nearly that the idea of a series should not be broken.

"We would pay for these papers, say one hundred dollars in gold for each, say one thousand dollars in gold for the series. We would protect as far as we can, your copyright here in the collected series, and of course that would be yours in Great Britain and the Colonies.

"We would pay for the papers, one by one, on the arrival of the manuscripts.

"P.S. I see that I have said nothing of the length of the papers I propose. It seems wretchedly carnal to measure them by a tape measure; but types do occupy fixed space even when they deal with the infinite realities. Let me say, then, that an average length of 7500 words each would be about the average of our philosophical papers in *Old and New*."

TO CHARLES

"*June* 12, 1870. We have taken *Old and New* from Hurd and Houghton, and are publishing for ourselves, under Roberts Brothers imprint. I suppose we may count the journal as just established, not firmly but hopefully. To the public we take a very imperious tone, and in New England, our sales are so large that all New England supposes that we have really gained the top of magazinedom. Our sales at the West and on the Pacific also are large, but in the Middle States we cannot keep the hold we thought we had. The magazine would fully pay for itself with a regular sale of 9,000 copies. We have often made that sale, but on weak numbers, I mean numbers which sell badly, we have fallen as low as 7500.

"I have this week ordered a correspondence with Sampson Lowe in London. If any accident throws you into colloquy with him, speak well of *Old and New*, and say we intend for it a wide popular circulation and a religious interest that will conciliate people of generous religious sentiments. His house is rather evangelical I suppose, willing to be broad church. You see I almost take it for granted that you mean to stop a little while in England, and follow your hand there."

TO WILLIAM B. WEEDEN

"*June* 18, 1870. I have been reading 'Lothair' with great enjoyment. We began in the middle, Emily reading it aloud to me, I am now reading from the beginning. I do not wonder that the English press dislikes it. It satirizes everything in England, so that you wonder that Disraeli dares go into a drawing room or any assembly after it is published. Observe that Godkin in the *Nation* follows this lead, — ut semper. Does Disraeli him-

self have any opinions? Or is he a general scoffer?
One does not think so much of a converted Jew.
You will like to see what Bellows says of Dickens.
Surely Disraeli has really the more power of the
two! I wrote to Emerson to do Dickens for us,
because I did not want a clear puff — see — "

TO WILLIAM B. WEEDEN

"*Dec.* 18, 1871. I have the article and have read
it with great satisfaction. I do not think it is the
best thing you have ever written. I think the Leg-
end(?) is. But it is good *criticism* of which I see
very little.

"I do not take quite so much interest in American
poetry, quoad American as you do. I have said
somewhere in *Old and New*, that it must take its
chance with American art, American manners,
American sermons, and American manufactures
generally. If they are good well, if they are not
good ill. As for protecting them because they are
American that is not desirable. A school of American geometry were as desirable as one of American
poetry. I do not think we ought to print Mrs.
Miller's letter or the allusions to it. Whatever
we can from the poems we may and will, — but
journalism must not, I think, inquire into the
individual writer's case and character and antece-
dents. In this case, I am in personal correspondence with Miller. I have printed a Christmas poem
of his in the *Locket*, and I enclose you a copy of
what he says of his wife's card (in a letter to Niles).
Now it seems to me that to review his poem in the

mere light of what we know of his wife-quarrel
would be to do what England did with Byron when
he deserted his wife."

TO WILLIAM B. WEEDEN

"*March* 31, 1872. It is late at night of this
stormy Easter Day. I wonder where you are.
I have had an exciting but fatiguing day. Collyer
helped me at the Sunday School, and this afternoon. Tonight I have been working like a beaver
to get ready for our grand expedition. Kidder,
wife, and niece, with Emily, Nelly, and me, start
tomorrow on a three weeks' lark, — perhaps shall
bring up at Florida. It has been a wretchedly
cold month, — and we are delighted with the prospect of warm weather. It is Nelly's first journey,
— never was in a hotel but once at the White Mountains (brother Greely's whom you remember). And
Emily has never been beyond New York. It is a
nice lark for all of us. To say truth I am tired to
death. See where my staff is.

"1. Williams has resigned

"2. Miss Tallant sick at Nantucket

"3. F. B. Perkins spending the week at New York

"4. W. H. Reed (treasurer and factotum) has
had his house burned down and can only attend to
his own affairs

"5. Even my errand man threw up his hat last
week in mid-career, abandoned his vocation, and
left me to carry my own letters!

"Do you wonder that I quit the wreck myself and
go southward?

"I enclose a copy of Martineau's nice letter. Gordon Street is beyond the British Museum as you go from Charing Cross. I wrote him at once, signifying my delight at his terms, — and all you have to do is to confirm him. *Mem. Very Important.* Ask him point blank, if I offered him ten dollars a page, or one hundred dollars an article? I kept no copy of my letter and I should be sadly mortified to make a mistake.

"I have *not* written specially about articles to Stanley, — rather preferring to leave that to you. You may offer him $10.00 gold a page for anything we may print on even date with what he prints in London. He had better send us MS. copies of his MS. That is vastly better than waiting for proofs. We will pay the additional charge of the amanuensis for copying.

"I had two nice little visits at Providence. I tried to persuade them to call Foote, who is wasted where he is in Boston. But they had not sense to do it. The babies were nicely and the boys in your absence condescended to play with me. Farewell, I am dreadfully sleepy and have to write my introduction to May before I go to bed. Much love to Grace."

TO WILLIAM B. WEEDEN

"*March* 8, 1874. I will own to being a good deal disappointed when 11:30 came Tuesday night and Emily and I could no longer persuade ourselves that Atkinson's eloquence was keeping you at the Club, — and so slowly and sadly turned off the gas

and went to bed. I am to this hour held to such
locomotion as my two-wheel chair gives me, — with
the variety of hopping up to bed at night and hopping down in the morning. I have read half the
Tichborne trial, — which is providentially designed
for such occasions, Coxe's Life of Marlboro, with the
parallels in the Spectator, Macaulay, Lord Stanhope,
Campbell's Chancellors and Thackeray. I have
written the leaders in *Old and New* and have finished
the copy for 'Workingmen's Homes' and on the
whole I have been quite happy. We are now
showering the foot steadily, which is, in my old
experience, the last stage before recovery, and I
hope to hop out before the week is over.

"Before that time is over I will make up and
send to you a parcel of books to notice, mixing
grave and gay, sour and sweet as best I can. In
the copy of my leader for the *Record*, I had named
you as the author of 'Coöperation,' — but I will
change that in the proof as you say so. It always
grieves me, — more perhaps than it does you, —
when you are annoyed about business relations.
To subdue the world — seems to me very great
— partnership with the Lord God, — though one
only make a nasturtium vine grow on a terrace at
Sybaris. But to discuss and debate with another
man how the world shall be subdued, — frets me
to the last degree. That is the reason why I avoid
Boards and Committees as I do, — and dread
partnership as I do. All which I do not and cannot
defend logically.

"To be shut up here reading and writing all the

time, when I am not receiving company, puts me up to lots of plans. I should like to combine with Tom Appleton and Quincy and Perkins, and you, and two or three very young men, say just out of college, — and boldly publish *daily* 'The Spectator' on just the plan of Addison's: — i.e. one essay a day on some matter of real interest at the time, a few advertisements and no news. I think we could make it as good (nay better) as they made theirs. I think it would be good fun, and could be made to go far and wide.

"Then I want to announce my *magnum opus*, 'The History of the Pacific Ocean and its Shores,' three volumes, very entertaining, big type like Prescott, quite a standard, for the next hundred years.

"Failing which I have put to press four Vacation sermons, and as I said 'Workingmen's Homes.'"

CHAPTER TWENTY-THREE

"TEN TIMES ONE IS TEN"

1870

MOST people think of "The Man without a Country" as my father's greatest story. He himself generally felt that "In His Name" was really more fully expressive of what he wanted to say to the world. But "Ten Times One is Ten" is in a way a more characteristic piece of work than either. It presents, in a literary form of course, the great prevailing conception of his life and his life work, and it resulted in the very sort of thing that he had in mind. Men have "builded better than they knew," as he used to say, and so did he. The results of his work were often by no means what he supposed they would be; sometimes they were not so good, and sometimes they were much better. But here the results were almost exactly what he himself planned, although undertaken without his direction and supervision, or indeed without his suggestion except as expressed in the book itself.

He said himself [1] that he had the plan of the story in mind while he was still in Worcester, and that in 1855 he told it to Doctor Francis Wayland, at that time President of Brown University. It is also well known to those interested that the chief

[1] In the preface to the edition of 1883.

figure of the story was suggested by Frederic Greenleaf, one of his earliest and most intimate friends at Worcester. These bare facts are worth noting if only to remind us that we have in "Ten Times One is Ten" no sudden fancy or anything of the sort, but one of the ideas that had long lain in the back or the bottom of his mind. A story which showed how a thousand million individuals could be organized to work together for good in this world, a story told by Frederic Ingham about Harry Wadsworth, a story which had ripened slowly in the years at Worcester and Boston, in the experiences of the War and of the "neighborhood" of the South Congregational Church, could hardly fail to be expressive.[1]

The Lend a Hand movement (which under Doctor Hale's guidance acquired a world-wide influence) began with the story "Ten Times One is Ten," which, as he tells us, was written because he needed a serial for his new magazine *Old and New*. This was in 1870, but the idea of the story had been in his mind for some years, and may be considered the best expression of the principles underlying his religion and life.

It was not so intended, of course, nor was anything farther from the writer's thought than the remarkable results which followed. It was just a story, written out of the fulness of his heart, to be sure, to meet an immediate need and to show how one good life may inspire many others, — $10 \times 1 = 10$, $10 \times 10 = 100$, — and how thus, as the numbers

---

[1] The remainder of this chapter is by the Reverend Christopher R. Eliot.

grew and the multiplying still goes on, the whole world might be converted at last to the religion of Faith, Hope, and Love, which by an inspiration is translated into the mottoes

> "Look up and not down
> Look forward and not back
> Look out and not in
> Lend a hand!"

Briefly told, the story is as follows. Harry Wadsworth is the hero, but it opens on the day of his funeral, when a few of his friends find themselves waiting together at the railroad station for the train, and fall to talking about him. He had done something, it turned out, for each one of them — something that had awakened respect, admiration, gratitude, and love. They tell their stories to one another, Bridget Corcoran, Caroline Leslie, quiet Mrs. Emerson, George Dutton, and the rest — how Harry had been the saving of Bridget's son Will, how he had changed the whole direction of Caroline's life, and how in a California mining camp he had faced an angry, howling mob and saved George Dutton's life. This was the kind of man he was, tender as a woman, brave as a lion, frail in body but so strong in soul. Then, though living in widely separated places, some one suggested that they form a club — there were just ten of them — to carry the influence of that life of sympathy and brotherly love to others, that life so honest, pure, and manly, always expressing itself best in friendly service. But the train arrived before they could settle anything, and they hurried away — ten individuals, men and women, — to their separate homes.

Nevertheless the seed had been sown, the idea had taken root, and "they all loved Harry with their hearts' love"; and so it happened that one of their number, Colonel Ingham, went through the train asking each one of the ten to write to him "if anything turned up which brought Harry to mind or which would have pleased him." And in the course of three years every one had written; the most interesting letters, delightful letters, and one may read some of them in the book itself. Every one of the ten had done something, and such different things, to carry on Harry Wadsworth's work, lending a hand, making people happier, building up a kingdom of love. The first Harry Wadsworth Club had been formed among a lot of workmen in the iron works somewhere down in Maine, transforming a gambling and fighting hell into a decent, happy camp. In fact, every one of that original ten had brought others together, boys and girls, students, newsboys, working men and women, rich and poor, and when the Colonel came to count them up, there were just one hundred and one — "Ten times Ten" and one to spare.

Yes, that's the way it went — the love-spirit, the love-purpose, and the multiplication table, Harry Wadsworth clubs springing up everywhere. One was among the skippers, rough customers, on Pelee Island; and one of the members talking about it said "No, it is not my philosophy, it is

my religion. But I don't like to call it so. Our
notion is that a man had better not talk much
about his religion, certainly had better not think
at all about saving his soul. We think he'd better
do what he can to save other people's souls, or if
he isn't strong that way, save their bodies, or keep
them from the devil some way; and forget he has
any soul himself, if he can't do better."

At the end of six years there were a thousand
people pledged by the mottoes; at the end of nine,
ten thousand; some in one city, some in another, all
over the world. Every three years a new reckoning was made, — a hundred thousand, a million,
a hundred million, — until twenty-seven years had
passed; and then it was a thousand million, which
proved to be the total population of the globe!
That's "Ten Times One is Ten."

Toward the end of the story Doctor Hale gave
the Lend a Hand mottoes. He had uttered them
for the first time that same winter in a lecture on
Hope, one of a course on "The Divine Order of
Human Life" given at the Lowell Institute, but it
may be of interest to note that we find him using
the words "Lend a hand" as early as 1843, in a
sermon from the text "Perfect love casteth out
fear" where, pointing out the mistake of considering as perfect love a man's "throb of good-natured
satisfaction," he refers to a man who refuses to
"Lend a Hand" when he had pretended to give a
heart. From that time on the spirit and the words
appear frequently in his sermons.

It is also interesting to note in this connection

that the Harry Wadsworth of the story was a faithful representation to those who did not know him of a young man whom he knew and loved in his Worcester days, and to whose influence, he would sometimes say, he owed his conversion from what he called "Brattle Street Religion" to that of "Lend a Hand." This was Frederic William Greenleaf, who was born in Williamsburg, Maine, on May 21, 1820, and died in Boston on July 28, 1850. His father was Moses Greenleaf, the geographer of Maine, and a descendant of Reverend Daniel Greenleaf of Braintree, Massachusetts. His uncle was Professor Simon Greenleaf of Harvard University. At the time when Doctor Hale first knew him he was at the head of the freight office of the Boston and Worcester Railroad. Later he held important positions in the service of other lines. He was married and left one son, Edward Hale Greenleaf. Among Doctor Hale's papers are a number of letters received from Mr. Greenleaf during his later years, all bearing testimony to the closeness and warmth of his friendship, to his sweetness and nobility of character, and to his intense interest in the progress of a liberal religion. Doctor Hale wrote to him as follows:

"And so good night now! When it gets warm and pleasant, pray take a walk to Wigwam Hill, and write me that you have done so. I shall imagine you looking toward the West with your eyes and the South with your heart." [1]

Such was the man, Frederic Greenleaf, whom

---

[1] Some of the letters to Mr. Greenleaf will be found I, pp. 213–224.

Doctor Hale cherished in his heart and made the hero of his "Ten Times One" story. Of him he has written as follows:

"Careless people speak as if such a life were cut off untimely, and as if its work were ended. Because I loved him, I could not but see that his power over those who loved him did not die. In different places, from different people, I heard him spoken of almost as a present friend might be spoken of; and what he said or what he advised was still held as a central and important direction. Now it was a doctor of divinity; now it was the laborer in an iron-mine; now it was the mayor of a city explaining to me his administration; now it was a sensitive friend whom Frederic Greenleaf had saved from agonies of morbid introspection, — who cited to me this young master of a freight-house, no longer living in this mortal life, as one of the authorities to be most respected. His body was buried; but in parts of the land, widely parted from each other, he was still a guide, and a helpful guide, in men's and women's lives."

Even before the story of "Ten Times One" was completed, the leaven had begun to work, and what was pure fiction soon became a living reality. The first Lend a Hand club was organized in New York by Miss Ella E. Russell among some street boys to whom she was reading the story. Letters began to come from people in different parts of the world wishing to be counted as Lend a Hand or Harry Wadsworth members, or to organize clubs. With unforeseen power the story seized upon the imagination of thousands and awakened their desire to be of service.

"In the beginning of 1871," writes Doctor Hale, "I had a list of fifty persons, in different parts of the world, who called themselves, more or less definitely, 'Harry Wadsworth people.'" As the years passed, the correspondence grew and a good many clubs were formed. Doctor Hale always said "the less fuss and feathers the better," and he insisted that the idea of a Wadsworth Club was "that is should be made of unselfish people, who met, not for 'mutual improvement,' but with some definite plans for other people." Every club was to be an institution for the education of young people in public spirit, the spirit of the three mottoes "which are the translation into modern life of the three words, faith, hope and love, representing the three eternities."

Fifty years ago this was, comparatively speaking, a new point of view. The ideal of life as *service*, though everywhere recognized, was not so generally emphasized as to-day, and there were comparatively few organizations of young people for that end. The hope of personal salvation, at best the idea of mutual improvement, prevailed. "To read one's title clear to mansions in the skies", to make earth a stepping stone to heaven, to save one's own soul, whatever might become of others, these were too common motives among young and old. Doctor Hale's appeal to unselfishness, to those generous and chivalric motives which make the hero, the patriot, the citizen, and better yet the loving friend and helper of mankind, was a timely one and greatly needed. That the world was ready for it was proved by the response. "Ten Times One" was only one of Doctor Hale's appeals in story form. It was followed by the "Harry Wadsworth Papers," "In His Name," and many others. His lectures and his life were but variations on the same great theme. To get people together, to inspire them with the Lend a Hand spirit, was his unfailing purpose. And so the movement gained momentum, until under different names, and often without each other's knowledge, thousands of people were enlisted in it. Without claiming too much, it is fair to say that Doctor Hale's story and mottoes were the inspiration not only of the Lend a Hand clubs, the Ten Times One clubs, and others closely associated with them, but also of those larger societies, the King's Daughters, the Look-Up Legions, the I. H. N. Clubs, the Order of Send Me, the Commerical Temperance League, and many more. The world was ready for such a Christianizing movement; and when we look at it broadly to-day, we rejoice to find that while the Lend a Hand name and mottoes may not be used always, every church has its Christian Endeavor Society, its Epworth League, its Young People's Religious Union, its Girls' Friendly, or some other union bringing its young people *together* for the purpose of serving the Kingdom of the King. "Ten Times One is Ten" was written, as men would say to-day, at the psychological moment: men would have called it then a *providential* book. At all events it was one of the many forces which helped wonderfully in the "Good-Will and Get-Together" movement of mankind, which is expressing itself in some new effort daily, organizing important societies, organizations of labor, looking forward to a Coöperative Commonwealth and the Federation of the World.

In 1874 Miss Mary A. Lathbury, having seen the four mottoes on the frieze of a parlor in Orange, New Jersey, proposed the Look-Up Legion, which soon extended with a charming enthusiasm through five hundred or more Methodist Sunday Schools, reaching a membership of more than six thousand children and young people. Doctor Hale, writing in 1880, says that he had never heard of it until that year, but then attended the first general meeting of the clubs at Chautauqua Lake, when the "Ten Times One" story was told again, reports given from clubs far and near, and greetings extended to all by Doctor Hale and to him in return. The Legion had its own badge, the Maltese Cross with the four mottoes on the four arms, and its own songs. It was pledged to temperance and kindness.

Another movement, the King's Daughters, was initiated in 1886 by Mrs. Margaret Bottome, increasing rapidly, until in 1890 it numbered one hundred thousand members. It was never closely associated with the Lend a Hand clubs, early becoming a religious order, but it was based on the four mottoes, with the addition of "In His Name." Doctor Hale was elected an Honorary Member of the Massachusetts Branch of the King's Daughters on April 8, 1892. It is also on record that Doctor Hale drew up the constitution for the King's Daughters.

The literature of the Lend a Hand movement includes the magazine *Old and New*, 1870–1875; circulars of "Ten Times One is Ten," 1882, 1883; *Lend a Hand, A Record of Progress*, 1886–1896; *Lend a Hand Record*, 1897–

Into *Old and New* Doctor Hale poured the wealth of his world-wide sympathy, splendid optimism, and eager desire for the coming kingdom. "The world advances and the good time is nearer." It was to be a record of progress; it stood for freedom, intellectual, civil and religious, "cherishing the memories of the past, to obtain from them a better and happier future, that we may squeeze from the Old its lessons for the New." Besides the story "Ten Times One is Ten," it contained many an article from the pen of its editor filled with the Lend a Hand spirit.

Lend a Hand was a "Record of Progress and a Journal of Organized Charity." It published articles by the leading specialists in charities and social reform, editorials and stories by Doctor Hale, and it has a special department for Lend a Hand clubs, including the Look-Up Legion and others. Into this department the enthusiasm of Doctor Hale and other Lend a Hand leaders was freely poured, and no one can read the record without realizing that this movement must have accomplished great good in itself and even more in awakening the spirit which is embodied in the social conscience and activity of to-day. When *Lend a Hand* was discontinued, it was merged in *Charities*, a new publication in New York, now the *Survey*, and the Lend a Hand interests were continued in the *Lend a Hand Record* issued by the Lend a Hand Society, Boston.

Of all these publications Doctor Hale was the moving spirit. His was the vision, his the inspiring faith. As he dreamed of a National American Church which should stand for "the free thoughts and the free life of a new world — not a new religion but an old and eternal religion newly interpreted and better understood, a faith for the first time married to freedom" — so to all these publications he gave the impulse of a great soul alive to the least as to the greatest of life's problems. He was the living Harry Wadsworth, never ceasing to look up, forward, and out, and ever ready to lend a hand.

To the list of Lend a Hand literature ought to be added "Mrs. Merriam's Scholars," which Doctor Hale wrote as a sequel to "Ten Times One"; "Four and Five," a story for boys; "Neither Scrip nor Money," and stories of hospital life in "Stand and Wait."

The Lend a Hand Society was organized informally as early as 1886, and it was incorporated in 1891. The purpose was to hold the clubs together, at the same time leaving them absolutely independent, and to encourage the formation of new clubs: also to undertake such Lend a Hand work as might be possible from a central office by coöperation.

As already pointed out large numbers of clubs, having received their original inspiration from the "Ten Times One" movements, had soon developed independent organizations. The Look-up Legion eventually became the Epworth League; the King's Daughters was more closely associated with denominational interests; the Christian Endeavor movement and the Girl's Friendly arose and enlisted the enthusiasm of the churches, taking the place once occupied by such groups of clubs as the Commercial Temperance League, the Order of Send Me, the I. H. N. Clubs and others.

But for years the Lend a Hand Society continued to be the rallying center, with Doctor Hale as its President and the *Lend a Hand* Magazine its official organ. Even after the number of clubs directly affiliated with it became smaller, as was inevitable, its work continued with enthusiasm. Doctor Hale remained its President and was its presiding genius to the end of his life. Since his death in 1909 a fund of over fifty thousand dollars has been completed to place the society on a permanent basis, as a memorial to its founder and to continue the work he so loved.

It would be impossible to give even a slight idea of the work accomplished by the clubs individually or collectively. Apart from the educational value of the clubs to their members, along lines of character and good citizenship, their work has been composed of an endless variety and succession of small services rendered to individuals or communities. In these Doctor Hale delighted. "The

Club reports do me more good than anything with which I have to do," he once said, and no one who ever saw him presiding at a meeting of the clubs could doubt the pleasure he took in hearing the simple story of "little deeds of kindness" told by the boys and girls. "Small service is true service while it lasts" he believed for others as for himself. One year fifty-two clubs sent him fifty-two stories of the Harry Wadsworth kind as a New Year's calendar. The ideal was that of the Master — "Whosoever shall give to drink unto one of these little ones a cup of cold water only" and "I have come that ye might have life." Next to the mottoes, the best expression of the purpose and work of the clubs, as in practice realized, is in Doctor Hale's sonnet "Send Me" —

"Be mine some simple service here below, —
To weep with those who weep, their joys to share,
Their pain to solace or their burdens bear;
Some widow in her agony to meet,
Some exile in his new found home to greet;
To serve some child of Thine, and so serve Thee,
Lo, here am I; to such a work send me."

CHAPTER TWENTY-FOUR

39 HIGHLAND STREET

1870–1876

IN the fall of 1869 my father moved into the house at 39 Highland Street which was his home till his death. For almost forty years he lived here, and he is, naturally enough, best remembered, as he was in those years that he lived here. It is not that in these years he did the best work of his life, — if we could estimate values, a good deal that he had already done might turn out to be better than anything he was yet to do. It is not that he had made his beginnings and his preparations, and now did the typical work which was to be remembered, — he was constantly working and growing and doing new things. It is not exactly that he had now the character which remains in mind when people think of him, for he changed much in those years, as he had in the years before. But the long period of years that he lived there is certainly more coherent and consistent and all of a piece than the years before. He had been a student at college and in the world, a young minister in a characteristic New England town, the minister of an active church in a growing and changing city, a leader in the resettling and reorganizing of a vigorous religious body: he was now

39 Highland Street, Roxbury

a well-recognized man, almost a public man, as one might say, who stood definitely in the public mind for an ideal in public life and public service, and who was known in a general way to many who had very little idea of the particular activities which took up his time.

However all this may be, the years of his life in 39 Highland Street are the years best remembered by his children and those who knew him personally. His youngest son, Robert Beverley Hale, was born in September 1869, while the family was still in Milton. In the Highland Street house his family grew together and grew up. This was for those years the family center, and he was the moving spirit of it. The "family" of the older generation had passed away. His father and mother were dead. Of the brother and sisters of earlier days, Jane, Sarah, and Alexander were dead; and Nathan died in 1871. Of the others, Charles was still in Egypt; Susan and Lucretia on their return from Europe had taken to apartments of their own. Here, then, was the family home where the aunts and uncles came for Thanksgiving and Christmas, from which people went for a longer and a shorter time, and to which they returned.

Roxbury, in those days, had just been joined to Boston, but it was still a pleasant countrified town, with plenty of large places in which stood handsome old houses. In one of these places stood the house that he had bought, a large square house in the midst of a good piece of ground. Unfortunately, perhaps, he had been unable to buy the whole estate, and in the course of a few years the house began to be hemmed in to narrower confines by the brick blocks which have since multiplied in the neighborhood. In the first years, however, there was little of this, and he had the freedom of the whole place; the house stood among its elms and apple trees very much as though it were really out in the country. It was but a few minutes' walk from Eliot Square, with Doctor Putnam's church on one side and the Parting Stone on the other. It was a mile and a half away from the church on Union Park Street, but the horse cars ran almost from the house to the church, and although they would not seem very fast nowadays, especially in winter, yet they served the purpose of rapid transport in those less demanding times. It was about three miles from the State House, so that one could get into town by the then Boston and Providence Railroad without much more loss of time. In the other directions the town stretched out toward Jamaica Plain and Dorchester. Perhaps my father, in thinking of the place, fancied that in these directions would be easy access to the sea at Savin Hill and to the open country. If so he imagined more than he carried out; he thought doubtless of the place as a country place, but more and more it became surrounded by the city, both close at hand and farther off, and as I remember him in those earlier years, his face and his thought were generally turned city-ward, and the house was really a breathing place in the midst of city work. For that purpose it was admirable; it had senting the Governor of the Commonwealth, Curtis Guild, he "paused to explain that in this designation of the State officially as 'Commonwealth,' Massachusetts had embodied in language the idea that every man and woman lives here for the common welfare." "The first time when words were so combined in the English language", he went on, "was when our own first governor, Governor Winthrop, wrote them in a pamphlet indited by him just before leaving this country for England." [1]

March 4, 1909. (This is one of the last entries in his own handwriting.) "The Inauguration. We waked to a heavy snow-storm — snow still falling. The streets were blocked as at any time this winter. The Senate had 'taken a recess' until 9:30. At 9:10 Dudley,[2] Nelly, and I went down. But my own service, the first act of the new V. P. did not come until 12:10. Then the whole 'chamber' was crowded and Mr. Sherman had been sworn. It had been agreed by that time that there should be no service outside but that all should be done in our halls.

"I had not known Mr. Sherman before.

"Mr. Fairbank's farewell was very cordially received and Mr. Sherman's inaugural. Then the C. J. administered the oath to Mr. Taft and he delivered his Inaugural. He said bravely that he was to continue the Roosevelt policies, and described them.

"I waited till the Senate adjourned and spoke to

[1] Historically not entirely correct.
[2] His grandson, the son of Herbert Dudley Hale.

Teller. We had to wait some time for the herdic, but were safely here before 4 P.M."

In the diary at this point is tucked a sheet of note paper with a few words of prayer written thereon, — not the whole, for it evidently lacks a little at the beginning. "Our Governors are from ourselves and our Rulers from the midst of us. Thy servants whom this people has appointed to execute their Laws need and ask thine Almighty help and blessing, as they oversee this People, as they care for the common life and welfare of the Land. We pray for them, for the People, that they may be that happy nation whose God is the Lord: — that every man may bear his brother's burdens and that every man may follow in our Master's footsteps."

On April 22, — he was a few days more than eighty-seven years old, — he left Washington for Boston. He wrote in his journal, "They are at work in the upper Chancelleries with the gold pens and gold ink on the record of the fourteen hours which followed. So I need not try what the newspapers would call my sketch of it. Suffice it to join the Pippa party and say, 'All's right with the world.'"

"*April* 23rd. — In a document as uneventful as this, Friday stands out as a *dies mirabilis*. Severely condensed is the record that I waked up somewhere and on schedule time that we pulled up at the South Station at 8: 13. Here was Phil with a wheel chair for me, and I took 37 inches from my car to his. So I was luxuriously carried to dear Cook's carriage, and Edward Hale Cook's driver ready for me, to bring me to the same old 39 Highland St. to which I brought Emily and the Baby Bob in the autumn of 1870. In the old class days we used to write quips on the number 39, and there were once people who knew their 39 Articles, not now. Here the day has passed cheerily and happily. [Dr] Temple was in to say that in the one billion, six hundred million people on the planet there was no one else in as good health as I am."

He passed the time quietly at the old house, — or "the old stand" he sometimes called it. The house has a large piazza to the south on which he liked to sit, and he could often walk about the grounds. In a day or two he was strong enough to take a drive, sometimes with Miss Freeman or some other friend. The day book he says is rather uneventful, yet he always dictated to Miss Abby or occasionally to Ellen, a running comment on the slight events. He constantly thought he might be able to preach but was not able to do so. He saw a few people, but he did no real business.

When Anniversary Week came around, he was able to be present at several meetings, — the annual Lend a Hand meetings, where he opened the meeting, the Convention of Congregational Ministers, where he made an opening prayer, the opening meeting of the A. U. A., — "rather a matter of sentiment with me. I believe the association and I were born in the same year, 1822, and since 1842 I have probably been at every annual meeting when I was in Boston." He had a desire to preach on Whitsunday and had hoped that he might be thought well enough to do so. Whitsunday was June 6th. He writes: "I did not leave the Island all day. Dr. Temple had forbidden my preaching to-day. The theory was that I should do too much talking if I went to Church. So it ended in my not leaving the house and my old mot of years by-gone that the miracle of Pentecost is not that they could speak in tongues but that they wanted to is fully applicable. The first White Sunday in the 65 years without a Whitsunday sermon." The entry on June 8 is as follows:

"They are curiously like each other, these days, and I do not even go around the Island. But we sometimes have a visit from the Doctor, and sometimes we do not. To-day was varied by a call from Mary Antin who has been in Boston for a fortnight. It was a lovely day and I spent all the time on the deck, from half past ten till five. Had a very good night."

On June 10 he died.

INDEX

INDEX

[For Dr. Hale's works see Hale, Edward Everett, Writings.]

Hale, Charles Alexander, and Arthur, ii. 85; death, ii. 91.

Hale, Edward Everett,

EVENTS IN HIS LIFE (for books, see under WRITINGS):

Birth, i. 5; childhood, i. 6–13; goes to Miss Whitney's school, i. 6; to Mr. Dowes' School, i. 6; to Boston Latin School, i. 6; first newspaper article, i. 196; goes to Harvard College, i. 18; graduates in class of '39, i. 51; reports legislative proceedings, i. 47, 59, 197; ii. 361; teaches in Boston Latin School, i. 56, 58, 63–65; 81, 127; studies divinity, i. 52, 132; first book, i. 68; articles for *Boston Miscellany*, i. 199–200, 205–209; articles for *North American Review*, i. 204; sermon at Mr. Barnard's Chapel, i. 153; ascends Mt. Washington, i. 89–102; ii. 72; admitted to preach, i. 155; preaches at Newark, i. 134; in New York, i. 134; at Berlin, Mass., i. 134, 159; at Sudbury, Mass., i. 134; for three months at Northampton, i. 136; visits Howe's Cave, i. 102–109; ii. 72; Trenton Falls, i. 109–113; ii. 72; preaches in Washington for a winter, i. 142; plans emigration to Texas, i. 245; preaches at Worcester, i. 147; ascends Mt. Katahdin, i. 114–120; ii. 72; ordination at Worcester, i. 164; plans trip to Palestine, i. 217–225; member American Antiquarian Society, ii. 3; called to First Church, Boston, i. 234–236; called to Brooklyn, i. 237; marriage, i. 237; interest in C. L. Brace, ii. 29; work with Emigrant Aid

Co., i. 249–265; interest in F. D. Maurice, ii. 30, 43, 44; called to South Congregational Church, Boston, i. 269–277; installed as minister South Congregational Church, i. 278; President of Christian Unity, i. 290; charitable work of South Congregational Church, ii. 32–36; first trip to Europe, i. 293–318; joins drill club, i. 323; dedication of Church in Union Park Street, i. 340; work in Civil War: Freedman's Aid Society, Emigrant Aid Co., Refugees Aid Society, Sanitary Commission, Soldiers' Memorial Society, American Unitarian Association, i. 363, 388; ii. 4; visit to front, i. 368–378; first National Convention of Unitarian Churches, ii. 6, 12, 13–16; work as trustee of Antioch College, ii. 8, 16–18; work for Richmond Schools, ii. 8, 21–23; work for Wilmington Schools, ii. 8; work for Hampton Institute, ii. 11; second National Convention, ii. 18, 19–21; trip to Washington, ii. 79–85; offers prayer in Senate, ii. 80; formation of Suffolk Conference, ii. 35, 36; Overseer of Harvard College, ii. 3, 87, 93, 94; writing for *Atlantic Monthly*, ii. 48; settles at 39 Highland Street, ii. 77, 134; establishment of *Old and New*, ii. 97–110; Lowell Lectures on Divine Order of Human Society, ii. 110; writes "Ten Times One is Ten", ii. 120–133; trip to Chicago, ii. 142; house at Matunuck planned, ii. 174; trip abroad with H. P. Kidder, ii. 152–169; first moving to Matunuck, ii. 176–179; first stories in *Harper's*

Rock, interest in, i. 32, 33, 45, 59–63, 360; early journals, i. 12; early life at home, i. 8; early newspapers, i. 13; early poem, i. 13–15; early excursions, i. 80, 87, 88; education of boys, on, ii. 150; Examiner Club, i. 366; ii. 3; family, devotion to his, ii. 76, 78; fiction, reading of, ii. 75; first mention of, i. 1; flowers, fondness for, ii. 72; football, plays, i. 43; Franklin MSS., testimony, ii. 259–261; friends Freshmen year, i. 17; genealogy, interest in, i. 4; garden at college, i. 40; German, study of, i. 21, 26, 31; habits of work, in the seventies, ii. 140–142; at Hampton, ii. 402, 403; at Harvard Class races, ii. 326, 327; Highland Street, house at Number 39, ii. 134; Highland Street, life at 39, ii. 134–142; history, interest in, ii. 74; House of Commons, visits to, ii. 160–163; 289–290; I. O. H., i. 21, 22, 23, 24; Hungary, visit to, ii. 166; Intervale, summer days at, ii. 393, 405; journalism, his view of, ii. 98; Lake Mohonk, conferences at, ii. 383–385, 390; Lend a Hand work, feeling for, ii. 326; Louvre, visit to, ii. 163–164; Martineau's, tea with, ii. 157; Massachusetts Historical Society, ii. 3; Matunuck, last letters from, ii. 404; life at, ii. 185–192; plan for life at, ii. 286–287; method in church work, ii. 205–207; at New Orleans, ii. 225–227; Newman Hall, calls on, ii. 87–88; organization, feeling for, ii. 9, 204; out-door life, feeling for, ii. 170, 215; oxygen, making, i. 46; Palos, visit to, ii. 298–300;

pastoral duties, ii. 2, 3; Permanent Tribunal, early forensic on, ii. 376–378; Permanent Tribunal, first sermon on, ii. 381; preaching in the seventies, ii. 212; Prescott, position with Mr., i. 53; *Reading mentioned:* Abauzit, i. 67; Alcestis, i. 72; "l'Allemagne", i. 64, 72; "Attila", i. 30; Bettina, Letters of, i. 143; Blackburne, i. 67; Blackstone, i. 70; *Blackwood*, i. 69; "Childe Harold", i. 50; "Chronicles of the Canongate", i. 48; Charlemagne, Old French lives of, ii. 189; "Vision of Don Roderick", i. 33; "Good Men of Clapham, The", i. 145; "Columbus", Rogers's, i. 70; "Excursion", Wordsworth's, i. 47; "Far from the Madding Crowd", ii. 281; "Flirt, The", i. 129; "Forest Life", i. 82; "French Revolution", i. 122; "Friedric", ii. 86; Grahame's "History of the U. S.", i. 39; "Hand of Ethelberta, The", ii. 282; Horace, i. 64; "Hyperion", i. 84; "Jane Eyre", i. 181, 182; Fanny Kemble's "Journal", i. 142, 143; Lockhart's "Scott", i. 30, 31; "Lothair", ii. 114; Mackintosh's life of his Father, i. 129; F. D. Maurice, ii. 43; "Nature", Emerson's, i. 122; Ossian, i. 33; "Pair of Blue Eyes, A", ii. 281; "Philo", i. 213, 216; "Rokeby", i. 33; Ruarus, i. 132; Sparks's Collections, i. 67; Sparks's Washington, i. 70; ritual, view of, ii. 216, 217; Roosevelt, inauguration of, ii. 401; Royal Academy, visit to, ii. 290, 291; Salon, visits to, ii. 293–296, 308; at San Antonio,

Percival", i. 210, 211; paper
cutters from, ii. 366; at Port-
land, i. 83; return from Europe,
ii. 135; mentioned, i. 5, 66,
91, 150, 233; ii. 112.

Hale, (Captain) Nathan, i. 3.

Hale, Nathan; death of Alexander, i. 230, 231; buys the
Advertiser, i. 194; church
relation, i. 9; death, ii. 76;
desires him to be a minister,
i. 125; early life, i. 1; editor
of *Advertiser*, i. 12; editor
of *Weekly Messenger*, i. 194;
exempt from General Muster,
i. 11; at exhibition, i. 25; at
installation, i. 279; as a journalist, ii. 98; letters to, i. 10, 236,
247, 250, 252, 307; marries,
i. 3; in Maryland, i. 191;
paralytic stroke, i. 254; in
Pennsylvania, i. 140, 141; his
politics, i. 243, 246; in the
Prescott matter, i. 53, 54, 59;
President Boston and Worcester R. R., i. 87; his printing office, i. 195; reads Horace,
i. 64; sends son to college at
early age, i. 16; settles in
Boston, i. 2; suggests first
newspaper article, i. 196; views
on education, i. 8; mentioned,
i. 244; ii. 135.

Hale, Mrs. Nathan, advice, i.
334; at exhibition, i. 25; her
death, ii. 23, 76; her German,
i. 195; her laurestinus plant,
ii. 345; her literary disposition, i. 66; letter from, i. 293;
letters to, i. 72, 77, 90, 129, 181,
273, 278, 357, 365, 367, 368;
ii. 48; marriage, i. 3; her publications with Carter, i. 68; one
of her rules, ii. 220; her spare
chamber, i. 125; visit to

Worcester, i. 191; other mention, i. 80, 337.

Hale, Nathan, Jr., and *Boston
Miscellany*, i. 205; ii. 97; at
college, i. 16; death, ii. 76;
experiments in sound, i. 22;
law office, ii. 330; letters to,
i. 72, 77, 129, 183, 237, 250,
255, 278; ii. 30; painting,
ii. 74; and *Old and New*, ii.
102, 108; social reputation,
i. 240; reads Ossian, i. 33;
at Worcester, i. 238; work at
night, ii. 140; otherwise mentioned, i. 5, 17, 51, 66, 74, 82,
84, 125, 132, 191, 192, 264; ii. 90.

Hale, Philip L., letters to, i. 4;
ii. 155, 292, 297, 316; at
Matunuck, ii. 177, 178, 183,
187, 191; at Niagara, ii.
393; and Robert, ii. 362;
mentioned, ii. 152, 321, 408.

Hale, Richard, i. 3, 5.

Hale, Robert, i. 2, 5.

Hale, Robert Beverley, born in
Milton, ii. 135; brought to
39 Highland Street, ii. 409; at
Class races, ii. 326; his character, ii. 362; and "In His
Name", ii. 241; at Matunuck,
ii. 182, 184, 187, 188, 193.

Hale, Rose Perkins, at Matunuck,
ii. 405.

Hale, Sarah, and Bunker Hill, i.
81; death of, i. 233; and death
of Alexander, i. 231; at exhibition, i. 25; illness, i. 191; at
Dr. Palfrey's, i. 54; mentioned, i. 5, 58, 66, 74, 78, 82;
ii. 135.

Hale, Susan, in England, ii. 154,
157; her painting, i. 238; ii.
74; return from Europe, ii. 135;
in Spain, ii. 288, 300, 301,
303; at Waterville, ii. 93; at

Homer, Peter, ii. 89.
Homes in cities, ii. 37.
Hooper, Mrs., at the Great Brewster, ii. 94, 95.
Horace, reading, i. 64.
House of Commons, visits to, ii. 160–163, 290, 291.
"How the Other Half Lives", ii. 28.
Howard, Frederick, i. 25, 27.
Howard Benevolent Society, discourse before, i. 292.
Howe, Julia Ward, ii. 314.
Howe, Mr., i. 103, 105.
Howells, his realism, ii. 60; talk with, ii. 327, 328.
Howitt, William, i. 190.
Hughes, Thomas, i. 314; ii. 30.
Hull House, ii. 28.
Humboldt College, ii. 8.
Hungary, visit to, ii. 166.
Hunt, Leigh, i. 153, 154, 201, 210.
Hunt, W. M., pictures in Albany, ii. 328.
Huntington, F. D., Bishop of Central New York, ii. 39; called to Harvard, i. 283; ministry of, i. 282; resignation of professorship, i. 319, 322, 323; second minister of South Congregational Church, i. 278; writes of the First Church, i. 235; writes of the South Congregational Church, i. 284.
Hurd and Houghton, ii. 108, 113.
Hurlbut, Dr., ii. 324.
Huse, Eliza, i. 4.
Huth, Mlle. E., ii. 336.
"Hyperion", i. 84.

I. H. N. Clubs, ii. 128.
Ingham, Frederic, author of "The Man without a Country", i. 358; tells of the Boothby's, ii. 63; plans the "Brick Moon", ii. 61; his experiences, i. 352; ii. 59; writes of Harry Wadsworth, i. 212; the "Ingham Papers", ii. 57; at Naguadavick, i. 347–350; interest in "Sybaris", ii. 50, 53; and "Ten Times One", ii. 123; and his wife Mary, ii. 244.
Ingham Peak, ii. 173, 175.
Intervale, N. H., ii. 356, 393, 405.
I. O. H., i. 20, 21, 22, 23, 24; poem for, i. 198.
Irving's "Capt. Bonneville", i. 258.
Isocrates, i. 183.
Israel's River, i. 89, 90, 92, 93.
Italian, study of, i. 34.

"Jack and the Bean Stalk", i. 13.
Jackins, guide on Mt. Katahdin, i. 115–120.
Jackson, Andrew, i. 32, 339.
Jackson, Dr., i. 91, 92, 113.
Jackson, Susan, i. 75.
James III, at St. Germains, ii. 310.
James, Henry, his realism, ii. 60.
James, Rev. Mr., ii, 184, 190.
Jameson, Mrs., i. 32, 136.
"Jane Eyre", reading of, i. 181, 182.
"Jasher", ordination charge to, i. 177.
Jefferson, Mt., ii. 72, 89.
Jefferson, Thomas, ii. 257.
Jerusalem Chamber, ii. 167.
Jesus, a man of practical experience, ii. 328; other mention, i. 162; ii. 15.
Jewett, S. O., ii. 406.
John, St., i. 158, 159, 183.
Johnson, Andrew, ii. 79, 80, 83, 84.
Jokai's Hungarian Stories, ii. 190.

Lesley, J. P., ii. 111.

Leslie, Caroline, in "Ten Times One", ii. 122.

Leverett, F. P., i. 10; ——'s Lexicon, i. 200.

Lewis and Clarke, i. 258.

Lewis, Dio, ii. 264.

Lexington, Centennial at, ii. 275–276.

Ley, Lady Margaret, Milton's sonnet to, i. 183.

Liberal Christianity, ii. 50.

Liberal Church in America, ii. 5, 12.

Liberty Tree in the yard at Harvard, ii. 78.

Lincoln, Abraham, assassination of, i. 382; calls out by draft, i. 330; epigram of, i. 380; letter to Fremont, i. 337; loyalty to, ii. 329.

Lincoln, E. W., i. 51.

Lincoln, Waldo, ii. 89.

Lind, Jenny, ii. 53.

Lintot, Fanny, ii. 227.

Literature, view of, ii. 354.

Little Gau, ii. 246, 247.

Little Pond, ii. 174.

Livermore, Isaac, i. 252.

Liverpool, museum at, ii, 155.

Livingstone, Edward, ii. 24.

Loan, pushing the, i. 334, 335.

Lodge, Senator H. C., ii. 394.

Logan, Mr., ii. 384.

Longfellow, Henry Wadsworth, call on, ii. 86; class in German, i. 21; death, ii. 315; first recitation with, i. 23; lecture on Dante, i. 34; lectures on "Faust", i. 26, 27, 31; "Hyperion", i. 84; "The Launching of the Ship", i. 214; in "The Modern Psyche", ii. 249; his professorship at Harvard, i. 21; resemblance to the Grand

Duke of Tuscany, i. 308; mentioned, i. 19, 22.

Longfellow, Samuel, article for *Old and New*, ii. 102; college comradeship with, i. 17, 18, 20, 21, 24, 25, 38; hymn for ordination, i. 165.

Long's Report, i. 258.

"Looking Backward", ii. 355.

Look-Up Legions, ii. 128–130; ii. 325.

Loring, Col. Wm., i. 329.

Loring, Judge, i. 261.

Los Angeles, ii. 345.

Lossing, B. J., ii. 265.

"Lothair", ii. 114.

Lothrop, Dr. J. K., i. 66, 67, 71, 279.

Louis XIV, at St. Germains, ii. 309.

Louvre, the, i. 297; ii. 163.

Lovering, Joseph, i. 19, 38, 39, 45.

Low, Sampson, ii. 114.

Lowell, James Russell, and the *Boston Miscellany*, i. 205; call on, ii. 88; Class poet, i. 199; Class poem not read, i. 42; college part, i. 27; editor of *Atlantic*, i. 346; friend of Nathan's, i. 66; law office, ii. 330; in "The Modern Psyche", ii. 249; otherwise mentioned, i. 74, 152.

Lowell, John, i. 194.

Lowell Lectures, ii. 64, 110, 124.

Lucerne, i. 302.

Luther, i. 139.

Lyman, Arthur, ii. 105.

Lyman, Gen., ii. 94.

Lyons, Lord, i. 338.

Lysias in "Sybaris", ii. 51.

MACAULAY, T. B., ii. 75.

McCleary, S. F., i. 40.

McClure, Capt. of the *Resolute*, i. 277.

McCormick, Dr., i. 377.

Macdonough, A. R., ii. 144.

McDougall, Senator, extols drunkenness, ii. 81.

McElroy, W. H., ii. 352, 365, 368.

McGilvray, David, i. 272.

Mackintosh, R. T., life of his father, i. 129.

Macomber, Mr., ii. 272.

MacPherson, Jr., i. 34.

Magellan, documents on, ii. 288.

Maggiore, Lago, ii. 323.

Magnin, M., ii. 313.

Major General Commanding, ii. 192–198.

Marco Polo, ii. 75.

Mardi Gras, ii. 334.

"Margaret", by Sylvester Judd, i. 214.

"Marjorie Daw", Aldrich, i. 208; ii. 60.

Marquand, Miss, in trip to Spain, ii. 288; her historical feeling, ii. 297.

Marquette, Father, i. 258.

Martineau, James, i. 209; articles for *Old and New*, ii. 117; letter to, ii. 112; tea with, ii. 157.

Mary, Virgin, ii. 215.

Mary and Martha, ii. 13.

Mason, James M., i. 339.

Massachusetts, the duty of, i. 138.

Massachusetts Hall, i. 18.

Massachusetts Historical Society, ii. 3, 250.

Mather, Cotton, i. 236.

Matunuck, called New Sybaris, ii. 56; character of country, ii. 171; first move to, ii. 167, 176–179; first visit to, ii. 171; General Orders at, ii. 192; house at, ii. 174–176; house

first laid out, ii. 174; last letters from, ii. 404; life at, ii. 170, 188, 193; Little Gau like, ii. 246; children's plan for life at, ii. 286, 287; sand congresses at, ii. 186; spends summers at, ii. 356; Susan in control at, ii. 77; trees and flowers at, ii. 73.

Maurice, F. D., influence of, ii. 29; on the Old Testament, ii. 43, 44; his Working Man's College, i. 314.

May, Samuel G., letters to, ii. 19, 23.

Meadville, ii. 79.

"Memorial History of Boston", ii. 258.

Merrick, Frank, i. 221.

Messenger. See WEEKLY MESSENGER.

Meyer, Mr., i. 21.

Mexican War, i. 246.

Michelangelo, i. 313.

Mill, John Stuart, i. 7.

Miller, Joaquin, ii. 115.

Miller, Mrs., ii. 115.

Miller, Ruth A., i. 182.

Milon, ii. 51.

Milton, John, his resignation from office, ii. 353; his sonnets, i. 183.

Miner, Mr., ii. 227.

Ministry, at Large, i. 281; ii. 28, 36; Christian, in cities, ii. 26; earlier views of, i. 127, 128; letter to a young man thinking of, ii. 204.

Miranda, Gov., ii. 276.

Miscellany, The. See BOSTON MISCELLANY.

Missionary zeal in Unitarian Church, ii. 5.

Missouri Compromise, i. 195, 248, 250.

"Puritan Politics", i. 361.
Puss, ii. 199.
Putnam, Henry, i. 139.

Quarterly Review, i. 202.
Quincy, Dr., medical advice of, ii. 146–149.
Quincy, President Josiah, i. 24, 30, 34, 35, 37, 41, 45, 50, 56, 57.
Quirk, Mary, ii. 177, 188.

RAMSEY'S HEIGHTS, ii. 175.
Raphael's pictures, i. 306; ii. 164.
Rathbone, W., ii. 398.
Raymond, President, ii. 266.
Realism, Christian, ii. 213.
Reconstruction, ii. 4.
Recruiting in 1862, i. 329–330.
Reed, W. H., ii. 116, 145.
Reform Club, dinner at, ii. 304.
Refugees' Aid Society, The, i. 363.
Regnault at Granada, ii. 300.
Rembrandt, ii. 164.
Renan, E., i. 193; ii. 65.
Reporting legislature proceedings, i. 46, 47; ii. 360.
Resolute, the, ii. 75.
Revere, John, i. 40.
Revue de deux Mondes, i. 142.
Rhodora, i. 363.
Ricasoli, B., i. 308.
Rich, Otis, i. 251, 252.
Richey, Mary, i. 4.
Richmond, England, view at, ii. 157.
Richmond, J. C., i. 42.
Richmond, Va., entry of black troops, ii. 14; schools in, ii. 11, 21, 22, 25; sending shirts to, i. 336.
Rifle Club in 1861, i. 324–326, 383.
Rigaud, ii. 163.
Rigi, i. 302.
Riis, Jacob, ii. 28.
Ritual, ii. 216.

Robbins, Chandler, i. 235.
Roberts Brothers, ii. 113.
Robinson, Charles, connection with Fremont, i. 264; leads emigrants to Canada, i. 249; Governor of Kansas, ii. 283.
Robinson Crusoe, i. 9; ii. 71, 245, 365; style of, i. 350.
Rogers, E. L., i. 51.
"Rokeby", i. 33.
Romance in real life, ii. 46.
Roncesvalles, ii. 190.
Roosevelt, Theodore, at Alpha Delta Phi, ii. 391, 392; at Commencement of 1902, ii. 391; of 1905, ii. 404; Forestry Address, ii. 400; inauguration of, ii. 400–402; letter to, ii. 385; probably elected President, ii. 397; otherwise mentioned, ii. 387.
Root, Elihu, eulogized by Roosevelt, ii. 392.
Rose Genevieve, Sister, ii. 333.
Royal Academy, visit to, ii. 290, 291.
Ruah, housekeeper of Edward Everett, i. 321.
Ruarus, i. 130, 132.
Rubens, enthusiasm over, i. 306.
Rudolstadt, i. 171.
Rules of life, ii. 218.
Ruskin, ii. 296; attacks conventionality in art, ii. 65; lecture at Oxford, ii. 159; at Workingmen's College, i. 314.
Russell, Ella A., ii. 126.
Russell, Mrs., i. 58.

ST. GERMAINS, ii. 309, 310.
St. Gothard Pass, i. 297, 302; walking stick from, i. 318.
St. Peters, ii. 158; impressions of, i. 312.

INDEX

Sales, Francis, i. 43, 44.

Salignac, drillmaster of Rifle Club, i. 324–326.

Salisbury, Lord, ii. 385.

Salm, Prince de, ii. 336.

Salon, visit to, ii. 293–296, 308.

Salter, Rev. Mr., ii. 271.

Saltonstall, Mr., i. 43.

Salvation Army, ii. 28, 306.

Salvini, ii. 315.

San Antonio, ii. 235, 237–239; ii. 335, 336.

San Diego, ii. 341, 343.

Sand, George, i. 171.

Sanger, Judge G. P., i. 271, 272, 293.

Sanitary Commission, i. 363, 365, 383, 384; ii. 4, 5, 7, 11.

Sargent, Dr. Henry, i. 220, 274.

Sarto, Andrea del, interest in, i. 305; ii. 164.

"Sartor Resartus", i. 202.

Saviour, The, ii. 205, 214.

Schofield, Gen., ii. 26.

Scott, Walter, account of Watt, ii. 398; and American copyright, i. 30; fiction his forte, i. 48; position in life, i. 31; remark of, i. 49; romance and realism in, ii. 46.

Scott, Winfield, letter on the "Trent" affair, i. 339.

Scribe, A. E., plays of, ii. 75, 190.

Scribner's Monthly, ii. 257.

Seal of the United States, design for, ii. 316.

Seaton, editor of the *Intelligence*, i. 336.

Senate, elected Chaplain of, ii. 394; prayer in, ii. 80; work as Chaplain of, ii. 395, 397.

Send Me, order of, ii. 128, 130.

Sermons, begins to print, ii. 200; early, i. 149–163; of the Seventies, ii. 210. For par-

Seville, ii. 297.

Sewall, Miss, i. 210.

Sewall, Samuel, ii. 373.

Seward, Wm. H., interview with, ii. 82–85; and Johnson, ii. 79; at Plymouth, i. 265; recommendation to fortify the Lakes, i. 338.

Shackford, Mr., i. 367.

Shakespeare, Bancroft's views on, ii. 317, 318; Club in Brookline, i. 322; his plays acted, ii. 315.

Shattuck, Mr., ii. 104, 106, 107.

Shaw, Chief Justice, i. 196.

Shepherd, S. A. D., ii. 272.

Sheridan, Gen., i. 381.

Sherman, Vice-President, ii. 407.

Sherman, W. T., ii. 86.

Sierra Nevada, crossing the, ii. 348.

Silliman, B., i. 43; *Silliman's Journal*, i. 45.

Simonds, Mr., i. 54.

Simons, Maria, i. 290.

Skalitz, ii. 86.

Sketching, fondness for, ii. 73, 74.

Slack, Mr., his reputation, ii. 17.

Slayden, Mr. and Mrs., ii. 239.

Sleep, views on, ii. 142, 147–149.

Slidell, John, i. 339.

Slidell, Mrs., i. 340.

Smiley, Albert, of Lake Mohonk, ii. 384, 387.

Smith, Gen. Baldy, i. 368.

Smith, Roswell, ii. 279.

Smith & Co., J. Stillman, ii. 369, 370.

Smithsonian Institution, the, i. 295.

Social Science in 1870, ii. 37.

Social Service, ii. 39.

Solander, Dr., i. 68.

large airy rooms and a large piazza which made it comfortable even in summer. It gave him a big study where he could work comfortably and in which he could store the growing mass of material which he carefully collected for the many objects that were interesting to him.

It is as living here that I remember him, so definitely that it never seems natural to think of him anywhere else, unless it be at Matunuck on vacation. As I recall, he did not alter much in the forty years that he lived here. Some changes there were: his beard grew gray, he stooped a bit as the years went on, the fashion of his clothes changed somewhat. But in the main his looks, his bearing, even his clothes were much the same, and his general manner of standing, walking, using his hands, and so on, hardly changed at all.

He used in those first days, generally, to dress entirely in black, with a long frock coat and a waistcoat cut low, wearing a standing collar with a narrow black tie in the mornings and a white tie in the evenings. When he went out he wore a black soft felt hat with rather a broad brim, and an overcoat which at first used to be cut with a long cape. All this, I suppose, was, or at least had been, rather a break from ordinary clerical customs. In older days the clergyman was clean shaven, wore what we should call to-day a dress coat, and put on a beaver hat when he went out. My father could not bear shaving (the monotony of it was too much for him) and he had gradually taken to wearing a full beard. When he came to Boston he still shaved his upper lip, for a moustache, though proper for military men and medical students, was not at that time considered suitable for the clergy. But he soon stopped this practice, and although his congregation were surprised, they became used to it. Instead of a dress coat he compromised for a long time on a frock coat. This used to be of black broadcloth. It was a good while after this that he first began to wear the cutaways and jackets which are universal now. In common with a good many clergymen he had long substituted the soft felt hat for the beaver or silk hat, just as so many men nowadays substitute it for the stiff felts once so common. His appearance as he stands in the statue in the Public Garden is pretty typical; it is about the way one naturally remembers him.

He lived in those years a busy life. We breakfasted regularly at half-past seven. In later years he commonly came downstairs a good hour before and began to write. He always believed it bad to work "on an empty stomach," as he used to say, and he generally got a cup of coffee as soon as he got downstairs. But in the first years at 39 Highland Street he did not come down much before breakfast, or if he did, he did little more than read the newspaper. This used always to be the *Advertiser*, in which, though it had passed out of family hands, he still kept a personal interest. Breakfast was more of a meal than it is to-day, and we all enjoyed it. There were in time beside my father and my mother, my sister and the six boys, each with regular place and silver cup, and I suppose the conversation was lively.

After breakfast we always had prayers: we each read a verse in the passage for the day, and in the earlier years we sang a hymn while my mother played on the piano and led the singing with her clear slight voice. My father used to sing too, sometimes, but as it remains in my mind his singing never had any relation to ours. It began and ended at odd times, and was neither the tune we sang nor in harmony with it. He had a splendid speaking voice and doubtless might have sung well. But he often told us how he had been discouraged from learning to sing in college, and said it was a pity. He always used to lead in prayer, for indeed prayer was with him simply a natural mode of utterance, and we ended our short service with the Lord's Prayer.

Then we boys had to put on our boots and go to school. My father, however, took his letters which had got around about this time and retired to his study, a good-sized room at the back of the house. It had an anteroom, as we used to call it, and therefore two doors. When both doors were shut, no one could come in. Having got his letters he settled down to work; about this time his secretary (or amanuensis, as she used to be called) appeared, and the work of the day began.

It was a little before that period that he had begun to have a secretary. Everything was written out by hand in those days, and though he himself sometimes wrote shorthand, he generally used long hand. Copies, if wanted, were usually written out in some copy book, although at this time he had already used, in writing to Charles and sometimes other people, a copy book in which copies were made on carbon paper. But in the main whatever was written in those days was written and copied in long hand. He often wrote his sermons and other things himself, although he got more and more used to dictating. His first regular secretary was Miss Carrie L. Tallant. She was followed in the course of forty years by Miss Mary O. Edes, Miss Martha Adams, and Miss Abby W. Clark. In those first years it used to be Miss Tallant who came every morning. Other people came too, constituting what my father (following perhaps the war-time custom) called his "staff." It consisted normally, I think, beside his secretary, of an assistant whose duties were commonly at the church, and an errand boy. But it varied a good deal: sometimes it all gave way, except the secretary; sometimes there were additional workers.

Beginning to work at about half-past eight, he used first to get at his morning's mail and the letters left over. He would manage these generally in an hour and a half or two hours. I do not think he did much original work in the first hours of the morning; he was not absolutely regular about these things, and he sometimes wrote or dictated at this time something he had in mind, especially his sermons. He would write anywhere, in trains or in stations, but he always disliked to work late at night, as Nathan and Charles generally did. He almost always had his ideas pretty well arranged, so that he could write at almost any time or at any place. In later years he was apt to write before breakfast. But in these years he did not do so, nor in the first hours after breakfast.

At about ten or half-past he left the house and went to the church, or down-town on some engagement. At the church he had also a study, and elsewhere in the vestry there was likely to be a good deal of more or less organized work, charitable and otherwise. He himself was apt in these earlier years to have some reading class, either in the morning or the afternoon, of the young ladies of the parish or sometimes of the young men. He often went on further down-town on some business or other. The mornings were a bit longer then than they are now, for we did not dine at home till half-past two. This particular hour was, I suppose, because school ended at two, and as the boys began to go to school that was a convenient time. Often my father did not get home to dinner; if he was kept down-town on business he would lunch at one or another place, and perhaps spend the afternoon making parish and other calls, and doing various things, getting home for supper which we had at half-past six. After supper he generally retired to the study. My mother used to read aloud to us children in the parlor — few recollections of childhood are more definite or more beautiful than those readings — but during those years my father was rarely in the parlor in the evenings. Frequently he was at some public affair, speaking at some meeting, as he often did, or lecturing now and then in Boston and elsewhere, or at a club meeting where he might have been for dinner. I think he did not often work in the evenings, but if he did we children knew little about it, for he went into the study and shut the door. He rarely sat up late. He valued sleep, and thought no work could be good which cut into it. Somewhat after this time he became very regular about taking a nap after our midday dinner; he used to sleep about three quarters of an hour. At this time, however, he had not grown to think of an afternoon nap as a habit, though he was apt to get one whenever he got a chance.

He traveled about a good deal, as he always had. He enjoyed seeing places, and the record of each year would probably show a dozen trips longer or shorter, perhaps only for two or three days, perhaps for a week. He liked the really longer trips: in 1871 he went to Chicago immediately after the great fire. He had been called on to speak at the Fanueil Hall meeting on October 10th and had made an appeal which moved everybody. A month later he went out to Chicago to see the city and be useful in the work of reconstruction. Such trips especially pleased him. He would have hated to feel himself limited by his parish, his city, or his part of the country, — or even, I suppose, by his own country, though of course he understood very well that nationality is a very real limit to ordinary organization.

In his plans of life in these first years he rather assumed that he should like to live in Roxbury through the summer. My mother always did like to live there. But soon conditions began to change, —Roxbury began to be built up rapidly, — and it may be that even had this not been the case, he would have found it hard to stay in town. As it was he was very often away, even before he had the house at Matunuck. But probably a man of his age and habits of life cannot do much in making summer visits or summer excursions. My father felt his regular arrangements rather a burden; he always wanted to get away from the postman and the doorbell. But when he was away, he always missed his study in a few days. He wanted some place where he could have regular work. He could and did write anywhere, but in a short time he began to miss the accustomed things and wanted to get back to them. A visit, he often said, should consist of three days — I forget just why; it was an old rhyme — and I believe that he rarely wanted to stay away from his books and papers a much longer time than that.

His letters to Charles are excellent illustrations of these years, though unfortunately there is room for only a few of them.

TO CHARLES

"*Feb.* 20, 1872. We were all delighted at receiving your good news last night at 10:20 just as we were going to bed.[1] The telegraph so often brings bad news that I think people are to be specially praised to whom there is given the grace of sending good by it. I congratulate you not simply for the success, of which I have been sure all along, but of getting over the miserable delay, through which you must have chafed in harness indeed. Of all

---

[1] Charles' appointment as Assistant Secretary of State.

places Washington is the most wretched when you
cannot give yourself up to the current of some
absorbing occupation.

"I think I have not told you how cordially Henry
Wilson spoke of you, just after you went on. I
thanked him for coming to the rescue, when so far
as we know, no one else did. When I was in New
York last week Sam Dana asked me how your case
was getting on (as a world of other people did).
Then he said 'if he wants anybody's help in explain-
ing Dainaise let him write to A. R. Macdonough,
New York City.' He has had some law-suit with
Dainaise and came to Dana saying, 'You are a
Boston man, and your Mr. Hale is in trouble with
Dainaise; tell him to write to me if he needs help in
exposing him.' I enclose a note of Dr. Storer's which
I thought had gone before. I did not send you
Macdonough's name at once because I then knew
that the committee had agreed on their report.

"I have been dining about everywhere, and am
rather overworked to tell the truth. I have been
twice to New York and once to Wilkes Barre, Penn.,
since you left us. By the way they spell it Wilkes
Barre with big B. You know the story of its name.
I am just sending through the press my last Antiquarian Report — with note of the last Columbus
speculation about Asia and America, a curious subject. The first time I find you in possession in
Washington, I shall lecture to you about the Khol collection of maps in the State Department. We have
tried for a year or two to have a catalogue with
notes printed, and I suppose it could easily be done.

"But I write simply to congratulate, really with the hope that you may not be in W. when this arrives. For I suppose you will have to come home soon. You saw my red right hand in Tuesday's *Daily*. Goddard consulted me and, tho' we had to act without your advice, I thought it best to say this.

"Fred Perkins, who you know works regularly for the *Advertiser* is a good belligerent fellow, is an enthusiastic advocate of yours, and wants nothing better than to expose in print the Kindeneco-Dainaise row if you ever mean to make public statement regarding it. He would do it dramatically and with a sting, if you like to put proper documents into his hands. I suppose you might prefer to have it done by another than yourself. Also, if best, Fred could probably produce it in some New York paper."

TO CHARLES

"*March* 21, 1872. I forget if I wrote you my standard delineation of the present state of my staff.

"1. My assistant has resigned.

"2. My amanuensis is sick and has gone to Nantucket.

"3. *Literally true.* My errand man gave up in despair in the midst of his jobs on Thursday, leaving half his letters and notes undelivered half way.

"4. His substitute fell on the ice Friday, and has been invalided ever since.

"5. Will Reed, my general man Friday, had his house burn down in the coldest weather, and has been wholly occupied since with Insurers, etc.

"It is a great pleasure to get your notes every morning. No human being sees your rough drafts except me, and they go directly into unseen keeping, so you need not be frightened. As soon as I have read my mail I sit at this desk to write to you. If it is an awfully cold day like today and nobody comes in, there is a chance for finishing a letter. If it is one of those days when a diffusive or centrifugal force sends everybody gadding, the despatch is short in proportion.

"If you took this letter before it was opened and threw it in your office fire, it would be two minutes before it was so burned that you could not rescue it with tongs. If you took a bag of such letters closely packed in canvas, and bade two porters make a fire with pine behind your office, and put the bag on, it would be two hours before it would be consumed. Even then adventurous boys would read fragments for weeks.

"But when a railroad car closely packed with some thirty such bags rolls down an embankment with a stove in it and takes fire, in presence of a hundred passengers and one or two agents whose whole business is to rescue the letters, 15,000 are so destroyed that no sign of them, bonds of the U. S. included, is ever heard of again. You might mention that to your confreres in the post office when you see them.

"If you have never seen our *March* you have never seen N. H.'s compliment to you at the end of it. I put up a copy yesterday which probably reaches you with this.

"It is horribly cold, but we are all well.

"The Rev. John Williams, a friend of mine interested in modern history, happened to inquire at the Spanish consulate yesterday about Admiral Polo's book. But though they seemed intelligent people they knew nothing of it."

TO CHARLES

"*April* 20, 1872. What surprised me in Quincy's letter of course ought not to have surprised me, for 'at forty every man is a fool or a physician' and Quincy must be near forty. Still I was surprised to see how nearly the regimen of life he had forged was my own, even in some details which I should have thought I could take a patent for. I forget whether I have sent you my essay called 'The Mind's Maximum'; it is just a skeleton of the course which a college professor on the 'Art of Life' ought to take up and carry through. When I came to deliver my Lowell lectures I opened rather farther on the same thesis, and made the first three lectures, 'Sleep,' 'Appetite,' 'Exercise.' I consider sleep the centre of the whole, as you do, and as Quincy does. I believe on the one hand that a man can secure good sleep and enough of it. And on the other I believe that if his sleep is not good, he has an absolute evidence that there is a mistake in his regimen, and that he is breaking down. I said last year to Olmstead of the Central Park and Sanitary Commission, one of the ablest men living, that I wished he would look at Dr. Hammond's little book on sleep. 'Oh,' said he, 'I am under Dr. Hammond's personal care. The trouble is that I will not obey the rules which he lays down as essentials.' This was frank enough, but with what he said beside, it corroborated a good many of my theories.

"There is no reason in the world why you should not sleep well. All of us, and you in particular, are of nature good sleepers. I never heard of any man in the world who could match your Mammoth Cave story in that line.

"I know all about the bromide of potassium for which Quincy sends you Clarke's recipe. It is an admirable addition which the most recent science makes to our resources. I have used it for my children again and again, should use it myself if I needed, — but I do not, because I am willing to obey Hammond's rules and had rather be independent of medicines of whatever name.

"I will not go to bed with my brain excited or tired, or with blood pressing on it, I may as well make the decision as anybody else, and I make that decision. This means that I will not work my brain within four or five hours of bedtime. This means that I throw my hard work into the earlier half of the day.

"Mr. Webster used to come down to your office and chat with Abbot and the other men of that time, about quotations from Virgil and Pope's 'Essay on Man' and other such stately small talk, as if he had nothing in the world to do. The truth was he had made his own fire at five, and written steadily from five to eight. You and I do believe in an hour's absolute quiet for digestion after breakfast, and then three or four hours of stiff work. It is clear to me that Quincy's whole plan is the same. That is what this flesh brush and dumb-bells before breakfast means, the dawdling in dressing, cold water bath, if you like it, if not, no; and that is what I mean by reserving till the working hours the hardest accumulations of the day before.

"I do not think you distinguished between sleep and lethargy. I told Hayward once that I always slept well on mince pie. 'I don't doubt it,' said he, 'but I should not like to say how near that sleep is to the sleep of apoplexy.' It is only within twenty years that it has been known, that in natural sleep the blood is largely withdrawn from the brain; in the sleep of lethargy the brain is overcharged with blood. The first is refreshing. The last gives headache and the rest, and is not refreshing. All which Hammond's book very curiously explains."

TO CHARLES

"*May* 7, 1872. Greely's nomination reminds me of an old mot of J. Q. Adams's who said of New York politics that New York always was one of the devil's own unaccountables. Mother was fond of quoting this remark, which was made I think when I was four years old, and which I have found true ever since. The first presidential election I remember was that of 1828. We voted late in Massachusetts, and I knew that we were defeated. Still, child-fashion, I supposed the tide might be turned by vigorous success in Boston. When, therefore, being led home from a party by Fullum near the head of

Avon Place, I heard two men cry, 'Hurrah for Jackson,' and only one cry 'Hurrah for Adams,' my heart sank within me. I knew as well as I know now that the first were cries of enthusiasm and the last only a cry of affectation. I understood — as well as I do now —

"1. The value of a Cry.
"2. The value of a Leader.

"You may not know that in the election of 1824, just before the vote, J. Q. A. wrote a letter which so disgusted his personal adherents in Massachusetts that they could not and did not vote for him."

TO CHARLES

"*June* 16, 1872. It is clear that Arthur has had a splendid time.[1] It is my first serious experiment in what has been in theory my system of education of boys, learned largely from our father. It amounts to this, that it is well to keep boys largely in the company of men, and well also to let them understand that there is no duty which they cannot do. It is evident that Sydney and Walter Raleigh, and I suppose most young men in chivalrous days, were educated on this system. People did not then herd a lot of boys together; they mixed them up with their betters, and let them learn by overhearing, by looking on, by trying experiments, and by example. I do not think Arthur a very bright or quick boy. But he is conscientious and affectionate. I am glad to see that he makes friends, and I think he will

---

[1] He had just been making a visit to his uncle in Washington, and was now with my father, who was going out to Antioch College in Ohio.

keep them. It is a great relief to have him with me in what would else be a very lonely journey. Ohio, with its matchless physical comfort, is the stupidest state to be trundled over which you could conceive, if you had never seen Indiana."

CHAPTER TWENTY-FIVE

TRIP ABROAD

1873

THE year 1873 was memorable for two matters, very important to him — his second trip abroad and the opening of the house at Matunuck. It would be hard to say which of these events was the more interesting to him at the time, although the latter was of most lasting influence. The trip abroad was arranged by his parishioner and old friend, Mr. Henry P. Kidder, who was taking his own family, and asked my father and mother to join them. As usual he was an excellent letter writer, though he wrote this time to the various children instead of to my mother as before. He takes a different tone, in subject and in style, with his different correspondents, from Phil and Berty who at this time were six and five years old, to his brother Charles.

"STEAMER SIBERIA; AT SEA.
"*May* 1, 1873.

"MY DARLING CHILDREN,

"If thinking of you does any good you have had a comfortable time of it for papa and mamma carry you with them all the time, and there is a great deal of time to think of nice good children, I assure you. Our last recognition was of dear Phil and Berty's faces. For the faces grew smaller and smaller, at last the eyes and noses died out of them and they became little white rounds in the sea of the black clothes of the people. So I could not distinguish the faces of the taller children, but Phil and Berty quite below the line of the others were distinguished to the very last. So it is sometimes well to be smallest of all, and that, dear Berty, will make up a little for being helped the very last of all at dinner.

"We have had the shortest passage out ever made by this boat, so there must have been some good angel or other on board. Till this morning we have had almost all sail set, which is very unusual, and means, of course, that the wind has been nearly fair all the time. Four days bring you past the banks of Newfoundland. Three days may be fairly called the English part of the passage, — there we see Fastnet Light tonight, if all is well, and do not reach Liverpool until Saturday morning. You will observe that three more days are left in the middle of the Atlantic itself. To this portion of the globe the sailors give the happy title of the Devil's Hole, and I am sure it is very well named. At least we found very rough weather there, and were all pretty sick till it got through, having started on our first four days with the idea that we were to be let off very easily.

"I have a copy of the ship's log, daily course and distance, which I will mail from Liverpool, and which I want Arthur and Edward to enter on some map or Mercator's projection. Perhaps they will need help from Nelly. They must do it the very day it arrives, better the very hour, or they may never do it at all. If Arthur cares to look in the lower drawers of Miss Tallant's secretary, I think he will find a chart made by me some thirty-odd years ago in which I entered some of the earlier steam passages. This would be a good map to enter this on. Perhaps he would like to copy that, without the old tracks. Or he may enter it on the Mercator's projection in Fay's Atlas, — Fay's is the rather new one.

"The proposal is that we shall all sit up tonight to ten o'clock to see the Fastnet light. This is the first light house in Ireland, not a very great way south of the Skelligs which are sometimes seen on this voyage. Tomorrow morning early we expect to stop at Queenstown and leave the mails, and such passengers as there disembark. The detention is not half an hour, and then we proceed up the Irish Channel to Liverpool, where, as I said, we arrive Saturday if all is favorable. I shall write from there so I will not go into farther plans here. But I shall at once write to Aunt Susy pressing her to join us at the Isle of Wight, where we shall spend a few days before we go to London.

"I shall try to write a line to Aunt Lucretia and Uncle Charles, but you may send them this note, as you may all my other letters that seem of importance enough. Of course mere directions for your own guidance need not be sent to them. We shall begin to hear from you on Monday, and that will be a great joy.

"Much love to all from
"PAPA and MAMMA."

"LIVERPOOL, *May* 5, 1873.

"DEAR PHIL and BERTY:

"This seems a very good country for boys, but I have seen no boys I like near so well as mine. We went on Saturday to a Museum which is like the Natural History rooms only a great deal bigger. We saw there a live chameleon. Now the chameleon is the beast who is one color at one time and another at another. He is not very big, about as long as Phil's hand. When we saw him he was walking up a little bush and he was greenish yellow. He had cabbage to eat. There were splendid peacocks and pheasants. When you go to the Natural History Society, I hope you will look for an Argus pheasant. He is called Argus because there was a king Argus who had one hundred eyes. Now this bird's tail is so full of beautiful spots that look like eyes that he is called the Argus pheasant. Is not that a good name?

"Then there were live fishes swimming among grass and stones in glass boxes so that we could see them. There were very, very old mummies from the tombs in Egypt. I laughed very much at some tortoises who were not alive but looked very funny. The people wanted to show their breasts, so they set them up in the cases with the breasts in front, and they looked as if they were jumping Jim Crow. Arthur will show you how to jump Jim Crow and perhaps will teach you how. Here is a tortoise jumping Jim Crow [picture]. As we approached the land after our voyage we saw a very famous light house, at a place called Holy-head. Holy-head is a cliff, or rocky mountain of which the sides run down into the sea. At the very end of the cliff is a little island and on this island is the light house all alone. There is a little bridge which crosses to the island. But when they carry oil and food to the light house, they do not carry them by the bridge, but in boats. And these boats sail into a deep cave under the light house. Then the people look down through a well into the cave, and lower down ropes and pull up the oil and food. Is not that a good way? All around the light house are ever so many gulls' nests, and the gulls lay their eggs there, and there the little birds are born. And no one is permitted to land or to meddle with the gulls' eggs at all, so they are not frightened. Why do you think they take such care of them? It is because they scream so and make so much noise that in the fog when sailors cannot see the light they can hear the gulls screaming and can keep away from the rocks. Is not that a good way?

"Now we are going to Chester, a very old city where you do not have to carry umbrellas, because the side walks have covers over them. Is not that a good way?

"Mamma sends love and kisses to all.

"From your own PAPA."

TO ARTHUR

"*May* 13, 1873. Our line of battle has been two days at Oxford, and then a ride by express train from Oxford to London in time to dine here at 7

Saturday. Then on Sunday we heard Mr. Stop-
ford Brooke, just now the most famous London
preacher, and in the evening we attended the service at Westminster Abbey, visiting Dr. Stanley and
Lady Augusta Stanley at the same time. After this,
at 8:30 we went to the Martineaus to tea. Yesterday was a perfect day. I went, with your aunt, to
the Strand to talk with Sampson Low & Marston
about the reprinting of my book here, and then by
rail to Hampton Court where we joined the others
who had gone in the carriages. I say the carriages
because Mr. Kidder began operations by hiring two
carriages for the company, and they are in attendance all the time. Nelly says you have got down
my old book [1] — which I think tells of Hampton
Court. Thence we went to the Star and Garter, a
famous hotel at Richmond. It is famous for many
reasons, but deserves its repute for the exquisite
beauty of its view of the Thames and of half a
county beyond, and we took our lunch as we sat
and enjoyed this prospect. Thence on the way
home, we came to Kew. Kew was a palace of
George III which he had the wit to give up for a
Botanical Garden, and for a hundred years it has
been kept as such. The palm-houses and other
green houses are magnificent, — high enough for
palm trees to grow erect in. So we added to our list
another of the wonders of the world.

"Of true wonders there were seven. If you know
without looking them up you may tell me briefly
what they are. If you do not know please look

[1] "Ninety Days' Worth of Europe," pp. 29–31.

them up and tell me. They are but a poor set. (I ignore the slang term by which you would describe them, but they were the best that could be had by those poor Levanters whom we call the Greeks.) Be that as it may I remember when I was first at Niagara with your Aunt Susy; she expressed her pleasure at seeing one of the things which everybody admitted was the first in its time. Of such things I have now seen in my life, Niagara, The Apollo Belvedere, the Venus de' Medici, St. Peter's, the British Museum, Stonehenge, and I think these Kew gardens belong in the same list. And this is not all, as your Uncle Alexander would say, because it is the last I have seen. I think the Chicago lifting engines, at their waterworks, belong there too, but of this I am not certain.

"I cannot describe to you the pleasure which Nelly's first letters gave us. Today I hope we shall get the Kimball parcel which will contain your first. There was a very well written letter by Berty in one of Nelly's and we were very much pleased to have it. Do not be frightened about postage; there is nothing we so gladly pay. I did mean to have a letter posted every day while we were in England, and I think a letter may be posted every second day till I say stop. With such paper as this, and you may go to Grover's and get some if Backup has none, you can bring within half an ounce all the despatches of the family.

"The party leave London for Paris on Friday. If I find my business is not over, I shall drop Paris, for which I care very little and shall join them at

Brussels. But I think I shall go with them. From Paris we cross to Cologne by Brussels, up the Rhine to Baden, and then across to Munich and Vienna. Do not fail to look these out in the German Atlas.

"London is in the full tide of what is called the season. They used to work Parliament in the winter, but what Trench calls the inevitable habit of procrastination has thrown things forward, so that the greater part of the business is done between Easter and the middle of July. At that time therefore the House of Lords, and the House of Commons are here, and that makes so much of the wealth and intelligence of England that all the rest comes. Of course all performers and entertainers and philanthropists come. Titiens is here and Nillson and Patti and are singing in rival opera-companies at Drury Lane and Covent Garden. All the galleries of pictures are opened. 4000 pictures are offered for the Royal Academy exhibition, of which they hung 1700, having room for no more.

"I heard Ruskin lecture at Oxford, as I wrote, and he cut up the exhibition terribly on the ground that it did not represent the great and critical points in the actual life of the people. But I do not believe that the criticism is very just, unless he means that these points, in the life of a great commercial nation of today, are not worth representing. Into such points you and I will not enter now. Goodbye. Love to all from

"PAPA."

TO CHARLES

"Paris. *May* 17, 1873. I spent my last night
in England in the House of Commons, and a very
interesting night it was. Mr. Herbert who is a
young man to whom Dr. Palfrey introduced me, an
extreme radical, the one person who divided with
Dilke on the question of an examination into the
Civil List, took me and got me an admirable place.
It seems absurd that with all the eagerness for
seats, four fifths of the gallery are wholly empty,
while the one gallery opened to most visitors is
crowded. I heard none of the most distinguished
lions, unless Disraeli made an interpellation, as I
believe he did, but a great number of men spoke
and I saw the forms of procedure to great advantage. They were going into committee once and
again, and they stuck to their work with a precision which is charming. The small size of the
room is an immense advantage, admitting of easy
conversation, back and forth about details. The
bill which took most of their time was their new
Jury Bill, which is of much more importance than
you would suppose from the report which I enclose.
But I am disposed to think that a custom has grown
up of not reporting discussions in committee. The
Bill as reported by a special committee proposes a
large property qualification for all persons, in the
hope of getting, by the English system, more intelligence on juries than they get now. At the same
time it sweeps away a very large number of the
exemptions which now exist. This is all very fine

for solicitors who argue before juries and judges, or
magistrates at quarter sessions who have to meet
them. But you will see in a moment that it is an
overturn of the whole principle. As a Mr. Mellen,
a very radical man, said to me, at the moment
when class quarrels are precipitated upon them,
they are going to say to every laboring man whom
they try, that by no accident shall a laborer be on
the jury, and to every Trades Union man whom
they try that by no accident shall a mechanic be
on a jury. In fact they relegate the business of the
jury almost wholly to the shop-keepers in the towns,
who, as a class, have been in all countries a conserva-
tive if not a bigoted set of people. But what was
to me very suggestive and pathetic, out of fifty
speakers on the bill no one said a syllable of what I
have said in the House. They merely discussed detail; if this was thus, such a county in Wales would
not have jurors enough, if that were so such a town
in Devonshire might not have enough. This very
Mr. Mellen, who was so scientific in private, said
coolly to me 'I don't care. I have saved my bor-
oughs, because their population is thus and so, but
it is a very bad night's work.' The bill as it came
to us had a large property qualification for grand
jurors. This affected the class which sends men to
Parliament, and it was fairly cried down. The
attorney general who had the care of the bill, said
from the beginning that he did not care much about
this, and they fairly compelled him to withdraw it.
That is to say, the moment their own class was
affected they winced and unanimously determined

that they would not be hampered by any such conditions. It seemed to be enough to say that the son of noblemen might not have in his own right property enough to entitle him to serve, and with that the question was decided.

"Now, it is just possible that they are so loyal to the theory of committee of the whole, that this refusal or failure to discuss the principle was due to the intention to discuss that when the bill was before the House. But I cannot believe that if they had felt the pressure of the bill on the laboring class, or had cared for it, the feeling would have affected a discussion so wide.

"Now, for detail of method. They are very prompt. The having whips helps very much in promptness, and the Speaker and Chairman of Committee of the Whole both understand their business. The Chairman of Committee is a permanent officer. In committee, and I think in the House, the method of putting a question is fairly dramatic. It seems like a bit of an opera. After the two sides have voted the chairman says 'I think the Ayes have it!' Then, if they want a division, the Noes cry in perfect time — as if they were intoning a response in the liturgy.

"'The Noes have it — the Noes have it!'

"He says again 'I think the Ayes have it', and they answer as before: —

"'The Noes have it, the Noes have it.' Then he orders a division. But this does not take place for two or three minutes, while the whips are telegraphing the clubs. Then the division requires two minutes more perhaps, the House meanwhile empty, excepting Mr. Kavanagh who has no legs nor arms, the clerks and the speaker. A clerk goes to him and asks him how he votes — and his vote is counted with the rest. I mean Mr. Kavanagh's vote."

TO ELLEN

"PARIS, *May* 31, 1873.

"My darling Nelly.

"Mamma gave you a little hint as to the Louvre last night, in a letter which she wrote when she was very tired, and which I posted this morning. This afternoon we agreed that we would go there again instead of trying the Luxembourg where are the modern pictures, the Rosa Bonheurs, Delaroches, and Meissonniers, and I am very glad we did. The second sight helps your memory vastly.

"Was it not a little curious that as we entered almost the first picture we saw should be by our friend Boucher? As lately as 1869 since I was here a Mr. Somebody, I think Cady, died and left his whole collection to the nation to be kept in the Louvre. The catalogue says that his ambition was to show that Watteau and Rigaud (name new to me) and other artists of the last century were the equals of the great names of the century before, and that whoever sees this collection will say he has succeeded. Be this as it may, so it was that mamma's first taste of a great world-renowned gallery, was of Watteau, Boucher, and Greuze by whom there happen to be pictures close to the door. And, not to waste paper on Boucher, there are a great many of

his pictures and they are very good and very interesting. I dare say you will live to see some renais-
sance or other — asserting that a little mysticism
or allegory is a very good thing, that you do not
want absolutely hard distinct expression, and that
Watteau, Boucher, and another man whose name
begins with F[1] are to be the great lights of the time.

"For a' that and for a' that the great men hold
their own. I like the Raphaels better than mamma
does, not better than I think she will. And I find
it very hard to tell you of the wonderful completeness of detail, in pictures which come in after the
masters. Once and again I stopped before some
picture by somebody you and I never heard of, to
say, that if anybody had given me that picture
alone and I had it in my own house for years I should
have constructed a theory of it, which would make
it for me absolutely invaluable.

"I am delighted to find my old enthusiasm about
Andrea Del Sarto more than confirmed. I found
Mr. and Mrs. Kidder shared in it and mamma does
entirely. There is a sort of homeishness about his
Holy Families that no one else's have.

"But, Nelly, you have no idea I think how charming the truly good portraits of all time are. Titian's,
Van Dyck's especially, Rigaud's, Mad. Le Brun's,
Rembrandt's and so on. Did you ever hear of a
man named Chardin? He is one of the Greuze crew.

"There, that is enough for tonight. I have one or
two photographs for you, but they do not say much.

"God bless you, darling, and all at home."

[1] Fragonard.

TO CHARLES

"VIENNA, *June* 8. Since I began this, I have seen the exposition. Today is the cheap day, and I was very glad to make my first visit this afternoon that I might see the people, the real people, who reserve themselves for this day. On this day the fee is fifty kreutzers, the new Austrian kreutzer, which is to say 24 cents.

"Well, I hasten to say that the whole is magnificent. It is interesting and instructing in the very highest degree, and even were I a penny-a-liner, as thank God I am not, feed to hawk and peck at it, I should find it impossible to do so.

"Its great strength, as I am told by a gentleman who has seen all the other expositions, is the completeness of its illustrations of the East. Vienna, you know, really has one foot in the East. Austria is more than ever Oester-reich, the Eastern realm. They have perhaps taken particular pains on that side, perhaps the Orientals have taken more time to waken, but the result is, whatever the cause, that the Orient is particularly well represented. Germany is, of course, very strongly represented. And those of us who were so occidental as to think England, France, and America the three great manufacturing nations in the world have a good deal put into our pipes for our smoking here. It would probably be a fair criticism on all these shows, if they were really to be held to their titles, of World Expositions, or Welt-Ausstellungen, that they give much more space than fairly belongs to the productions of the country in which they are. But this is a result so entirely of course, that it is preposterous to find fault with it. For I am very glad it is so. I have not come a quarter round the world to Vienna to regret that I see the manufacture, agricultural, and mining industry of Austria and Vienna now that I have come here.

"This was a mere coup d'oeil visit, and yet in three hours we did not go into one tenth part of the courts or galleries. I think we spent more time in the Hungarian department than any other. They have taken special pains to exhibit the popular manufactures, little quaint national things, than any other nation of which I saw the show. England and France, for example, exhibit specially choice manufactures such as you might live months without seeing in either country.

"There is a special pavilion devoted to the German school system. By pavilion I mean building as large on the floor as the City Hall. A wonderful collection it is, of apparatus of every kind, and makes one think that the model of a slab school house from New England was the less necessary."

TO CHARLES

"RIVER DANUBE, below WIEN. *June* 15, 1873. I am at this moment on my way to Budapesth, as I like to call it, with Mr. John Fretwell, whom I believe you met at my house last year. He is commissioned by the British Unitarian Association, and I go with him as a representative of our people, to meet at Pesth the Bishop of the Hungarian and

Transylvanian Unitarian Church, which you know still survives, and is the living monument of the zeal of the old Polish Unitarians of the 18th and 17th centuries. There was a set of men of whom the world proved itself not worthy, who in their day did one of the best works for God and the Right that ever got itself done. Among other things Blandrata, one of them, came over to Transylvania and by pure force of his preaching converted the whole county from Roman Catholicism into a sensible Unitarian religion, the first and last time in history that that thing ever got itself done. Of that Transylvanian church the Bishop Cusa, comes up from Claudius-polis (New Clausenburg or Colosvar) twenty hours to meet me and Fretwell at Pesth. We go down from Wien to meet them. The occasion is fairly historical and I am glad to have a share in it. Of which I shall of course write after it is over."

He had to leave the party early in order to start the new household at Matunuck. My mother continued with Mr. Kidder and the rest of the party.

TO MRS. HALE

"LONDON, *Sunday*, July 13, 1873. At the end of Henry the Fourth or the beginning of Henry the Fifth as you remember the old king dies, and Prince Hal takes the crown from the pillow. You will remember, what I had forgotten, that this took place in the Jerusalem chamber. When the King is told that it is the Jerusalem chamber, he says he had been forewarned that he should die in Jerusalem.

Now believe this which follows. I took tea by chance in the Jerusalem chamber last night. The old fire place, before which, for warmth, the dying King lay, is what it was, — and through the same old glass the light shines in as then!

"This happened of course, from my own luck.

"After a very successful, but rather hard working day, I took a cab and drove to the deanery at 5 : 30 to make a p.p.c. hardly expecting to get in. The servant said the Dean was out, but when I took back my card to add p.p.c. he said the Dean was showing the Habbey to some friends, and if I liked he would take me to him. After it dawned on me what the Habbey was, I said he might. Do you think I found Stanley going round with a party of fifty working men from government workshops, explaining the statues, windows, and other wonders of his own Abbey! Was not that a good chance? He was very entertaining and the whole thing was dramatic in the extreme. When we had gone all round he led the way to the Jerusalem chamber and there was served tea for the crowd. Lady Augusta Stanley appeared and we had a very good talk. She invited me to dine there today at 5 : 30 and I am going; going indeed first to hear the Dean preach in the afternoon."

TO MRS. HALE

"QUEENSTOWN HARBOR, *July* 16, 1873. By the way of travel presents for the children I have a butterfly net for Nelly, some drawing books for Arthur, a corkscrew knife for Edward (and a paint box for Arthur's birthday), I have two little school knapsacks for Phil and Berty, a box of letters for Harry and a box of blocks for Robby. When I thought for 12 hours that the trunk was bone-fide *lost*, imagine my grief for Arthur's opera-glass and my Vienna portfolios. The Vienna things we bought together I have with me. To say truth beside these things the trunk had comparatively little of value.

"Well here closes the European correspondence of 1873 on my side. My next letter will be an American letter. Has it not been an expedition of ideal success? When I consider how entirely the path of it has been smoothed even from the smallest bumps and delays, how at every point we have used time to the very greatest advantage always pulling at the best point of the lever; when I consider how many of the real wonders of the world we have seen, and seen thoroughly well, I am fairly aghast to think that in less than 'Ninety Days' so much is possible. When we come next we will come with Nelly, Edward, and Arthur, as soon as Edward is big enough for Scotch or Swiss tramping."

CHAPTER TWENTY-SIX

MATUNUCK

1873–1880

ONE of the great elements in my father's later life was his summer place at Matunuck. From the summer of 1873, when he first moved down there to live, it was for twenty-five years and more an invariable source of delight and recreation. From the very beginning it was just what he liked and just what he had always longed for. It satisfied much of his craving for outdoor life. In earlier years he had climbed mountains; in later days he had felt, in his slight glimpse of army life, how much pure delight there was in living as near to nature as possible in our sophisticated days. He also appreciated being at a place seven miles from the railroad, where there was but one mail a day and in a house where there was no doorbell. It was before the day of telephones.

His friend, William B. Weeden of Providence, owned a considerable estate in South Kingston, Rhode Island. His property lay not only on the south side of the Post Road, where the old farmhouse stood, and the meadows stretched a mile and more down to the sea, but also on the north of the road where the low white oaks and the huckleberry and sweet fern cover an irregular group of little hills dotted with many little ponds. My father

first saw the place in the summer of 1867. The
following letter to my mother describes his first
glimpse of the country.

"Kingston, R. I.
"*Aug.* 25, 1867.

"My dear Emily:

"I shall deliver this with my own hand, or arrive
before it, but I like to break the spell which leaves
the last day of an expedition always unrecorded.

"We are here a mile from the Sea beach, three or
four miles from Pt. Judith light, — in an old farm
house which was a tavern a hundred years ago, when
this deserted Post Road was one of the thoro'fares
from Boston to New York. I have adopted the
house as the scene of

'Franklin one night cold —— to the skin
Stopped on his journey at a country inn.'

Here the lady of the house today, is Miss Elvira
Weeden, aunt of William B. W., herself cruelly
deformed. She is bright, thoroughly well informed,
perfectly bred, and a most agreeable companion.
The farms here stretch from the hills to the sea,
much as Connecticut River farms stretch from the
hills to the river. They are kept rich by the sea-
weed drawn up from the beaches, — and what with
hay and native flowers, and the softness of air which
I always rave about as Gulf-Streamy, the air is
deliciously fragrant, heavy with fragrance you would
say, were it not so bracing. Queer enough this
fragrance of the North American coast is constantly
spoken of as remarkable by the early voyagers.

"Here we arrived by a charming morning drive

about 10, and after our hospitalities ran down to the beach for the daily bath, here without company or bathing clothes, as it pleased God to make us. Oh it was splendid. Breakers just high enough for surf and the temperature perfection. Dinner as soon as we came home, then a short nap — an hour's slop with water colours,[1] — a visit ending in tea from a bright Mrs. Hazard, — a walk to the hill opposite to see a splendid sunset, — and so night and bed."

I do not know just when the plan was proposed that Mr. Weeden should build a house for my father, but no plan that ever came into his life gave him more pleasure. In those days it was the custom of the family (in 1867 with five children and in later years with seven) to spend the summers at Milton as has been seen. When he bought the house at 39 Highland Street, he had some idea that it would be possible to spend his summer there. But Roxbury was actually as well as legally a part of Boston, and he never found there the real rest which he always longed for. Whenever it was that Mr. Weeden first suggested to him that he should come to Matunuck for his summers, they settled the details in the summer of 1872, during a visit which my father paid Mr. Weeden, who had for several years been spending some time in the summer in the old family farmhouse, which he had begun to make over.

I do not find record of other visits until the following:

[1] Still kept in the parlor at Willow Dell.

"WILLOW DELL: — *Aug.* 30, 1872. Edward is very happy, — quite too busy, I fear, to write, but I will try to put him up to it. The only writing he has done is about six lines of a drama on the subject of Der Freischutz. He calls this his 'resource', recurring to it when the weather does not permit his playing out doors. I thought he would get his fill of the 'resource' last night, for we had a tremendous storm lasting into this morning. But just as we all got our sitting clothes on the rain ceased, and we all went to ride to see the surf which was truly magnificent. We have been on Ingham Peak this afternoon miles away from the water you know. But from there you can see those solemn lines of white pouring in from the gray, almost black sea.

"I have determined not to take Edward to New York with me. I do not know whether we talked of it, but I had a feeling that he might be homesick alone. It is evident that there is no fear of that, and he likes the idea of staying over Sunday. I take the Stonington boat Sunday night, and am now minded to spend Monday morning in New York. If, as I suppose, Susy sails on the 10th, I shall come home on the 7th. If she sails earlier, be sure to let me know, and I will come back earlier. I am having a perfect time. The climate is peerless, — and I get all the time I want for writing, not more than an hour a day, — but that I like to have regularly. Edward is learning to row very well. I take him out on the pond every day."

During this visit my father and Mr. Weeden settled the matter of the new house. One Sunday afternoon they went up on the hill to the north of the road, and laid out the general arrangement of the house and grounds. The hills come down to the Post Road, just there, and south of the road the meadows run a mile or so away to the sea. The house was placed on the edge of the hills, overlooking a wide stretch of country; the meadows and salt pond toward Point Judith on the southeast, the meadows and woods to the Sound and Montauk Point to the southwest, and straight in front, to the south, the meadows reaching to the sea, which extended away to the south, east, and west, broken only by Block Island, which on some days was but a cloud in the horizon and never really broke the harmonious stretch of the sea. The house stood on a hill that rose abruptly from the road, so that it commanded a remarkable view; behind it the country was hilly and covered with woods. Among the hills and woods were little ponds, sometimes very small, sometimes a mile or so long. One lay right behind the house, so near in fact that when stone steps were built down to the water from the house, a fence had to be built to keep the children from falling into the water. One could row across the pond, land at the other end, where there was another called the Little Pond, and walk up into the hills, where at that time there was hardly a house for miles. It was a succession of scrub oak woods, upland pastures, old meadowland covered with sweet fern and huckleberry and laurel, varied by these

little ponds here and there, and now and then a
farmhouse. Into this hill-country Mr. Weeden and
my father, with a following of friends and children,
would walk on an afternoon, so that soon the main
details were familiar places. They gave names to
the favorite spots. Ingham's Peak was a mild elevation of perhaps two hundred feet in height: I
do not think that we children thought there was
anything out of the way in calling it a peak; at
least it was the highest land round about. Emily's
Knoll, Ramsey's Heights, The Vatican, were other
places of which the remembrance has now passed
away. The pond behind the house was most difficult to name. My father called the house the New
Sybaris and the pond Sybaris Lake, but the names
somehow could not stick. Halcyon Lake, on account of the kingfishers, Lake Surprise, and others
were suggested, but no name ever displaced the old
country name of Wash Pond. Like a good many
other ponds in the neighborhood it served for the
sheep-washing in the early summer and so, like a
number of other ponds, it was called Wash Pond.
At first there were no boats upon it except a large
and clumsy ship's yawl that had come ashore on
the beach below in a wreck. But as time went on we
built and bought canoes, and in later years my father
was especially fond of paddling about in a canoe.

The house was finished early in the summer of
1873, and my father, as has been said, left the
European party to move the family into it. My
mother continued more slowly with Mr. Kidder and
the others.

TO MRS. HALE

"*July* 31, 1873. Here I am in the new home. You cannot think how charming it is. I have come in from the piazza with its view as wide as yours in Switzerland, and with the serene infinity of the stars in half-heaven, with new wonder at the world's beauty. I had just been up stairs, and had heard the Lord's Prayer in the four versions, as to language and expression, of the four older boys. They have been good boys all day, and give in their loyal manly work in the morning good promise for our holiday.

"As for the house itself you cannot think how nice it is. In the first place it is pretty. Nelly and I must try to send you a little sketch of it. It is completely finished, to the last iota, and finished more thoroughly than any country house I ever saw. It reminds me of Susan's house at Beverly, but is in every way more comfortable. The furniture is ample, and particularly pretty, new ingrain carpets of charming colors all over the house, pretty wicker furniture in the parlor, and in short everything you could wish and much more than you expect. The furniture alone must have cost two thousand dollars. It has been very dry, so that they have been sadly disappointed about their grass. But you know this hillside made no great pretences that way ever, and the prospect for next month seems better. I hear the surf of the sea as I write, and the moonlight and stars are delightful.

"Friday morning. I have begun on the new

dynasty by setting them all pretty well at work.
I do not know but they will think me a hard task-
master. I set Phil and Berty on shelling peas, which
was a way mother used to have of keeping us out of
mischief. We are bringing things into order fast.
It is like a first day in Milton, — but much less so,
because so many things were here. And the Weedens
had adjusted all questions of milk, eggs, ice, and
fish and such like before we came.

"The final Hegira was made by Arthur, Nelly,
Ellen the new table girl, and Marnie Foster, coming yesterday morning at 7:30 with Edward. Marnie Foster is to cook. Ellen is a trump, a very nice
womanly person, and all hands are very fond of her.
At two I brought up the rear, locking up 39 Highland Street and bringing with me the four little
boys, Katy, Mary Quirk, Bruno, and endless hand-
baggage. We were a little short for leaders, as
Bruno required my presence in the smoking car
where he was tethered. But we got through without accident, and lost and left nothing. The inci-
dents of the journey however will serve to make you
laugh when you hear them. On arriving at the
station here we found that all the crockery and
bedding and trunks which should have arrived by
Wednesday morning early, had just come at 4
P.M. Thursday, so that my advance working-party
had had nothing to do all day but pick blackberries
and dine at the Weedens.

"I got here just at sunset with my party, found
all hands briskly at work, and met a hearty welcome from Weeden, Mrs. Weeden, and Mary Bel-

lows, who is here on a visit. And it did seem a haven of delights. The servants are delighted with the place. Indeed they were all eager to come, and ten more would have come had I let them. Arthur distinguished himself by his pluck and skill with tools. When Mr. Goodchild, the factotum, came round to open the cask of crockery, he found Master Arthur had done it, and that half the things were in their places on the shelves.

"It was beautiful to see Phil and Berty as we drove through the woods, — so eager were they about the flowers. And what tempts me to write this is that Berty appears at the window offering me a bouquet. They watched the woods on both sides, and reported every blossom as we did on the Alps. And they were mightily pleased when one of the Goodchild boys handed in huckleberry bushes for them to browse on.

"I am already distressing myself about your arrival in New York. It will probably be on Saturday. Of course I shall be there to meet you. But your boat may tarry as mine did, and arrive on Sunday. To be ready for that I now think I shall preach in New York that Sunday. You would not want to wait on Sunday before seeing the children, and if you arrived Saturday I could send you here to them, while if you arrived Sunday we could come on together, Sunday night. Nothing need delay you, only I might have to stay there Sunday while you come here in advance. It is a convenience that this is just half way between the cities.

"If the light at Pt. Judith could be seen 60 miles

— as they pretend it can, it would really be sighted by the steamers coming in, as it is not.

"I have said nothing of your letters. Monday arrived that from Luzerne. I do not wonder that you felt knocked up by those terrible hot days. How provoking that my omission of the word *Belle-vue* cost you my letter at Andermatt. I do not know how I could have been so oblivious. You know I have your route, and I trace you from day to day, imagining that you hold steadily to it.

"Your mother went yesterday to Mrs. Claflin's. I think she feels rather tired from her spring and summer responsibility, but she is in good spirits and well. She goes to the mountains in about ten days. You should hear how enthusiastic Katy's nurse is about her.

"I am just fitting off the troop and myself for the sea. Goodby and God bless us."

"NEW SYBARIS
"Address PERRYVILLE, R. I.,
"*Aug.* 4, 1873.

"DEAR C. & L.

"We are safely here, after a very easy Hegira. I think every one was surprised to see how easy was the packing and moving. All my women wished to come, and I have locked up 39 Highland Street, and cut off my retreat as far as I know how.

"It is lovely here. I look out, as I write, on the pretty pond close behind the house. From the piazza, at a distance, is the eternal sea, not so far but we hear its unrhythmed laughter at night, and see the white lines of the breakers. Just at the left Pt. Judith light flashes — as we sit at night on our piazza, and I believe Block Island [1] light has been seen on the right.

"I have been young and now am old. I am ashamed to say what a relief I find it that I have no *visitor's duties* to discharge. The oversight of the children and the presiding at dinner are as nothing in the comparison. As for the oversight of the children, the freedom and the open-air of the place are all in all to them, and in such solace nineteen-twentieths of the ordinary care vanishes. As for eating and the provision for it, we are yet living on the feudal homage of our new neighbors, and I cannot yet tell how hard it is to be. I know this, that Wednesday in Boston I lugged out two boxes of blackberries literally five miles on a tired arm to treat my children with, having paid 95 cents for them, and that the next night here I found many more and much finer on my table which they had picked themselves on the hill-side.

"Meanwhile they have set to repairing our church, so that by good luck it is not to be open till Sept. 7th. If I am not called to Boston by some exigency I shall not leave this place till I go to New York to meet Emily on the 5th.

"I think even you, Lucretia, will return to your allegiance to the sea-bath when you get here. There is none of that shock, which people say brings on a

---

[1] Long Island. The light on Montauk Point could be seen from the house in good weather. The Block Island lights were directly in front and easily seen.

glow, which shock I hate. It is simply to walk into
an element all charged with elixir vitae — and to
stay as long as you like, to dress slowly, and ride
home in the most delicious air. For me, I found
out long since that I was the slave of climate, that
if the climate suited me I cared but little what the
books were, or the chairs or even the people or the
duties. I am only afraid that Emily and you, when
you come, may find a life very stupid, which has
nothing to plead for itself but that it is never too
warm and never too cold.

"I enclose Emily's last, and Susy's last. The last
is probably not so late as you have. When will
you like to try us here? My mail is wretched so
you must give me notice fully two days in advance
and better thrice.

"Much love always."

TO MRS. HALE

"*Aug.* 4, 1873. For me I cannot tell you how the
life is more than my fancy painted. For it had not
occurred to me what a relief it would be not to have
to discharge a visitor's duties when one was at the
seaside. The days are only too short.

"I ring them up at six, when I do not sleep on,
as today I did for the first time. Breakfast is at
seven, and Marnie is prompt and full early. Then
there are prayers, nail-cleaning, and the Officer of
the Day and I do what we think you would do if
you were here. The boys are not permitted to have
their boots on or to go out till this time. At eleven
or earlier Goodchild's wagon, with an old white horse

comes round for the bath. We get back by one-thirty and dine.

"Then Nelly and I see to Harry and Rob till Katy is ready for them. I try to arrange some party for all at four or after, and of course tea comes before we know. The boys go to bed by twilight. Nelly and I sit up quite gravely till nine-thirty, but ten is apt to see us all in bed."

TO MRS. HALE

"SYBARIS, *Aug.* 6, 1873. We have your letters from Luzerne to Berty and to me. I wish you could see the quiet full pleasure the boy took in it and in the picture, the attention with which all of them absorbed the letter, and the pride of Berty at having it, for his own. It arrived very fitly. For Berty's birthday celebration had been postponed till a more convenient season, and this season was appointed for today. So that the house was full of whisperings and preparations, and your present seemed to come just in the nick of time. It came yesterday afternoon.

"Our life here is absolutely perfect. I was going to say Arcadian — but it is more and better than Arcadian. It is simply what a good God, who loves his children meant and means in his infinite grace that his children shall have, pure enjoyment if only they will take life simply. There is nothing to tell, one day is just like another, but the days are crowded full and perfectly bright and happy. You will delight to see how the children enjoy it.

"There is a patriarchal side to it which has an

element of humor. The older children are constantly talking of Swiss Family Robinson. As we came, five of us from the Beach the other day, they said papa was 'I', Nelly the good Elizabeth, Arthur Fritz, Edward Ernest, Philip Jack, and Berty Francis. Then they seemed conscious that Edward and Ernest did not fit well and tried to recast their characters. You will guess that the whole imagination originated with Edward. But my great triumph was Monday, when we came up all eight together from the beach, Nelly and I on the back seat with Berty and Harry in laps, — Arthur, Edward, and Phil on the front seat with Robby in laps, — and the three older boys taking turns in driving. Then in the afternoon they all had their first row on the pond. I do not let them go without me, Phil and Berty rowed us round. I felt as grand as our old hen with all her chicks. The boat is an old ship's yawl, which we could not upset if we all hung on one gunwale together trying to. The rate when well rowed is between one and two miles an hour, which, as the pond is small, is better than if she were larger.

"I am writing serenely while Katy and Nelly are making the lunch preparations for the picnic by which Berty's Birthday is to be celebrated. Nelly made the cake this morning, and at five o'clock (now) we take it to pic-nic grove, which is 1000 feet across the pond as I sit here, the other side of the pond to take our tea. The greatest triumph in the cuisine, I think was yesterday. The four boys went out and picked huckleberries, with which Nelly made the pudding, a perfect success from Miss Tallant's receipt book. This was our third in five days, today we had the fourth. We have at last got them big enough which we found difficult. We ate ten pounds of oat meal and ten of sugar in our first four days, but for all that house keeping is very cheap, and I shall make money by the operation.

"This birthday rather takes up the time of all hands or you would have with this a letter from Edward, who had a great deal that he wanted to tell you. I brought from Liverpool birthday presents for Arthur, Berty, Harry, Rob, — and a general present — a sort of coach-building toy for the crowd of the others. I have, rather weakly, produced Rob's with Harry's today. Harry's birthday also having been postponed, and the presents take up a good deal of their time. Rob's is a sort of dissected puzzle, and Harry's a good game.

"We have at the other house Bellows and Annie, — with Mr. James, the minister of Bristol, England, who is spending his summer with Bellows. We always meet at bathing and practically we are together every evening. But tonight they are going to some festivities at Wakefield, to which fortunately I am not bidden. Bellows is as jolly as he always is when he is off duty, and Annie very well and happy. I hear no more of her young doctor. What a pity he did not know his own good fortune. Your Aunt Katharine would have told him! Oh today's *Independent* has verses by Rose Terry Cooke, but neither Nelly nor Arthur know anything about her marriage, and I did not think to ask your mother.

"I get very pleasant letters from Charles and Lucretia who were at Bethlehem when I came home, and, having to give up their rooms there went to the Waumbek house, where they now are in one of the cottages, having a very pleasant quiet time. They are to the last degree silent about any plans, — perhaps have none, but I think they mean to stay there two or three weeks longer. They found all the world there including Ann-Caroline and Lizzie Guild. Lucretia had never been on that side of the mountains before. Some letters slip through to us very quickly, this one did, others are several days in coming from Boston so that thus far there is no particular mail now and one expects nothing and is never disappointed.

"Nelly announces that the pic-nic is ready so I start, I shall probably be back in an hour, so intelligent and sensible is the whole plan of the entertainments. Leila Weeden is here rushing round, she being the only company at the party, which is well.

"Berty was very much pleased with the soldier hat sent him.

"Much love to all

"P.S. Evening. The picnic went off very successfully. We were absent from the house perhaps an hour and a half, the distance for the walking party being rather more than I had calculated. I forget if you went to what they call Picnic Grove. It is a pretty place, just in sight from this window on the other side of the pond, with only this difficulty, which I have noticed in other picnic grounds, that as it slopes toward the water there is a certain ten-

dency to coast down, which all the pic-nickers and
their provisions feel, which they are obliged to con-
ceal, as far as they can. The children enjoyed the
whole expedition to the top of their bent. Katy
went with us, to keep an eye on her chickens.

"I am particularly pleased with the pluck of all
the four older boys. I made a mistake in landing,
and missed the path, so that we had to work our
way for some distance through the heaviest tangle
you can conceive of clethra and laurel. It was very
hard work. But neither Phil nor Berty winced nor
complained. We had to leave them while we went
forward to discover the way, and they had a wait
till we were ready, but they were thoroughly brave,
obeying orders promptly, and in all regards showing real manhood. For which you may be sure I
complimented them thoroughly.

"Nelly made and frosted the cake very nicely.
We dressed it with some sugar plums I found at
the apothecary's at Wakefield. Mine had a certain
hore-houndy taste, — but I found the youngsters
did not care. They are all in bed now, sleeping
soundly.

"I have just been fitting out a wax paper in oil
in the red Bohemia glass for an entry light."

"Good night. Ever yours,"

Few hours in my father's life, at this time (1870–
1880) can have been happier than those he passed
on the beach at Matunuck, sitting on the sand after
the bath, and talking with Mr. Weeden, Doctor
Bellows, and Doctor Hedge. It was not that the
talk was so brilliant or so intellectual; doubtless,

talk as good could have been heard in many other
groups on many other beaches. It was rather that
these three men preëminently had been his co-
workers in the work which for a dozen years had
absorbed the best of his life and energy. We children, as we played about on the beach, did not
understand that. To our minds Mr. Weeden was
of course the person in general authority in the place,
the Sachem, my father liked to call him; Doctor
Bellows and Doctor Hedge were kindly old gentlemen, who came for visits now and then, one a bit
more genial than the other, who could tell amusing
stories if one cared to listen, but were otherwise unin-
teresting. To my father they were fellow soldiers,
fellow captains in fact, in the battle of life. The
battle was still going on all the time, and they all
had their stations, but (in the kindly fashion of
older campaigns) the war gave leisure now and then
for easy-going recuperation and rest of the soul.

TO MRS. HALE

"*Aug.* 10, 1873. It is a lovely Sunday morning
and I am down stairs a little before my chicks. I
can hear Harry and Robby having a great frolic
with Berty and Phil up stairs.

"We got yesterday your very nice letters from
Berne, with the picture of the bears for the children.
I have the Baedecker's Switzerland out from the
Fellowes Athenaeum, so that we can follow your
route there. I hope you may meet, in the semi-
weekly (*Advertiser*) of yesterday I believe, my letter
of the Over-Alp Pass. The children are desirous, of

course, to know the story of the English officer who was devoured by bears, which I did not remember. You will have to give up your plea that you do not write letters well, for no one ever made a journey so distinct at a distance.

"Harry comes in, brown as a berry, and very handsome. I compliment him on having gone into the sea yesterday which till then he has refused to do. But yesterday afternoon Katy and Mary Quirk went down to the beach with Marny Foster, and both Harry and Rob volunteered to go in,[1] if they might have their stockings on 'so as not to be wet.' But when they arrived, Harry abandoned the stockings and went in as far as they wanted him to, and played in the water very happily. This is a great triumph. As for Robby, he said it wet him as it undoubtedly did. But Katy got her bath for him which is what she wanted. They are all burned as brown as Indians, but you will not care for that when I tell you how perfectly well they are.

"My heart is harassed because I fear that the berries will be gone before you come here, and I cannot bear that you should not take in the profusion of our first week. We have berry pudding every day. The blackberries are splendid and very abundant, and every night and generally at breakfast, we have as many of them as I will let them eat. But yesterday when dear Nelly, who is perfectly well and very jolly, wanted to make huckleberry cake, it was with difficulty that enough were found for the purpose. Unless some new pastures prove

[1] Harry was five years old, Robby almost four.

to be richer than those here, they will be all gone before you come. The drought has been very bad for them. It is equally bad for the grass, which does not grow at all. Yet the morning fogs are heavy and should take the place of rain.

"Nelly likes taking the advantage of the simple kitchen proximity and has had very good success in cooking. She made our first huckleberry pudding — rolling the paste with a bottle — because we had then no rolling pin. She has made nice Indian bannocks from a Nantucket receipt, birthday cake for Berty's birthday, and huckleberry cake for last night. She always confers with Marnie about the breakfasts and dinners, and the girls all adore her.

"*After Breakfast.* I am surprised at the evenness of our temperature. Today is a cool day, so that I have just now retired to put on flannel drawers. But after all it is not cold. They went to Newport from the other house yesterday, and reported, when they returned, that it was the hottest day of the season there. But we had not been conscious of heat. I brought down a thermometer, but it was blown down and broken the first day so that we have no more accurate register than our own feelings. I think I have slept without blankets one night.

"The time goes mysteriously. I thought I should be tempted to write too much for want of other occupation. But after ten o'clock there is seldom any chance. I do get a little reading in the evening when we do not sit out on the piazzas. I have with me some of the Old French lives of Charlemagne, which are very curious and interesting, especially after what we saw in Bavaria and Austria. Had I found out while we were together that Oester-reich meant the Eastern realm of Charlemagne's Empire? The battle of Roncesvalles dwindles into a very insignificant skirmish on the Spanish frontier. One of the only things I read coming over was Galien le Restauré, one of my beloved romances, with the Romance account of it. One wonders more than ever what the truth of history is.

"The Bellows party leave tomorrow and of course we shall all miss them very much. Mr. James to whom I have alluded is a very lively, gentle, unsophisticated Englishy man, unmarried, and about Bellows's age. He has not been well, and Dr. Bellows, who likes him, I think, better than he does any of the English Unitarians, wrote over to invite him to spend the summer with him. He is very fond of our boys, and is constantly offering to them to take them back to England. I do not think he more than half understands Bellows's fun, which indeed needs to be mitigated a little in the presence of a person so slow-moulded. We always bathe together. Poor Bellows came over here for some books on Friday. You know he reads at least one a day. He was in despair when he found little here besides my guide books and dictionaries, the Greek Testament and Horace. You know my summer tastes all too well. I offered him Jokai's Hungarian Stories and a volume of Scribe's plays. It ended in his taking a French history of the Calendar which I bought for Charles, and the Report of the Weather Bureau. That night Fred sent us quite a parcel of books, so that I am ready to lend to people who do not see the charm of the anonymous life of Charlemagne.

"I am going to Mr. Goodchild's Sunday School at 9:30 and at 10:30 we shall have a service at Willow Dell as we did last week. Arthur and Nelly have practiced 'Awake My Soul,' 'Joy to the World,' 'The Lord is my Shepherd' and the Italian Hymn, so that we can have some singing in which last week we failed. The boys are writing to you and I shall enclose their letters. I shall try to strike you at Liverpool or Queenstown. Think of being so near the end!"

TO LUCRETIA AND CHARLES

"*Aug.* 5, 1873. I have your notes of July 31st and August, announcing your change of base. Observe that my mails are of the worst, (for my purposes the best,) and though we get some papers from Boston in twenty hours, we have to allow seventy-two for anything. It is just lovely here for the patriarchal simplicity of life; rode up from the beach yesterday, driven by Phil and Harry and Arthur in turn in a wagon which contained me and my seven children. In the afternoon we all took a sail on Sybaris Lake as the children have christened Wash Pond, the boat rowed by Phil and Berty who rowed very well. Bruno the dog followed, not being permitted to enter."

As soon as he reached Matunuck with the family, motherless for the moment, of one girl and six boys of whom the oldest was thirteen and the youngest three, my father's mind naturally turned to the need of some sort of arrangement which should turn the probable chaos into a possible cosmos. The experience and the interests of the Civil War, still fresh in all minds, led him to form a military organization. To carry out this plan, he devised a series of General Orders in which he promulgated whatever ideas and directions he desired. He used to read the General Orders at breakfast. We children accepted the plan, as children are apt to accept the phenomena of family life, as being a normal way of doing things and entered naturally into the spirit of it. The theory was that the household was a military post. He was himself the Major-General Commanding. Mamma was the Field Marshal. We children had different ranks, and were gradually promoted. There were no privates, except the dogs, of whom we had a varying number. The military organization did not go much beyond the arrangement of the day's occupation. The Officer of the Day had to make arrangements for this and that, and had certain privileges, like driving to the beach. I cannot find the earliest General Orders, — probably they were not kept at first, but the following of later years preserve the original spirit.

GENERAL ORDERS

New Sybaris, *July* 3, 1877.

1. The M. G. C. calls the attention of the Command to the hour of rising on National Holidays.
2. The Junior Officers may get up when they like,

on Holidays or on any other days, on the following conditions, and with the following restrictions.

3. They must get up at the rising bell whether they like it or not. Those who do not like it will copy the passage from Marcus Aurelius in their adversaria at school.[1]

4. If they get up before rising bell they must not disturb their senior officers, of whatever grade.

5. In the celebration of National Holidays torpedoes and caps are forbidden except at the ice house and summer house, and fire crackers wholly forbidden except in presence of M. G. C.

By the M. G. C.
E. E. HALE Officer of the Day.

Password   GENERAL ORDERS   *Countersign*
Bob.   Major.

NEW SYBARIS, Sept. 5, 1877.

1. The energies of every officer of the line and staff will combine for the happy celebration of this auspicious day.[2]

2. Major Bob will himself take the general command of the enterprises set on foot for the celebration, in co-operation with the Officer of the Day.

3. His commission as Major will issue dated this day.

4. In the gradual progress of time, and the pro-

---

[1] "School" was the hour or so after breakfast, in which those who did not have "policing" or something of the sort, studied moderate lessons. The adversaria were blank books in which we used to write and copy all sorts of things.

[2] Robert's birthday.

motion of deserving officers the command is
thus left without Captains. There was a time,
within the Major General Commanding's memory, when officers of genius, now prominent
members of the staff ranked even as privates,
and when in this whole command no commissions had issued of higher grade than that of
Captain on this auspicious day disused.

5. The same progress of time, however, has gradually made unnecessary the office, by the gradual
abolition of the privates of the line. There are
now but three privates in this command.[1] Two
of them, although drawing rations regularly,
and adding to the nominal strength of the garrison, cannot be counted among the effectives
as they are always under arrest. The remaining private, of wayward character, somewhat
unreliable even as a sentry, and never understanding the watchword, is now left without a
company standing, — by the gradual promotion
of the Captains.

6. Under these circumstances the M. G. C. pro-
motes Private Bismarck to the rank of Corporal,
in the hope of getting rid of the grade of privates
altogether. So soon as privates Pusheen and
Kitty Clover show themselves capable of boot-
blacking, a company will be organized from
these recruits. Till that time they will be spoken
of as recruits, in the same grade as Cock a
Doodle, Partlet, Partlet's sister, Partlet's sister's
friend, Chick a biddy, Little chick, and Pullula.

[1] The three dogs, Bismark, Disraeli, and Andrassy.

7. Of the relief of seeing a garrison without privates the M.G.C. will say nothing.

8. The Regatta, with infinite difficulty, resulted in two successful heats, Ingomar and Charles Wager winning one each. It will be resumed immediately after the morning parade.

9. The Command will parade for bathing at 10.30.

10. The completion of the Frigate is an era in the history of this command reflecting great credit on the garrison. The thanks of the M. G. C. and the staff are tendered to the chief of staff.

By the M. G. C.

CHAS. BARRY, Officer of the Day.

Password	GENERAL ORDERS	*Countersign*
Kappa		Victory

NEW SYBARIS,
June 28, 1878.

1. After a series of combined movements, of the greatest intricacy as of the greatest importance, the Major General Commanding has the honor of announcing his return to this garrison, and personal assumption of the command. The precision of the combination made at the Kingston Station between the two columns which moved from the West and the North deserves a permanent record in Military History.

2. Officers will report in detail to the F. M. the parts borne by their regiments in the series of skirmishes of last night, skirmishes continued till daybreak, and assuming the proportions of a battle. Victory achieved by our army, exhausted

by long movement and hardly accustomed to its new positions, assumed new value, — and every regiment engaged is permitted to mark upon its colors the name of the Battle of the Trumpets.

3. Following the policy of F. M. Joshua, in the case well known in the books of the fall of Jericho, the enemy announced his presence in all parts of our camp by the sound of trumpets, blown incessantly. Without discussing in these orders, the propriety of the movement as executed by that distinguished commander, the M. G. C. warns his junior officers in this command of the danger of accepting that isolated case as a principle.

4. The instance of last night is a sufficient illustration of the danger of such an error. At the post where the M. G. C. had stationed himself the winged hosts of the enemy encouraged by darkness rushed forward to the attack with gallantry worthy a better cause. Their bodies lie at this moment where they sounded their wild alarm. And morning, as she waked, beheld the M. G. C. asleep among the hosts of slain!

By the M. G. C.

Password   GENERAL ORDERS   *Countersign*
Beaconsfield   Independence

No. 2

POST NEW SYBARIS, *July* 4, 1878.

1. The M. G. C. resumes his command in person on this auspicious day with feelings of particular satisfaction.

2. If, as men be, it is so that they must cut the tie,[1] — the M. G. C. rejoiceth that he is far distant from the points where that cut tie is commemorated, by public demonstration.

3. In deference, however, to the superstitions of one hundred years, and with a view to the conciliation of the autocthons, lessons will be omitted today. In the place of them, each intelligent officer of this command will furnish three lines for a sonnet on the "Peaceful Celebration of Victory." The rhymes will be furnished by the Chief of Staff on application.

4. The Command will have observed, with regret, that the exigencies of distant service have removed from us all the officers of that sex, without whom it has been supposed Earth was a desert. It is for the officers of this command to shew, that that popular impression is fallacious, which supposes that, under such circumstances, life fails in the decencies and dignities.

5. To avoid pain, however, to those whose services are well intended, officers will not wash their own linen, cook their own food, mend their own clothes, or make their own beds, until further orders from these head-quarters.

6. Punctuality at meals is especially to be observed.

7. Till otherwise ordered Col. Arthur will act as chief of staff. Maj. Phil will act as officer of the day today and will find some proper badge for this service.

[1] This was a paraphrase of the Declaration of Independence in words of one syllable.

8. On other stations the M. G. C. has observed with regret the growing practice of bossing among officers. He alludes to it to condemn it. Even to a private, orders should be given without austerity. Among officers the intimation of a wish is to be so conveyed that no suspicion of rank shall be carried by the manner. The junior officer, — indeed, shews his ingenuity and re-source best, by anticipating the wishes of his senior, before they are spoken.

9. Capt. Rob will write to mamma today.

By the M. G. C.

TO MRS. HALE

"MATUNUCK BEACH, *July* 2, 1877. It is beyond language how much I enjoy this place. I remember my old first letters to you when you were in Europe. I suppose it is all the better from the awful randan before we came. Today has been a very tranquil and a very successful day. I am working like a dog on the history, but I have plenty of time. I have to grind out sixteen pages a day. I am sorry to say that I have done all the interesting part, which is poor La Salle's life and death.

"This evening till half past eight we have been capping verses. Strange to say this is a favorite amusement of Charles's, who brings in his old Latin lines with great freshness. He has entered into life here very heartily, and you might see him for a day or two without thinking he was ill. He will not touch a pen, but he rows in the boat, reads, gets up to breakfast, generally, and is even talkative. I am very much encouraged about him. But it seems very queer here without you. Because you were real estate. Whoever was not here, you were, and I constantly catch myself thinking that you will come downstairs, or that I will run up to your room to shew you something.

"Goodchild has a new beach wagon and a new saddle all ready for us. The Weedens have a pair of new horses and a phaeton to take the place of the defunct Puss. These necessitate a new coachman who takes the place of Jerry. The new coachman has a dog, the dog is a slut, and has four little puppies. I need not say that they are an important part of the establishment. We had a very homelike service over there yesterday. If I can find a copy, I will send you my sermon on Sunday in the Country."

CHAPTER TWENTY-SEVEN

PREACHING

1870–1880

TOWARD the end of the seventies my father began to print his sermons more or less regularly. "Every parish minister," he wrote in 1881,[1] "will understand that there is a certain convenience in having in print a few copies of a sermon, which he may wish to send to some who did not hear it. This convenience has been enough to justify the continuation of this series. For the additional convenience of preservation, a few copies are now bound and published together, — not because they are on one subject, but rather because they are not. They simply represent the affectionate counsel which a minister who has spoken to one congregation for a quarter of a century has a right to offer on every theme to the people who come to hear him, — people most of whom have heard him long, but who are, in general, younger than he is." It can hardly be that such a series, or we might say several such series, will not represent the body of theological convictions of the preacher. Theological doctrine we need not say, for often the stated doctrine ex-

[1] In a preface to a volume which included the fourth series which he reprinted: "June to May: The Sermons of a Year, Preached at the South Congregational Church in Boston in 1880 and 1881."

presses imperfectly the convictions at heart. Yet
even the theological doctrines of my father might
with certainty be gathered from these volumes. He
was not indifferent to doctrine. He believed absolutely what he did believe. He belonged to a Church
which feels that beyond the limits laid down by the
necessities and circumstances of human association,
the particular religious convictions of the individual
are matters which lie between him and God. He
could have fellowship with anyone who wanted to
work with him. Whatever his own body of doctrine was, therefore, he could never have felt that
he could insist upon it as the creed of his Church,
but on the other hand such body of doctrine as he
did have he was bound to declare to those who
heard him.

He was a believer in theological doctrine. I do
not see that he ever changed his mind in regard to
the opinions which he expressed as early as 1848 in
a sermon preached to the Charlestown Unitarian
Book and Tract Society. In the beginning of that
sermon he remarks that the Unitarian rarely takes
in a discussion of mere doctrine the same interest
that will be taken by one who really feels that
eternal happiness or eternal misery depend upon
theological opinion, belief, or knowledge.

"Now it is quite too late," he goes on in that
sermon, "to attempt to account for this difference
by saying that the Unitarian does not care for his
own religion, and that he has so little of it that he
does not care to seduce others to his views." He
speaks of earlier Unitarians and goes on, — "It is

too late to say this of a faith which is tested every hour in the patient, faithful, hopeful, sublime death-bed scene of those who have lived by it here on earth, and have been taught by it how to begin the life which is heavenly. Care-wrung men, fear-worn women, cling to this exposition of their relations to God, and to one another, more dearly than they cling to anything beside — to life itself — it is all that makes life tolerable. Their first prayer and their last of every day is gratitude to God that he has made clear the mystery of godliness, that they are children at his feet, that they have a world of brethren of his love, that they hear the whisper and see the heavenly life of the Brother — the chosen son of his affection, — and that there is no magic veil, no chasm of mystery to keep them longer asunder."

Doctrine, he held, was not unimportant to the Unitarian; it was, as one might say, of the first importance, for it was a means and not an end. Unitarianism made no claim that its creed was an entrance ticket to the gate of heaven. "With us religious doctrine is not the end, it is only the first step of the beginning. It is the first means of life, of true life, but only the first. We look upon doctrine as being the means of true life, but not as its object. We look upon the object of true life as being this — its own enlargement, its own advance, its own improvement forever." As I remember my father's preaching as I heard it regularly for almost twenty years, as I see it now in the records of this preaching, it seems to me that this early statement

THE SOUTH CONGREGATIONAL CHURCH
Union Park Street

made at the very beginning of his career as a preacher
was the foundation on which he stood for the fifty
years and more of his subsequent ministry. It seems
to me, as I look over the pages of this early sermon,
that save for some difference of style, it fairly repre-
sents his later ideas, not only in its fundamentals
which have been given, but in its development of
those fundamentals.

Undoubtedly his later experience furnished him
with many ideas for explanation and illustration.
As he felt that doctrine must always work itself
out in life, so he was always seeing in life the evi-
dences of the doctrine. And although he rarely
formulated an inclusive statement of belief, yet it
cannot be difficult for one who heard the sermons of
these years or who now reads them, to understand
the convictions which gave life to the different things
he did and would have others do and made them a
harmonious and organic whole.

He must have had more belief than he would ever
have tried to formulate for the Church of which he
was a minister. His feeling for doctrine was much
the same as his feeling for organization. He knew
that organization was a necessity in life, but his idea
of organization was in making an organism (as we
call it, though I think he never did), and not in
making a machine. We have seen of late (as he
would have rejoiced to see) the break-up of a great
organization; we have read of the Russian Empire
which had gradually in the course of centuries
grown to take in such a great number of different
political bodies that the chief aim of the bureau-

204 EDWARD EVERETT HALE

cracy which governed it was to form a complete
centralization of the whole machinery of State
organization — "to reduce everything to one uniform pattern." Such a social structure my father
could never have approved, for he felt instinctively
that such an order was a denial of the individuality
which was his dearest possession. In like manner
he felt that no central authority could express any
detailed creed so as to be sufficient for all people in
all places, for all times. He was doubtless a Catholic
in his all-including charity, but he could not accede
to such Catholic creeds. He preached a sermon
somewhat after this time called "What it is to be
a Catholic." One will easily imagine that the
Catholic religion was not that of which the creed
was believed by everyone, everywhere, and at every
time, but that of which the plan and influence
went out to everyone and took in everyone in its
range of benefit.

He was often content to state the essentials of his
religious belief in its simplest terms. The following
letter, written in answer to an inquiry, is one of his
own statements on the subject.

"BOSTON, *Dec.* 14, 1874.

"MY DEAR FRIEND;

"As I hope I may call you;

"I am very sorry to have delayed so long my
answer to your note of the 18th of November. But
I have had to let all my letters go, while I was finishing a little book which I had promised, and which
I shall hope in a few days to send you.

"I can tell you in very few words what I believe.

"I believe that God is here now, and that I am one of his children whom he dearly loves.

"I believe a great many more things than this. But when you ask me such a question as yours, namely what is the belief that makes me a happy man, and resolute to do God's work in the world as well as I can, this answer is the real answer. It is what your ministers would call the essential or fundamental answer.

"For the truth is, that what a man needs is to *live* as much as he can. 'Life more abundantly,' as the Savior says, is the great object. That I may live more earnestly and vigorously and efficiently to-day than I did last year. Now in this matter of *life*, what I do or do not happen to think about one thing or another is of very little consequence, if only I have the infinite help of God's Holy Spirit, which does come to any man who believes God is, that God loves him, and is eager to help him as being indeed his child.

"Instead therefore of hunting round, as I think you are doing, for verbal expressions of the truth, I try to live by such truth as I have, quite certain that I shall get more. Suppose I were a blacksmith and wanted to strike stronger blows. The best thing I could do would be to strike my very best, and my arm would get stronger every day. But if I went off to read books about the structure of the arm, and other books about vital fluids, and others about medical theories, why, my arm would be growing flabby all the time.

"If you will *use* what faith you have you will be sure to get more faith. That is about what Jesus says. If you only have as much as a grain of mustard seed, *Use it.* That is, the grain, *if you use* it, will swell and grow and become a tree, with ever so many more grains. But if you keep it in a box to look at it, and handle it, and talk about it, and are all ready when the minister comes round to show it to him so that he can say it is all right, why it will not grow at all, and you will not have any more.

"Live with all your might, and you will have more life with which to live.

"Now all that will show you why I am afraid to send you any books which will tell you what Unitarians believe about Christ or heaven or hell, or other things of interest. Because I see from your letter, that you think you can *read* or *study* your way to faith, and more faith. Now, as Paul says, the letter killeth, and only the spirit gives life. And although I think the Unitarian books have the truth in them, yet I think a man makes a great mistake who studies those books or any other books, with the idea that *Faith* is a matter of the intellect, any more than a matter of the digestion or appetite. The body and the mind are both of them merely tools of the soul, and you and I must see that the soul keeps them under.

"For faith, the soul needs to pray simply to God.

"'Father — help me,' that is quite enough; and to act bravely on what faith it has already. That faith will certainly grow and the soul will get more.

But you can no more argue a man into faith with
the best of arguments, than you can whip him into
faith with the best of whips.

"You are quite right in thinking that I have
faith in my faith. I certainly have. Our religious
armor or clothing among the Unitarians is very
light and it does not chafe us. Because we are
children of God we thank him very heartily for his
Son, his Word, his Spirit, and, though there are
many things we cannot explain, we do not think
it is our business to explain them.

"If, however, you will determine to take the
books I send, for what they are worth *and no more*,
I will send you a parcel of Unitarian books. You
shall pay the express, and you need not pay any
more. I shall have to pay nothing for them. But
I beg you again not to think that any verbal statement of truth that you may find in them is of any
consequence compared with the solid *faith* that
will grow in your own heart in proportion as you
do God's will, and ask him to help you.

"Very truly yours.

"EDWARD E. HALE."

One could go farther thus in saying what he believed, but I believe one should not try to formulate
fully his theological belief from the sermons of these
or other years. It would be entirely against his own
will and feeling, even were it possible for me to do
so. It would certainly seem to him far too much
like the estimating or summarizing of the system
of ideas of a literary man. I do not believe he had

any great faith in such estimates and summaries.
If one wanted to know what anyone thought, there
was no shorthand way of finding out. He did himself occasionally make some summaries more inclusive than others. He once preached a sermon on
Unitarian principles. Unitarians, he points out,
were first so called (in Hungary, 1563) because they
believed in the unity of religion for all Christians,
whatever their especial creed, whether Lutheran,
Calvinist, or Socinian. The word was applied with
other and not inappropriate meanings, and now
stands for the "oneness of God and the consequent
oneness of man, who is the child of God." And as
the central statement of Unitarianism was that all
men are children of God, it was for them especially not to adopt any partisanship, sectarianism,
phariseeism, which should keep others away from
them.

"All the same, however, Unitarians exist, and
have a religious life, parted as far as the poles from
the religious life of people who believe in sect and
rely on dogma. I have some times found myself
in correspondence or in conversation with persons
relying on creeds, and as sure of their doctrines as
the high priest Caiaphas was of his, who did not
seem to me to have the faintest idea of what I meant
by the word 'Religion.' Thus, if you train a man
to consider that forms are the essence of religious
life, you cannot make him understand what you
mean by 'spirit' or 'spiritual communion.' The
religious life of Unitarians and what is popularly
called their faith, cannot from the nature of the

case be defined in a creed. For a creed is limited and means to be limited, and the religious life and faith of Unitarians are unlimited and mean to be unlimited. Still truth is true, life is life. The divine life, shown in human order, will show itself in ways resembling each other. And so it is that, even without a written creed and without any authoritative statement of form or dogma, the position of the Unitarian Church is probably more intelligible than that of any other communion in Christendom."

He goes on to note the points of the religious system. Based on the central doctrine that God is Father and that men are brothers, it goes on with the duty of men to help each other, to build up God's Kingdom in the world, to expect a continuance of spiritual life, to worship in the spirit rather than the forms, to gain strength from the truth wherever found. And he goes on "It is thus that the Unitarian Church, naturally recognizing Jesus Christ as Leader and Lord of the whole Church, makes him the most real being in history, while the church of the dark ages has succeeded in making him the most unreal. As God visits every soul and gives help to every child, how certain is it that this Son of God, who receives the spirit of God without measure, who shows in his energy, his purity, his tenderness, and his unselfishness, the fulness of every attribute of life, — how certain it is that he will be able to exhibit to us God's will and law completely. There is nothing unnatural in such an exhibition of perfect manhood. It is, on the other hand, perfectly natural."

I should not think it right to attempt any such summary of my father's faith, even were it otherwise the thing to do.   I could never satisfy myself that I had got in everything that ought to be in, and that the things I had left out were unimportant and unessential.   But one thing I ought to say, — that his preaching seems to me to be like a beautiful and perfect sphere, perhaps of crystal, of which every part demands every other part, and from any part of which one may imagine or infer the whole.   There was a great consistency in his preaching; it all hung together.   This was not because he had a remarkable intellectual grasp, which infallibly saw the whole when he was called to speak of a part.   I cannot think this was his consistency.   It came rather from his perfectly developed belief in his central propositions and his feeling that thought and action, if rightly inspired and caused by that underlying idea, must be not only consistent with its origin but with every product of its origin.   We do not compare all the leaves on a tree or a plant to see whether they are alike; in fact they are not all alike in every detail, and sometimes they have material differences. But we know that like forces will produce like results, and that the oak leaf, or even the mulberry leaf, will always have the true characteristics of the oak or the mulberry, unless it be for accident.   So with my father's sermons.   I seem to read them all in each one.

It may be because they were the sermons that I heard every Sunday, winter and summer, one year after another during these years, that I think that the sermons of this decade are the most characteristic of him. We children always went to church. We used generally to walk in to church and out, and when Sunday school was in the afternoon we walked in and out again. We were always allowed carfare one way, but we preferred to walk and save it. Some time before, my father had said in a letter to William Weeden that he meant to have his children glad when Sunday came around. To be honest, I must say that I do not think we liked Sunday as well as we did Saturday. But in the main we liked it; there was nothing burdensome about it. We sat in our pew, my mother at one end and my elder brother Arthur at the other. As I remember it, there were six of us at one time, till my brother Harry died in 1876, but I suppose that the two little boys did not come. We were allowed to read Sunday-school books during the sermon when we wished, and up to a certain age we did so. After giving up the Sunday-school books, or perhaps when Sunday-school was put in the afternoon, I used often to follow my own thoughts and imaginations instead of the sermon, but this was to a great degree because the sermon rarely seemed to me anything new; it was of the same stuff and substance that I used to hear otherwise from my father; it was his natural utterance. I do not think, however, that having got to the age of intelligence, I really neglected the preaching, for I have very particular recollections of sermons which must have come in 1875 or '76 and I find, as I look over the printed or the written sermons, that the expressions are very

familiar though the especial development of thought
may be forgotten.

In the pulpit my father always wore a heavy black
silk gown which the ladies of the parish used to give
him.   In this heavy full-sleeved gown, with his
tall figure and massive head, he made an impressive
figure, and needed, as one might say, a large and
massive pulpit to preach from.   At any rate the
pulpit was large and massive.   It was not merely a
reading desk or an open platform, nor a small erec-
tion on a column.   It was a fine massive pulpit,
appropriate to the large man in it and the large
ideas to which he gave utterance.   He usually had
his sermons written out and read them, but so practiced was he in this sort of writing and of delivery
that it had much the effect of extemporaneous utterance.   His sermons were simple in structure, but
they generally expressed the development of his
own thought.   It was not that he had an idea and
looked up a text that would be appropriate.   He
was very apt to take for a text some words of Jesus
or of Paul, and he was by no means neglectful of the
actual meaning of the particular words in the actual
circumstances under which they were uttered.   These
he often spoke of, doubtless always had in mind.
But in nine cases out of ten the saying and the circumstances are of interest to him because they are
broadly typical, because they express not something
particular and exceptional, but because the thing
they express is universal and belongs as much to our
day as it does to the days of the Bible, because they
show God expressing himself in those days in ways

that one can see in our day. Perhaps this is always so of a good sermon. It was so of his sermons because he thought of no essential difference between our time and Bible times. God the Holy Spirit, the world, men and women, are existing to-day and active as they had existed and been active then. Whether he also included Jesus Christ the Saviour among the unchangeable verities, I do not find definitely stated. I suppose, however, that he did, although many of the things he said might seem to imply the contrary. He says on the subject himself in a sermon on "Christian Realism," preached Feb. 6, 1876.

"I read those passages, and I would gladly read more, that I may ask if it is not better thus to consider what Christ did for the people who knew him than to ask what his nature was, or what we should call it, or how he did what he did. It is clear enough that somehow he moved the world.

"Can it be a matter of much import what name we give to this person? People try to make me think so; but I do not think so. One set of people tell me it is his divinity. I assent at once, and I say, 'I also am divine then; I also am a child of God.' Then another eager set says that all that is wrong; it is his exceeding and perfect humanity. Have it your own way. Call it what you will. I like to think it is his humanity; for I know I also am a man. Surely the power of his personality makes clearer what he meant, when he said we are not creatures of God but his children. It shows what he means, when he says God's spirit shall inspire us.

And we, if we will look at him more and repine about him less, if we will obey him more and question less, if we will follow — that is his word — we shall be more sure to find the worth of the lead and the certainty of the power of him who goes before."

Thus one may take almost any sermon and one will find that he is realizing the circumstances then or now.

"That is the reason why they are to repent: Repent ye for the kingdom of God is at hand. The reason is forgotten by many of our modern exhorters. But it was distinct when the Saviour spoke and when his apostles spoke. Yes: and when they prayed, as he taught them to pray, their first prayer was for this 'Kingdom of God.' 'Thy Kingdom shall come.'

"What he taught them, and what they believed, was that a real Kingdom of God was to come in this world that they lived in. And when the Christian Church, in any of its simpler and more intelligent moments falls back on the foundation truths, this is what it teaches now; that God can reign in this world, and that he is to reign here. It does not so much discuss the origin of evil, as proclaim the overthrow of evil. All things bad, mean, cruel, painful, distressing, unjust, unclean, untrue shall cease to be. God shall reign. God's Kingdom shall come. Just as, in the heavens above, planets move as his law directs, — comets come and go, suns and worlds revolve, in precise obedience, — so the time shall come that in this world, which we choose to call the world of man, everything shall obey his purpose. Why not? Man is his child, and like him. Man

and man's doings, the earth in all his methods, shall
obey God. God's Kingdom shall come."

All this is doubtless a part of his sincerity and
consistency. He spoke sincerely, as he believed,
and he achieved consistency, and found it. Some
separate points may be noted, which do not seem
to have as necessary a connection with his religious
thought as with his personal character. Thus he
always was apt to lay stress on the outdoor element
in the Bible because he himself loved the great
outdoors.

"No man reads the four Gospels, indeed, with a
true sense of their flavor, or I may say, an adequate
comprehension of their language, unless he sees how
much of that language and the scenery and illustrations of the story belongs to open-air life. Shep-
herds feeding their flocks by night, the weird caravan
of the astrologers wending their way across the
desert at the bidding of the strange conjunction in
the sky, — these are the very beginning of the story.
Among the thousands of pictures which the life of
Christ has furnished there is not one more suggestive than that in which, under Mary's palm, the
heaven-eyed boy sits at midnight on the knees of
his mother who has herself succumbed to sleep,
while Joseph, too, is sleeping on the ground; the
child, wide awake and without a thought of earth,
looking up at the glories of the infinite stars. Fit
illustration of the beginning of the life of him who
preached from the mountain and the deck, on the
sea-side, at the lake side, and in the corn field, and
finds his lessons in lilies and birds' nests, in sunset

and in storm. The religious lessons of the Gospels
are thus all couched in language which belongs to
what people used to be so fond of calling 'Natural
Theology.'"

In like manner his individualism and hatred of a
lifeless uniformity led him naturally to definite ideas
on form and ritual. Form and ritual he liked, —
that is, he was expressive and he wanted other people
to be expressive also. If people were to express
themselves it must be in some way, and the mode
of expression, the form of the service, the ritual, in
other words, was a matter of importance and interest. Thus he says in a sermon on "Ritual":

"Ritual must never be small or mean, hurried or
apologetic; people must never carry it through as
something of little consequence, which is to be got
out of the way. I have heard people call the worship
of a Church 'the introductory exercises.' The newspapers are too apt to call them so. The truth is
that the worship is what we come for, — the sermon
is an accident or incident, not essential. Yet I
never go down town but I see two or three signs, on
as many chapels, saying that 'preaching' is at such
a time. One guesses that those signs are ordered
by the minister and that he thinks more of himself
than of the God who calls the worshippers together."

It was this communion of worship that he liked.
His own preaching he liked, but that he conceived
was merely his own part in the service. He liked to
read the psalms alternately with the people, or sometimes alternately with the choir. He liked to feel
that the choir were not merely strangers who had

their Sunday work at his church, but were as much
a part of the church as himself. It was partly this
that made Mr. Lang, and Mr. and Mrs. Winch, Mr.
John Winch, and Mrs. West so admirably representative of the spirit of the church. But better even
than fine singing by the choir did he like good singing by the congregation. That was the best kind
of ritual.

"Ritual must give opportunity for common worship. When we read the psalm it is good ritual for
all to read, — to read slowly and with the heart. A
congregational hymn sung with life and spirit is
admirably good ritual."

Such being the general principles, that God was
father and men brothers, that men should work to
bring in the Kingdom, that to do so they must hear
one another's burden, that the spiritual life is for
now and always, that it is spiritual and not a matter
of form, ritual, doctrine, or creed, — these being the
important points of his religious belief, there were
also other principles and beliefs characteristic of him
that ought somewhere to be stated, principles and
beliefs which seem secular and to have little connection or point of contact with his religious doctrines
though not inconsistent with them.

Here, then, I may say a word or two of my father's
wisdom, as we may call it, for he had a great knowledge of the conditions and causes of life. His religious ideas he gained from revelation. It is not
that he believed that a natural theology would result
in the same ideas, but the fact was that his own
religious ideas had come, chiefly of course, from

revelation transmitted by the Church. Spiritual
wisdom it was. But he had besides a secular wisdom
which was also of importance. There was current
about the house for quite a time a picture of an
Arab Sheik, which Charles got in Alexandria, who
looked exactly like my father. My father was
always amused at the resemblance and once projected a publication called, I believe, *The Story
Teller*, which had for a cover illustration a picture
of this Arab telling stories to a group of children.
My father had a good deal in him like the Eastern
story teller, but he had a good deal more about
him like the Eastern man of wisdom. His wisdom
was in one respect Oriental: he was apt to put it
in short sayings. Perhaps he thought more commonly in these short, somewhat detached ideas and
attained his end by them rather than by the more
systematic, regular, and discursive arguments of
western philosophers. However this may be, he
had often in mind certain "mottoes" as he used to
call them, or "rules." Proverbs like those of Solo-
mon they were, sentences or gnomic sayings. Some
he made up, but he liked best those which had a
traditional origin. He liked for instance to ascribe
these sayings to one or other of the family, like our
grandmother, or Uncle Edward, or Fullum, the old
family servant, or other such people. We boys got
pretty familiar with this traditional wisdom, for
though he seldom used it in advice he often used the
phrases. We paid but little attention to it at the
time, but one or another bit of it has often recurred
to me as life has gone on, and as I look back I see

that most of it was very wise, and of a wisdom generally in entire harmony with the doctrine and gospel which he so firmly believed. When he had some saying which seemed out of harmony with the teachings of our Lord, he generally quoted it with a word of comment. Thus in his very last days: "How true," he wrote, April 24, 1909, "is Mr. Everett's cynical remark, — if you want a secret kept, you must keep it." Why was the remark cynical, if it were true? I never asked him that; if I had, he might have said that it was because it recognized a foolish popular characteristic which really did exist, but which one might as well ignore if one meant to accomplish anything.

But as to his sententious wisdom. It would be idle to try to put it in systematic form, for its very essence was that it was not systematic. But the following express in various ways much the same characteristic kinds of conduct.

One of the earliest of these mottoes was: "Do the duty that comes next your hand." This he took from Carlyle, who took it from Goethe, of whom my father had no very high opinion. "Noblesse oblige," he used to say in earlier days. "It is better to do a thing than not to do it, — other things being equal." "A man who is good at excuses is good for nothing else." "Personal presence rules the world." This he used always to ascribe to Eli Thayer of Emigrant Aid days, but he used also to quote Franklin's saying, "If you want your business done, go: if not, send."

"Get the men forward, anyway" and "March on

the sound of the firing" may have had a Civil War origin. "Get along as well as you can every day," was one of Grandma Hale's rules for bringing up a large family. Another was: "Brave boy quick, hands through the flames:" this used to vex us boys very much; I never knew exactly what it meant, but am pretty sure that it came out of Miss Edgeworth's "Harry and Lucy." "Stare decisis" he probably often had in mind, sometimes in Napoleon's form — "If you want to take Vienna, take Vienna." [1]

[1] See "Ninety Days' Worth of Europe" (quoted on I, p. 316). "This I did first on the great principle of life which Napoleon expressed when he said, 'If you want to take Vienna, take Vienna.'"

CHAPTER TWENTY-EIGHT

THE TEXAS JOURNEY [1]

1876

MY father was the best traveling companion in the world. I have often thought, when people were praising his talk and his social charm, that no one really appreciated that side of his personality who had not passed alone with him those evening hours, on a long railroad journey, when it is too dark to look out of the window or to read. His philosophy of travel was perfect. While he was most careful of the health and comfort of his companion, there was deeply fixed in his mind what he early fixed in ours, the noble doctrine that if you cannot stand the discomforts, or even the dangers of a journey, you had better stay at home. He was of a most adventurous spirit, his love of Nature was lifelong, he was a good landscape sketcher, and he knew America, past and present, as few other people did. The Texas journey, which his letters in this chapter describe, was, as he says in one of them, the realization of a wish which had been his ever since he wrote his first pamphlet on Texas in 1845. It enabled him to make the final researches for his novel of "Philip Nolan's Friends," in Louisiana as well

---

[1] This chapter is by my sister Ellen, who was with my father on this journey.

as in Texas, and his little book called "G. T. T. or The Wonderful Adventures of a Pullman" commemorated a part of it. I have been with him on many delightful long journeys since those days; we never enjoyed one more than this.

The first of these letters expresses what was always one of the charms of traveling to him, the release from the horrors, known to all travelers, of winding up one's affairs at home. The reader of this book will have seen pretty plainly that my father was occupied with many affairs beside his personal ones, and the rest of spirit in settling comfortably down in Section Five or Section Six, made, even at as unwearied an age as fifty-four, one of the joyous moments of his life.

> "*March* 29, 1876.
> "LITTLE MIAMI R. R. 30 MILES
> "NORTH E. of CINCINNATI.

"DEAR MAMMA:

"We are very well, thank you, and are very happy. I was too lazy yesterday even to read. Much less did I want to write. My dear, it was luxury enough for me to see the country reel by us, to see N. happy and to do nothing. I could not have stood that chaos of the last fortnight much longer. Even now, I do not quite understand how it came on, save that as any opera draws near its close, all the people get on the stage together, all try to outsing each other, and all the fiddlers try to outfiddle all the singers.

"We had some snow, and some rain, 'areas of snow' the prophet said, and said truly. And the darkness closed in so soon that N. saw but little of the blue Juniata. What she did see was very clayey and yellow, very angry and full. We took our supper at Altoona, where I posted your letter, and we slept from there to Dresden junction, a place you may not know. It is about midway between Ulrichsville and Newark, if that helps you. I slept wonderfully well and N. says she did, but she waked earlier than I. We have had the best section, or one of the four best. For as I told the boys on my last journey, 5 and 7, 6 and 8 are the four best, being the four in the middle. N. prefered to sleep above, so I slept below, as I prefer to do. I believe I have come to that stage that the slight motion lulls me as a cradle's rocking might do. I say that of the Pennsylvania Central which is very steady. I doubt if I should say it here, where as you may see the motion is more frantic.

"You may see also that there are not many events for discussion, even by the pen of a ready writer. We had a good breakfast at Columbus, and I should have said before that we have eaten all the chicken but one leg, and he has been very good, and so was the bread and butter and the gingerbread, of each of which one small piece remains. They have served us admirably at times when the high powers gave us no chance whatever to live upon the country. When they do, the Salons have much improved since I first knew these regions. All the same am I glad that we are going to stay in private houses. Early in life I laid down the rule that the worst house was better than the best hotel, and I have never changed it. It is true that I have had some special advantages.

"It is still very cold, as cold as any weather we have had for a fortnight. In the car, of course, we are as warm as we want to be. The country is a very little greener than with us, where it has a chance, but snow still lies on all northern slopes. I think they must have had a good deal of snow yesterday, and perhaps you are in the same wave or tide or storm or influence today.

"We are nearing the city, and I will fold my note to take a chance to post it at the station."

My father was quite right about the joys of staying at private houses. We were most happy in our stay at Mr. and Mrs. Kebler's in Cincinnati, and at Doctor and Mrs. Heywood's in Louisville. We made the journey between these cities in a small river boat, and enjoyed our voyage so much that we were sorry we had not arranged to continue it to Memphis, where we were to take the *Charles Morgan*, an ideal river steamer, to New Orleans. But our first sight of the Mississippi was so wonderful that it put all regrets out of our heads. It was in flood, and higher, they said, than ever before. The sunset of that evening, which my father has described in "The Wonderful Adventures of a Pullman," was one of the events of our journey; so was the premature arrival of the *Charles Morgan*, which he has described there with equal truth and spirit.

Then followed several strange enchanting days. We were equally happy sketching on the guards and in the pilot-house, where we were made welcome. We sailed, as my father has said, through a profound solitude, for the most part, and through the slowly advancing spring. "This travelling on the river," he wrote, "is admirable. It is the ocean travel with the disagreeables left out. You have no post-boy, no telegraphs, no beggars and no business; per contra you have no sea sickness, no close quarters, you are in an immense hall, and can go out doors any minute, and every few hours you can run ashore if you want to. As for its being monotonous it is the most exciting and eventful life. . . . The leaf enclosed is from a plantation which we backed into by accident this afternoon. It is the best we can shew of spring. There are good coal fires in the cabin which is perhaps a little too warm. The decks are good to walk on but not to sit on save in the middle of the day.

"But at Natchez they brought red roses on the steamer, and when we landed on the levee at New Orleans the air was sweet with summer scents."

TO MRS. HALE

"NEW ORLEANS, *April* 8, 1876. If I had come here, rather than to Washington when I was twenty-two years old, I should have lived here ever since. Where we are, is as perfect a representation of my own Sybaris, as if Mr. Gould had taken it for his theme or study. And the ride out from the city was ludicrously like the ride described there,[1] even to the change of mules for steam power, by a system known, I think, nowhere else in the world.

[1] "Sybaris and Other Homes," p. 31.

"It is just the weather and the aspect of a lovely June or May day in Anniversary week. I mean there is that laughing freshness of the leaves and the garden: the look as if nature were not yet tired of summer. But you can hardly compare season with season in that way. Great bouquets of roses, Solfaterre, Lamarque, La Reine, Marshal Neil, drunk with delight, and hanging heavy on their stalks, are what we do not cut at all. I think the perfume is what knocks me most. They apologize because the oranges are past bloom. One occasional orange of last year hangs on a tree, where it has been left so that people may see: but the storm of last night beat off the last blossoms from these particular trees, and they are covered thick as cherries with little green oranges about the size of cherries. The perfume therefore with which the air is loaded comes from magnolias, just coming into bloom, the large magnolia, from the smaller ones, which have been in bloom, and largely from roses.

"We arrived at the levee about 8, just before breakfast. We walked up to Mr. Gould's store at 9, and met a very hearty welcome. . . . I feel terror-struck now, lest in the excitement of this Mediterranean life (that is what it is, not semitropical), we should never write you about the Mississippi which is one of the Wonders of the World. What we did write to you I do not know. But it is a series of interests and surprises which one might well write a book about. And time and war have changed things so that whatever else is true, the stage notion of a Mississippi steamer or that of romance is absolutely unlike all that we saw in the *Charles Morgan*."

Our stay at New Orleans meant a great deal to me personally, for it was my first foreign town, although everybody in it was my fellow citizen. In those days you constantly heard French, and good French, spoken there, and the whole aspect of the place seemed miraculous to both of us. Old and new friends of my father's were kind to us, his classmate, Mr. Christy, and our kind hosts, Mr. and Mrs. Gould, among the former, and a young and modest literary man, whose stories I had read and admired, Mr. Cable, among the latter. My father found much valuable help in the studies of early Louisiana and Texas which were his main object here. But the hospitality of which New Orleans was full did not cease when we left the city. We passed a night or two at the plantation of Mr. Miner in the Têche country. Mr. Miner and his sister were near relations of that Fanny Lintot who was the young wife of the historical Philip Nolan, and who died of grief after his murder, and it was they who first showed us the charms of plantation life. But we had more time to enjoy that life at Belmont, the plantation of Mr. Stephen Le Bourgeois, on the Acadian Coast, north of the city.

The reason Mr. Le Bourgeois asked us to visit him was so characteristic of that very great feature in Southern life, its hospitality, that I venture to speak of it here. Miss Montgomery, his children's governess, had known some friends of ours in Boston, and had once heard my father speak.

That was enough for Mr. Le Bourgeois; he wanted to give Miss Montgomery pleasure, and he certainly gave it to us.

My father has described, in the little book I have quoted, our arrival by steamer, late at night, at Belmont. I remember our anxiety before getting there; the captain seemed to have very little idea as to where we were going to stop, and to be divided in his mind between several estates belonging to planters named Le Bourgeois or Bourgeois. At last, as my father says, of the heroines of his book, "Far, far away as the boat rushed on was a speck of light. This the ladies were told was the signal on shore which Mr. Le Clerc had lighted to direct the pilot.

"There was a fascination for a minute or two in watching the speck. Then the girls went back for their traps; and, with shawl-straps, umbrellas and the rest, stood waiting. The boat rushed toward its goal faster than ever, it seemed. A few minutes more and they could see a white shed and dark figures moving to and fro. Nearer and nearer! A gentleman with a lad behind him is visible, and three or four larger Negroes. Nearer and nearer! The great landing-plank of the larboard side swung round and hovered about the shore. 'Ting! ting!' The pilot stopped the engines. Flash! From the depths appeared two great pine-knot torches, which, with the pine fire on shore, made the whole as light as day.

"'All ready!'

"'Good-by! Good-by, captain!'

"And the ladies ran on shore."

We were met by Mr. Le Bourgeois and his son, just as they were by the Mr. Le Clerc of the novel. Then followed days packed full of interest. The problems of a great sugar plantation, only eleven years after the Civil War, were attractive enough to my father, and his admiration of our host's energy and intellect in dealing with them is apparent in the letter which follows. As for me, the picturesqueness of the cypress swamps behind the sunny area of well cultivated plantation rivaled in my heart the joys of my rides with the young daughter of the house. After forty years, I have but little scruple in printing these extracts from my father's letter as it stands, describing the beginnings of a friendship which has lasted for many years now.

TO MRS. HALE

"STEAMER ST. MARY, *April 23*, 1876. You have before this come to the conclusion that we are decided 'Children of the Public.' There never was a better illustration of this, than the change from Belmont to this steamer. Whether the state of society and civilization which reigns at Belmont is to continue or not, is an open question. I look more favorably on its prospects than they do themselves, and they do more favorably than they did a year ago. However that may be, it is, on the whole, the most finished feudalism now to be seen in America. It is more like the life I saw at Lord Hatherton's [1] than Nelly is like to see anywhere, and in many regards it is more feudal than that was. Mr. Le

[1] See I, p. 300.

Bourgeois is one of the most satisfactory men I have ever known. He is an accomplished gentleman; I think I said before that he is four days older than I. Now observe that this man, like all sugar planters, has to be a farmer on the largest scale, say 800 acres under cultivation, a manufacturing chemist, in the most delicate of processes known to manufacture, a merchant whose combinations may result in a profit annually of $75,000 or a loss of the same amount. He is requested, at the same moment, by philanthropists like you and me, to supervise in its detail the greatest social problem of the age, which changes untaught negro slaves into voters, and to adjust the labor problem which results from this, without losing one day's work on his farms, or the proper bubble on one of his great sugar kettles. At the same moment, under our system, he is of course expected to attend to the politics of the parish, state and country, to thwart the Kelloggs and Warmoths when they need thwarting, and to encourage them when they need encouraging. For recreation he has five sons and two daughters, ages much the same as our children's. Of course he could not approach these duties, but that he has a cheerful, active, intelligent, prudent, careful, spirited wife, who is also very pretty. For visitors, as we have often been taught, the life is delicious. Perhaps the life of all visitors is, if, as that poor soul said, they have a house to start from. I think we were favorites. Certainly, we staid but three days, but while we were there the school was pretty much suspended, and Mr. Le Bourgeois must have given his directions to his foremen somewhat on the sly, though I must declare that I did my best to keep out of his way.

"I did not mean to get into such a moralizing vein, but what is written is written. So soon as our plans were made, Mr. Le Bourgeois went to New Orleans to engage our berths on this steamer, and to have her call for us on Saturday night. All hands but Mrs. Le B. and her mother sat up to see us off. Whist till 11 P.M., star-gazing and sentiment with the ladies till 12. Nelly asleep till she was called. Religion, philosophy, and literature with Miss Adele till 1 A.M., all the time walking in the verandah. Improvised lunch with great frolic till 2 A.M., then the whistle. Coats and cloaks, bags seized, bonfire on shore, weird steamer rushes up and puts out her landing stage, ten black men rush out and seize the trunks. Goodbyes and handkerchiefs, and we rush on board, and find our staterooms.

"Children of the public still. I tell Nelly, en philosophe, that it is a pleasure to live in a country where the humblest emigrant going to the frontier has such good conveyance. But it is no longer the palace of a Baron, it is a small stern wheel steamer, curiously well provided by the law of selection with what everybody wants, and with, let us confess, but few luxuries beyond, but Nelly and I always come back to each other with infinite satisfaction, after our grandeurs, which have compelled us to rotate on our own axes instead of working in common. We have slept well in our modest state rooms, beneath our cotton quilts. I confess mine was a little warm. There is a beam at the end of my berth, which compels me to separate my feet in sleep. But fortunately they were not fastened together when I was born. The boat is not as swift as the *Morgan* was, but fortunately the scenery is much more lovely, the spring advances so rapidly. She is a stern wheeler, which means a smaller boat, and fortunately the jar in writing is much less. I shall be able to bring up my lost stents of Philip Nolan before I leave her. And we have a nice letter from you and are very happy."

TO MRS. HALE

"International R.R., Texas,
"Between Troop and Jackson,
"*Thursday, Apr.* 27, 1876.

"Unless you put up with the jar of the train I am afraid you will get no letter by today's train East. Only think it is a month today since we left home. Looking back upon it, it has been a marvellous month. It is the realization of a dream, not to say plan, of mine for years, and now it has come, I hardly knew how. I have enjoyed every hour not to say every instant. I believe I have already said that I do not see how a month in any country can bring together such constant variety and novelty, and there certainly is an amazing advantage in being master of the language. (And yet, when on the boat one day, I asked a young gentleman by me, what the fish was, at table, he said: 'Not understand any English,' and I had to ask him in French:

'qu'est ce qu'on appelle ce poisson ci,' to get an intelligible answer, and we fell into a French conversation. And this man was my countryman, born under the American flag, and I had done my best to drub him back into it when he flagged in his allegiance.) As you see, a good deal has opened to us which we never thought of. The visits to these sugar-plantations, as you see, have been a great enlargement on the original plan, and a very pleasant one."

TO MRS. HALE

"AUSTIN, TEXAS, *Sunday,*
"*April* 30, 1876.

"Nelly and I have been taking our early walk to see the Sunday morning market, and I begin this at the breakfast table as they get, or pretend to get the breakfast ready. This is a curious place. We have cut so wholly loose from New England associations that it does not seem so queer as it would, but really, in architecture, in costume, and in the things offered for sale, it is as queer as Linz. Only a lettuce and a chicken must be much the same everywhere. Still, if when you buy a pair of chickens for your dinner, the chickens are alive in a nest, in a tall coop in a cart, and you and the vendor and a number of interested friends stand round the coop while a little trap is opened near the top, and the chances of your dinner depend on the chances which dictate which particular chickens shall first escape, to be caught by you and the man and the friends in waiting; there is so much novelty in the method of the purchase, that the similarity of species and genus does not so much impress you.

"When I looked over my pile of Texan letters yesterday, I found but one here, which was to a banker, of whose historical firmness I doubted. I was left, therefore, a good deal to my own resources, which have not failed me. Indeed I never was in a place where what men call cheek went farther. Which being interpreted, means, I suppose, that in an absolutely new country, where every man's own bowie knife has carved out his destiny, previous acquaintance or position has little or nothing to do with a man's status, and he is left very much to try placing himself. I know I walked into the Sec. of State's office, told them what they had and what I wanted. They said they did not think they had it, had not been in office long, but would be glad to oblige me. I looked round, said if they would give me a step ladder I would examine some docketed files myself. They said they should be glad to have me, and I returned from my ladder with 'San Antonio Bexar archives 1801–1820.' I cut the red tape, opened the file and the first paper was Vidal the Spanish consul's report to Nacogdoches of the fact that Phil Nolan had started on the expedition which our novel describes.

"I am quite at a loss about our movements tomorrow, from the difficulty of getting exact information about trains etc. I want to go to San Antonio Bexar, but it is almost as difficult as in Inez's time, and we really have not the time."

My father's difficulty in arranging our journey

to San Antonio, which he mentions in the last of these letters, was a more serious one than he cared to tell my mother. The best way to get there was to drive eighty miles over the prairie, a method which commended itself highly to us both. But the stage had been robbed on this road some weeks before, and both of us had learned this, by reading the posted notice of a reward, for the apprehension of the highway robbers. My father was planning to engage a private conveyance, what was then called an "ambulance," for the journey. He thought I might feel uneasy if I knew about the highway robbery. The same thought struck me in regard to him. It was some time before we confided in each other; when we did, we found we were quite agreed, and we decided that, as one of our advisers said, it would be safe enough, as they didn't know we were coming. My father thought of leaving our watches at Austin; as for money, we seldom had much with us, and as he thought it most improper for a Christian minister to carry a pistol in peaceful times, we thought a hold-up, if one came, would be simple enough. But it never did come. Some echo of the relief he felt may be seen in his next letter.

TO MRS. HALE

"In the ambulance,
"On the prairie,
"Above San Marcos.

"MAY DAY: Is not this date marvellous? Of all the ways to spend May day commend me to this.

You have no idea of the loveliness of these rolling prairies. Our catalogue of flowers only begins to tell, and the abundance is such, that they would have to be recognized in the broadest and most dashing water-colour. I never made a decision with more doubt than that which brings us here, and I have never been so glad of anything as that we came. Nelly is as happy about it as I am. We are to stop in a few minutes to see the wonderful springs at San Marcos. But I want nothing more wonderful than I see all the time. Only we are so grieved both of us that you are not here. The road is as good as from Roxbury to Brookline, and the driver and team perfect."

That May Day really was a day of rapture to us both. We were sketching whenever we could, and I remember my father's writing on a distant area in one of his pencil outlines, a memorandum that there was a small lake, where no lake existed, only a wide expanse of blue verbena. I have seen the California spring flowers since then, the glory of that State; but that country was no longer so untouched as the rolling Texas prairie in 1876. Such an army of cattle as my father describes in his next letter might pass through to the northward, carrying all before it; but in general, these lovely tree-dotted slopes, which everybody rightly calls park-like, still retained the "enamel of a thousand colors" which good Bishop Diego Marin celebrated in his Texan poem long ago.

TO CHARLES

"San Antonio de Bexar, Texas,

"*May* 2, 1876. I am almost as far from you as
we can go in the United States, as you and I remember the United States. No, that will not do either,
for I rather think we got California by the same
manifest destiny which got us Texas. I refreshed
my memories as we rode, by telling Nelly the history of that annexation. The whole of it is in my
memory: although I cannot say I was a part of it,
few men now living heard so much of the debates
which accompanied it. Yet to Nelly the history
was as little known personally, as the wars of the
Roses.

"This place is wonderfully satisfactory. In the
first place it is completely foreign. The hotel I
am in, a very good one, is much such a hotel as I
was in in Linz and at Pesth, built round an open
square in which the people have tables and their
meals in summer. The town is built on both sides
of a lovely, narrow river, full of rapid water, and
overhung everywhere by willows and mesquit, and
acacia which looks like a willow. Over this river
go no end of bridges, some broad, some only foot-
paths. The streets are not wide, but let you now
and then, just where you least expect it, into great
Spanish plazas. The Americans do their best to
introduce their own style of building two and three
stories high. But the Spanish is so much more
sensible that even in the new buildings it holds its
own, while the old ones were so solid that they are

still occupied, and are indeed, in many cases, hard to pull down. The whole aspect of the town, therefore, is like Buda, if you crossed to go there, and I guess rather like what you found in the cities lower down on the Danube. The notice to people to cross the bridge on a walk is in English, German, and Spanish.

"The Alamo, the scene of the horrible Famine massacre, is still standing close by this hotel. The Cathedral, like that in New Orleans, has been modernized and in part rebuilt. But in many many instances you see stone gargoyles projecting to let water off roofs, without the least suspicion on anybody's part that they are picturesque or old-fashioned.

"As for costume, no two people by any accident are dressed alike. There is a large enough number of Mexicans to make an evident Spanish look in costume, and some of their customs prevail over the Yankees. Thus they have a peculiar felt hat, with something like a serpent coiled round it, and we saw yesterday that herdsmen and drovers who are not at all Mexicans wore these, got up in a very showy way, I have no doubt at some New York factory. Think by the way of meeting a herd of 1800 cattle slowly walking towards Brighton and death across the prairies, driven by two or three men, who simply walk their horses (or gallop them) back and forth at right angles behind the line of march to hurry up stragglers. The rest, if they think, like many a poor devil, suppose that because they go to destruction slowly they do not go at all.

My father says in another letter from San Antonio, "They claim that this is the healthiest place in America. I should think it might be. It is certainly the most picturesque." I am sure it was the most picturesque. If New Orleans was my first foreign town, San Antonio was, to both of us, our first Spanish town, and nearer to old Spain than some Spanish towns we saw later. In those days, they drove their Mexican cotton across from Chihuahua in ox-carts with solid wooden disks for wheels. You could see the small stone hand mills, on which the Spanish women ground the meal for the tamales we had for breakfast in the morning market. You could see Spanish sun, and Spanish architecture, still noble, in the three or four great Mission churches within driving reach. Everybody was kind to us, in the town and outside it, at the military post. But I find myself regretting that our very best San Antonio friends of later years could by no possibility have been living there then. Mr. and Mrs. Slayden would have made any wilderness a garden of pleasures; what would they not have made of a paradise like San Antonio, in 1876?

We passed a few more days in Texas, spending the next Sunday at Hampstead, where one of my father's letters records that he happily finished his novel, and also preached in the Presbyterian church. It was there that the kind friends with whom we dined, planning to take us for a drive, were unable to find their horses on the open prairie; but they were consoled by finding their cow, which had been lost for some time. Such accidents were precious, for they showed that we were actually sharing the life of that Southern frontier of which my father had dreamed so long.

We traveled through what was then the Indian Territory, made a stop at St. Louis, and went directly home. Some of my father's happiest letters of this happy journey are clouded by anxiety for those we had left behind. I am tempted to think that he had some premonition of what was to follow; for when we arrived, my little brother Harry was already ill with the diphtheria which ended his life, and which was nearly fatal to my eldest brother.

CHAPTER TWENTY–NINE

LITERATURE

1870–1880

MY father generally thought of "In His Name" as his best book. Some twenty years after this time, he wrote of his youngest son, "It occurred to me only this morning that Bob was the first person to share with me what came to be eventually my chief success in letters. He is the first person who ever heard my story of 'In His Name.'" Expressions of literary excellence are so vague and confusing that it is not worth while to try to be perfectly definite as to which was my father's "best" book or story, or which he thought was best. When he spoke of "In His Name" as his chief literary success he must have meant the piece of literary work which most nearly accomplished the particular end that he had in mind. He can hardly have supposed that the tale was more widely read or more highly esteemed than "The Man without a Country," nor can he have supposed it had had a greater practical result than "Ten Times One." But it will have been seen that his first great story which was written during the war to influence the election of 1863 did not attain that end, and indeed was at first generally admired merely as any clever story might be. And although the practical results of "Ten Times One" were remarkable, and probably exceeded very much his own expectations, yet the story has never (probably in his own mind even) been regarded as of great literary value. But "In His Name" seems to have as nearly attained his ideal as is possible with works of literature, and he always felt and spoke of it as being the book of his that he liked best. At about the time of its publishing he received a note from Doctor Andrew P. Peabody which gave him great satisfaction. Doctor Peabody among other things said: "You have not only performed the higher office of a spiritual teacher, entering into the inmost heart of the Divine Teacher; but you have succeeded in the lower, yet more difficult task, of fidelity to the date and scene of the story." My father may have thought that in one way this says too much, and in another too little; but he must have felt that in the statement he had an appreciation of the two things that he wanted his literary work to be. He wanted it to be good literature and he wanted it to be an active factor in the hearts of men. He saw that "In His Name" was both of these things and valued it accordingly.

I do not know when the story first came into his mind; the general idea must have long been thought of, the particular form and setting may not have been thought of till he went abroad in the year 1873. He told it to us boys one Twelfth Night: in what is quoted above he thought especially of Robert, in the book itself he turns at the end to Philip; I rather think that he told the story to all of us together in the evening after we had got back

from the Twelfth Night celebration that in those
days we used to go to at the Orphan Asylum. It
is not very important just who heard it first; the
important thing is that the story — as he presents
it himself — is one of the examples and illustrations
that were continually coming to his mind of the prevailing power of the love of God and the love of man
as dominant factors in human life.

With the conclusion of *Old and New* my father's
work as an editor ceased. I nowhere find any expression of his feeling in the matter, though probably it may be easily imagined. But one result of
the cessation of such critical work was that he
turned his attention more to creation or invention
or imagination, whichever it be best called.

During these years, between 1870 and 1880, he
wrote much — not only sermons and addresses on
matters which belonged to his profession, and historical studies of which he was interested in a number, but stories and novels. These latter were sometimes expressive of some social or other idea, — like
"Back to Back," but many of them had little "purpose" in them save the purpose of amusing or entertaining those who were pleased with imagination,
invention, or whatever else we may name the quality
which creates stories and people and places.

This is no place for literary criticism, if one understands by that term an estimate or judgment of
artistic value. But my father's writing was so
much a matter of natural expression that these
stories are immensely interesting to those who will
look through them to the author. Perhaps no

literary criticism can really do much better than that, better than to let us see who and what sort of man this was and how it was he wrote what he did. At any rate such biographical material forms something of a foundation for any kind of literary criticism unless it be very abstract and absolute indeed.

In the March number of *Harper's Magazine* for 1877 is the story of "Ideals." It is hard to say what the uninstructed reader may have thought of it, though as it was one of the first of a long series, it may be presumed to have been popular, but to one who knew my father's life it was full of reminiscence. It concerned four men and their wives.

Felix and Fausta Carter
Frederic and Mary Ingham
George and Anna Haliburton
George and Julia Hackmatack

Of these the first two were the Children of the Public of whom he had thought twenty years before and of whom he had written in 1863. The second pair were, of course, the Sandemarian clergyman and his wife. Frederic Ingham since 1854 had seen a good deal of life in different capacities, but now he had settled down in Boston on his half-pay as a retired brevet officer in the patriot service of Garibaldi in the year 1859. George and Julia Hackmatack were the South American Editor and his wife from the days of long since. The Haliburtons I do not trace. Of all it is said that in a general way they lived for the good of the world. "Perhaps the happiest period they ever knew was when in different subordinate capacities they were all on the staff of the same magazine. Then they met daily at the office, lunched together perforce, and could make arrangements for the evening. But, to say true, things differ little with them now, though that magazine long since took wings and went to a better world." Even since the end of the magazine they got a good deal out of the world, and yet they were not satisfied, and on one occasion, being rather downcast over an election that had gone wrong, they amused themselves by striking a balance of good and evil, in the manner of "Robinson Crusoe," their lay gospel and creed.

What was there of good and what of evil? Of good there was much; they had good children and friends enough; they had health and enough to live on, and they seemed to be of use in the world. But there was evil too; the doorbell rang all the time, they were behind in their calls and social engagements, the plumbing and the furnace were always getting out of order; the gas meter told lies; the children's schools were never what they really wanted, — the little worries of life all these, — and meant to be little — and probably no more felt at 39 Highland Street than in some other places.

The remedy for their familiar condition was of course a wonderful invention. All eight put their children to school (Antioch College) and went to a place in Mexico on the side of a mountain such that when it became too hot on a lower level they had only to go a quarter of a mile up the mountain and there find a good climate. When that got too

hot they went up again.   Before they got up to the
top of the mountain it was summer, and they came
back, took the children out of Antioch College, and
passed three delightful months at a place called
Little Gau, which was very like the New Sybaris
at Matunuck.

When they first went to Mexico they asked the
counsul about the valley they wanted to find.   He
said there were lots of them and introduced them
to a friend who knew.

"Was the friend quite sure that there were no
plumbers in the regions he named?

"'Never a plumber in Mexico.'

"'Any life insurance men?'

"'Not one.'   The prudent friend did not add
'Risk too high!'

"'Were the public schools graded schools or district schools?'

"'Not a public school in six provinces.'

"'Would the neighbors be offended if we do not
call?'

"'Cut your throat if you did.'

"'Did the friend think there would be many
tramps?'

"The friend seemed more doubtful here, but suggested that the occasional use of a six-shooter reduced the number and gave a certain reputation to
the premises.

"'If what the man says be true,' said Ingham,
'we must be very near heaven.'"

But we do not have merely an absurd and impossible caricature (shall we say? or is it really not

absurd or impossible?) of the small worries of life;
the end of the story is as ingenious as the rest.

Life in Mexico and at Little Gau was perfect and
they had arranged to go back to Mexico in the fall.
But on the eve of the journey Julia Hackmatack
went for a farewell call on Mrs. Blake. They talked
about all sorts of things, among them such minor
troubles as Mrs. Blake's poor eyes, the dust in
Gladstone Street, the failure of Rupee and Lac, the
new anvil factory on the other side of the street.
Mrs. Blake was not troubled by any of these things,
and when asked how that could be she said, "Why
Julia dear, we do not let these things trouble us,
don't you see. If I were you, I would not let such
things trouble me."

"George Haliburton laid down his knife as Julia
told the story. 'Do you remember Rabia at Mecca?'

"Yes, they all remembered Rabia at Mecca.

"'Oh, heart, weak follower of the weak

That thou should'st travel land and sea;

In this far place the God to seek

Who long ago had come to thee!'

"Why should they not stay here, and not let
these things trouble them?

"Why not indeed?

"And they staid."

The critic will certainly have his interest in this
tale, especially if he compare it with some other
short stories of the time, or we ought to say of the
time before and the time after. But to the biog-
rapher it is invaluable. No one can understand
how my father did his work at 39 Highland Street

without remembering this humorous reckoning up of doorbell, mailman, furnace, plumbing, calls, and parties, — or some equivalent. No one can understand how he enjoyed the days or weeks that he snatched as vacation at Matunuck or elsewhere unless he had in mind the life at Little Gau or something like it.   No one will understand the real energy of the man who pursued his course despite such humorous satires as this or such humorous growls as we have on p. 270. But further, no one will understand the spirit of the man who cannot comprehend the necessary conclusion — "Why not stay here (where 'we seem to be of some use in the world') and not let these things trouble us?" He could not always keep these things (and worse) from troubling him, but he did pretty well. There came a time in later years when he would enter in his diary—"Did not leave the island all day," or "Did not leave the quarterdeck." He was then at this same 39 Highland Street where the telephone was added to the doorbell, though schools and life insurance men were of the past. I believe in those days, as thirty years before, he was glad he had stayed.

One cannot say that all of the many short stories of these years are, like "Ideals," some whim or fancy dressed in the garments of experience and real life. But a good many of them are of much the same sort. Two years before "Ideals" appeared "The Modern Psyche." Miss Psyche Varney married Edward Ross, but on marriage Edward asked her not to ask him what his business was nor who his friends were. She did not, and their life was

EDWARD EVERETT HALE AND HIS GRANDSON NATHAN
AT MATUNUCK

happy. He went to his study for a couple of hours in the morning and at eight in the evening he disappeared, telling her not to sit up for him. All went well till a visit from her sisters made her feel that she must unravel the mystery. It turned out that he was the editor-in-chief of the *Argus*. So far he had been able to keep his business life and his home life separate. But now their life changed; instead of the halcyon days they had spent together, there came days clouded by doorbell and mail man, axes to grind, and calls to pay.

Those who remember 39 Highland Street in its early days will have recognized an idealized form in the account of the young couple's first home.

"It was in Roxbury, so it was half country; and there was a pretty garden, with a little green-house such as Psyche had always longed for. Nay there was a fernhouse, with just the ferns she loved, and with those other Himalaya ferns which he had talked of in that lovely first day."

But more interesting are some accounts of the way one might spend one's time in Boston, and the way one actually did:

"Bloody Mary was literary, and she had said at breakfast that she hoped that they should see some of the Boston literati; that she should be ashamed to go home to Painted Post unless she had seen Mr. Fields and Mr. Lowell and Mr. Longfellow and Dr. Holmes. And the second day, Edward said should be Polly's day, and they should see the book-shops and the libraries. So this day he did not order the ponies, but two open barouches came up and they drove first to the dear old corner of Hamilton Place, and went up to the pretty 'author's parlor' of Fields and Osgood.   And Mr. Fields came in and told them some very pretty stories, and gave Bloody Mary an autograph of Tennyson.   And Mr. Osgood and Mr. Clarke came in and showed them the English advance sheets of the new Trollope, and some copy of the new Dickens in manuscript.   Then Edward took them to the Historical rooms and they saw Prescott's sword, and Leutze's.   Mr. Winthrop happened to come in, and they saw him; and Dr. Holmes was there looking at some old MSS., and he was very courteous to the ladies, and showed Miss Polly the picture of Sebastian Cabot.   Then they drove out to the College Library, and while they were looking at the old missals and evangelistaries it happened that Mr. Longfellow crossed the hall and spoke to Edward.   And Edward actually asked Agnes and Polly if he might present Mr. Longfellow to them; and then found Priscilla and presented him to her and to Psyche.   And Polly slipped out her album and he wrote his name in it, and said he was sorry that he could not stay longer; but he pointed out to her some of the most interesting autographs there.   And then they started for the Museum, and by great good luck they met Mr. Lowell in Professors' Row.   And Edward stopped the carriage actually and asked if he should be at home in an hour; and when Mr. Lowell said he was engaged with a class, Edward arranged so promptly!—that they should all go and hear his lecture.   And then they went to the Museum, and by the same wonderful luck Agassiz was going out as they came in; and he turned back and shewed them everything. That was a day indeed. They came home to the most beautiful little family dinner, and in the evening they all went to Selwyn's Theater, where was another play."

Such was the possible literary life; the actual life began when Psyche had unveiled her husband's secret and learned his name and occupation.

"It was not till they went back to Roxbury that the real change came. Then it was that before breakfast the doorbell began to ring, and women with causes, and men with inventions, began to wait in the ante-room till Mr. E. Ross came down stairs. Then was it that he poured down his hasty cup of coffee and ran to be rid of them. Then was it that the councilmen came out as soon as breakfast was over to arrange private schemes for thwarting the aldermen; and that while the councilmen arranged, aldermen called and waited for Mr. Ross to be at leisure, because they wanted to make plans for thwarting the council. Then it was that, from morning to night, candidates for the House and candidates for the Senate came for private conferences, and had to be let out from different doors, lest they should meet each other. Then was it that men who had letters of introduction from Japan and Formosa and Siberia and Aboukuta sat in Psyche's parlor six or seven hours at a time, illustrating the customs of those countries, and what Mr. Lowell calls 'a certain condescension observable in foreigners.' Then was it that Psyche received calls from wives of Senators

and daughters of Congressmen, to say in asides to
her that if Mr. E. Ross could find it in his way to
say this, he would so much oblige thus and so. Then
was it that trying to screen him from bores, she received all the women who sold lives of Christ, and
all the agents who exhibited copies of maps or helio-
types. Then was it that, when the ponies came to
the door, railroad presidents drew up, who just
wanted a minute to talk about their new bonds.
Then was it that, after the ponies had been sent
back to the stable, grand ladies drew up to send
cards to Psyche and to persuade her to take tables
at fairs, and to be vice-president of alms-houses.
Then was it that every Saturday Psyche gave a
charming literary dinner, not bad in its way. And
the counterpart of this was that Psyche and Edward
dined at other people's houses four days out of the
remaining six. The sixth day Edward was kept
down town for some of the engagements these
wretches had forced him into. Thus was it that in
the end, the moths ate up the camel's-hair pencils,
and no one ever found it out, that the upper G
string in the piano rusted off, and no one discovered
it, that Bridget Flynn put ten volumes of Grill-
parzer into the furnace fire, and nobody missed
them; and that all the ferns in the fern-house died
and nobody wept for them."

It would be a great mistake to lay too much stress
on these pictures of the great battle with the bores
and the axe-grinders and the crazy people. There
are enough of them in his stories from "My Double"
and "His Level Best" down. But they are really

little more than his humorous way of recording his protest against the unnecessary inflictions of Society. Very rarely was he other than kind and civil, at the very least, to those who wanted him to do something for them. In many cases I am sure he felt that they would do better if they would look after their own interests. But he rarely told them so. Sometimes he thought of some good way to make them realize that they were taking a busy man's time in a purely selfish way. Once he got a printed request for an autograph; he had an answer printed, signature and all: "I am glad to comply with your request in the same convenient form in which it comes to me. Edward E. Hale." Things like that did good; in this case the man appreciated what he possibly had not thought of. My father felt that the possibilities of life were so wonderful that with fair play all round people could help each other and enjoy themselves too. That was the way it should be in the perfect world, and if it were not so in this, there was no harm in showing the difficulties on both sides. He had a splendid overflowing nature, and his sympathy went out to thousands. But he had also a very keen eye, and he saw often that it was not sympathy that his visitors really needed.

He wrote many short stories during these years. It is better to give something of the spirit and manner of a few than to try to give an account of them all. They were by no means all veiled records of experience. Some were little more than whims or fancies in the realistic form that was natural to him, like "Susan's Escort" or "Crusoe in New York."

Not a few, however, had a far more definite purpose. In 1877 he published in *Harper's Magazine* "Back to Back." This story gave his idea of the possibilities of coöperation; he wrote it with frequent interchange of ideas with Mr. Weeden, who was a large woolen manufacturer. He did not drop the idea, — the student of his writings sees how tenacious he was of what he felt was the real thing, — and how he turned it and put it into very different forms often with the interval of years. Ten years afterward he developed this idea again in the form of "How they Live at Hampton: a Study of Practical Christianity applied to the Manufacture of Woolens." The preface is characteristic:

"The author supposes that this Essay on the Christian relations of the capitalist and the workman will be more generally read if it is presented in narrative form.

"It is proper to say that the details bearing on the business of manufacture have the authority of a well-known and successful manufacturer of woolens.

"I am myself the person who was invited in 1873 by the proprietors of three different woolen mills, to take them and carry them on on the plan proposed. I received these invitations because I had blocked out this plan, or rather a manufacturer of large experience had blocked it out for me, in a story which I published at that time in *Harper's Magazine*, called 'Back to Back.'

"Unfortunately for me, I was not trained to the woolen manufacture and could not take, therefore, the difficult part which Mr. Spinner takes in this book, as Max Rising took it in that. But in this book, as the reader will see, I have supposed that Mr. Spinner accepted one."

My father wrote a good many of these essays on practical subjects. He evidently felt very definitely that such an essay would be "more generally read if it was presented in narrative form." At any rate he often did present such ideas in narrative form, just as he often presented them in other ways. "Our New Crusade" is a temperance story; "Tom Torrey's Tariff Talks" is a conversational presentation of an economic question. I should be the last to try to judge the value of these books; but it is not hard to see some at least of their particular and characteristic qualities.

"My Friend the Boss" is one of these pieces of entire realism, so reasonable that one wonders that people will not give it a trial. John Fisher, "my friend," a rich manufacturer, manages the town of Tamworth, its sport, philanthropy, art, even its politics, — or at least he sees that those things are well run instead of ill run. He had large interests in the town, and he found that the town was being run by a ring of adventurers, bartenders, horse jockeys, gamblers, and so on.

"Well, I set myself to considering this thing. I said to myself, 'Suppose I had a fancy for yachting. Or suppose I wanted to buy folio Shakespeares and original Miltons. Or suppose I had taken to Corots and Calames and Meissoniers, like your Mrs. Morgan or Mr. Vanderbilt. How much should I gladly spend a year in that business? Why, I should readily

spend a hundred thousand dollars the first year for
my yacht, and fifty thousand a year afterwards.'
I laid aside these amounts in my plans for the next
six years. Of course I never bought a man or a vote.
But I put the money where I thought it would help
in the good government of the city. I put it in
readingrooms, and boys' institutes, and music-clubs
and libraries, and Sunday-schools, and galleries, and
law-and-order leagues, and a thousand other agencies which enthusiasts are constantly inventing.
The consequence is that I am the friend of the enthusiasts and they are friends of mine, And,
Mellen, it is always the enthusiasts who win in the
long run, if they have a man of sense behind them.
Nothing ever succeeded in this world, which had not
a crazy man hitched on somewhere.

"'That was the first consequence, I say. The
second, if you ever choose to go into the same line of
business, was this. When I began, my taxes to
this city were sixteen on the thousand; I paid sixteen dollars on every thousand of my assessment.
Now I pay eight on the thousand, just half what
it was, and the government is much better than it
used to be. They assess me for about two million.
So I save in my own taxes rather more than a hundred and fifty thousand dollars a year. Practically
it costs me nothing to run my yacht, and I enjoy the
fun of sailing her.'"

An especial word should be said of "Philip Nolan's
Friends," a story of which something has already
been seen in the letters of the trip to Texas. He
wrote of it himself:

"I remembered, when I was collecting material for my story, that in General Wilkinson's galimatias, which he calls his 'Memoirs,' is frequent reference to a business partner of his, of the name of Nolan, who in the very beginning of this century was killed in Texas. Whenever Wilkinson found himself in rather a deeper bog than usual, he used to justify himself by saying that he could not explain such or such a charge because 'the papers referring to it were lost when Mr. Nolan was imprisoned in Texas.' Finding this mythical character in the mythical legends of a mythical time, I took the liberty to give him a cousin, rather more mythical, whose adventures should be on the seas. I had the impression that Wilkinson's friend was named Stephen, — and as such I spoke of him in the early editions of this story. But long after this was printed, I found that the New Orleans paper was right in saying that the Texan hero was named Philip Nolan.

"If I had forgotten him and his name, I can only say that Mr. Jefferson, who did not forget him, abandoned him and his, — when the Spanish Government murdered him and imprisoned his associates for life. I have done my best to repair my fault, and to recall to memory a brave man, by telling the story of his fate, in a book called 'Philip Nolan's Friends.'"

The story was published first in *Scribner's Monthly* in 1876–1877 with illustrations by Mr. Abbey, of which some mention appears on p. 279.

At least a note should be made of my father's historical writings, though most of them come somewhat after this time.   In the later seventies, he wrote a number of chapters on the "History of the United States," which had been projected under the editorship of William Cullen Bryant and Sidney Gay.   Bryant's work on this book was slight; he died before it was finished.   My father wrote a good deal on those parts of our national history which concerned the Southwest and the Pacific coast, matters which just then were vivid in his mind.   In 1880, when Justin Winsor planned and carried out the "Memorial History of Boston," my father was one of the historians of the city called upon to take part in the enterprise, and provided chapters on "Boston in Philip's War" "Bellomont and Kidd," and "The Siege of Boston"; three views of Boston respectively in the colonial, the provincial, and the revolutionary periods.   A few years afterward, when Mr. Winsor extended his view and planned his great "Narrative and Critical History of America," which like the earlier book depended on the coöperation of many scholars, my father contributed studies on "Hawkins and Drake" and "Magellan's Discovery."   These were the beginnings of the great study which he always liked to think of as his *magnum opus*, the "History of the Pacific Ocean and its Shores."   Perhaps he never really thought that he should write such a history, but from the early days, when he detected the mention of California in the old romance of "Esplandian," [1] he had felt that this was something that he should immensely enjoy studying, working, and

[1] See "The Queen of California" in the *Atlantic Monthly* for March, 1864.

writing about. Being in Paris in 1883 with some time on his hands, he found some opportunity for study in the libraries. On May 23, he wrote to me: "I have sunk into quite a regular life, I write my letters and read my paper till eleven, and then go to one of my libraries. I am well forward with Magellan, which is the first of my papers for *Harper's*, and will begin my 'History of the Pacific Ocean and its Shore.' Today I am going to the Genevieve, which is the great working library, on this side of the river, of the Sorbonne and the College of France. Yesterday I was in the Library of the Marine, and on Tuesday at the Société de Geographie where Mr. Jackson is very good to me."

About 1880, or perhaps before, Mr. Henry Stevens offered the United States a large collection of Franklin letters and other papers, belonging chiefly to the period of Franklin's life in France. My father had known of this collection for a good while, and he had also known Mr. Stevens. He appreciated the value of the papers and desired very much that the government should buy them. In 1882, while in Washington, he appeared before the Congressional Committee which was looking into the case.

TO MRS. HALE

"WASHINGTON, *Feb.* 23, 1882. The business at the Capitol was to urge the Committee on the Library to buy the Franklin papers which Henry Stevens wants so sell. Stevens has a bad reputation for bargaining, and the committee has therefore been afraid that it had a damaged lot offered it.

But the State Department, Dwight their Librarian, and we historians believe in the value of the papers. Mark — I did not volunteer to go — nor wish to, indeed. But Frisbie Hoar of the committee, summoned me and Mr. I. R. Bartlett. Bartlett gave his view very briefly and pleasantly, but knew very little about the papers. I had read through the report which Mr. Winthrop lent me, before I left home and again yesterday. I knew something about Franklin's letters before, having had to read them all for historical work. So when I began to testify (or to talk) I saw at once that I understood much more about it than any of them did. Mr. Voorhees, the rather eccentric Democratic member of the committee, asked an intelligent question, and I said that if he pleased I would explain it to him on his own copy of the public document, so I crossed the room and sat by him, and the examination took the form of a personal conversation between me and him, — interrupted by him with ejaculations of 'This is excellent. Now I begin to understand. This is just what we have wanted. This makes it clear. I see now why this has been left so. Pray go on Mr. Hale. This is very interesting. Now turn to p. 49,' and other such, which were very satisfactory. To tell the whole truth, I think the officers of the State Department understand more about the papers than they did at this time yesterday, and when, after ten minutes, my examination was over, Mr. Voorhees said, 'To tell you the truth, Dr. Hale, you have converted me,' and Hoar said that they had learned more in five minutes than they had learned in six months before. All which was sufficiently pleasant, because I really thought it was true."

When the papers were finally purchased, my father formed the plan of editing them, or some of them, in a book which should present Franklin's life in France. This he did and made use of the chance to visit Washington once and again, where he not only carried on his studies in the Franklin papers in the State Department, but met old friends and made new ones in the city which after Boston he was always most attached to, and which he regarded as being in its later days most representative of American life.

CHAPTER THIRTY

TRAVEL AND BUSINESS

1873-1882

OF course life was not entirely taken up with editing *Old and New*, writing "Ten Times One," "In His Name," and the many stories that followed, going abroad, living at Matunuck, going to Texas, or even preaching to the South Congregational Church. There were all sorts of other and very important things going on. But of these one can give but a general and indeed a chance notion, by picking out what seem particularly typical or characteristic letters. As time went on his letters grew shorter and there were fewer of them. When he lived at home he was very apt to write only the particular thing that was required. His real letters of this period are likely to be those written when he was away from home making a visit or traveling. He liked to travel, and as he wrote with perfect ease he generally sent back a letter a day. Especially did he write on the Pullman cars, when they were introduced, and in the leisure he found here, he got somewhere near the tone of the letter writer of former days. There follow a number of letters illustrative of the different occupations and interests of these years, but not much connected in subject.

TO MRS. HALE

"VASSAR COLLEGE, *April* 30, 1874. We leave here at noon having steadfastly resisted the most pressing invitations. I am in love with the place, — not with the girls or Miss Terry, the Lady Principal, though they are very nice. I have torn myself away from two seniors and a junior, all very pretty girls, that I may write this line to post it as we go down.

"The address seemed to pass off very well, and I have found out what Founder's Day is. The 29th was Matthew Vassar's birthday, and this fête is a celebration of it, which originated in his own time. Ever since then it has been kept as a holiday, and to most of the girls, I suppose, the great feature is that it is a holiday, when they can do as they please and receive their friends. There are, however, certain fixed ceremonies. One is the decoration of Vassar's grave with flowers, one is the address in the chapel, and then the day closes with a party and collation in the great dining hall. Yesterday it poured all day or nearly all day, so the decoration of the grave was done very quietly.

"I am not drunk, most noble Festus, as you may well have supposed from the passage above. It was an attempt to write in the car as we came down, but as you see, was not very successful. The truth is that their hospitalities on the spot were quite too pressing to enable one to write, unless he tried it after twelve at night or before breakfast in the morning.

"The impression of the whole institution is very agreeable. I shall write a formal letter to the *Daily* about it, which will give the grand statistic, but to you I can tell rather more of the personal detail of our times. Meanwhile I hope you understand that I am using this paper not because it is elegant, but because I have no other. We are, since the pencil above, at Aunt Katy's[1] but I am in my room, with only my own stores.

"Here is, you see, a colony of near six hundred persons, in a building larger than almost any hotel, three miles from Po'keepsie, and rather indifferent as to intercourse with the greater part of the world. In this colony there are more men than I at first supposed, the President, certainly four professors, the steward, the head-waiter, the master of the riding school certainly being men, their children having a share of boys. I doubt if there are more than ten males to five hundred and fifty women. The building is handsome, the rooms light and airy the whole is well furnished and is quite free from that barracky air that all colleges I had ever seen had, those in Oxford and Cambridge excepted. The girls look well, their bearing is good, thanks to thorough gymnastics, and they are right well fed. On this, see my printed letter.

"The first night we went to the gymnasium, and saw the exercises of the seniors for half an hour in light gymnastics. Quite what our dear Dio Lewis had used you and me to — and done very well, without too much precision. Then I went to my

---

[1] Mrs. William C. Gilman, my mother's sister.

bed room, which is the Founder's room and is re-
served for visitors, and the three girls were carried
off by their friends to their rooms. And our three
girls are beside themselves with delight and satisfaction at what they have seen, heard, and done.
They did not breakfast till 8. I found afterward
that this was because it was a holiday; 7:15 is the
usual time. We were put at the Faculty table.
The dining hall is immense, broken up into small
tables, like a large hotel. The fare is abundant and
excellent. The girls all testify to that. The beef-
steak was simply perfect, as I believe I said yesterday.

"Observe the ground was deep with snow, and
the storm was still raging. We heard nothing, therefore, of the going to the grave. But we spent our
morning very pleasantly in the Library, and in the
Art Room. They have a large and very good collection of water colors, and a large and quite good
collection of modern landscape. Some of the girls
are at work copying, and among the photographs
are some copies from drawings by the masters which
Nelly was glad to see. In the library, I met and
talked with Lossing, the author of the Fieldbooks
of the Revolution, which the boys like so much; he
is one of the trustees of the college, and an interesting man in his way. I also got an hour for working
on and studying the address, which on the whole I
like pretty well, though it is perhaps not very well
arranged. After dinner I got a nap, and we made
our calls, first on Mrs. Campbell, Mrs. Reed's niece
who had invited us to be her guest. She is wife of
the steward, and they have their separate house in

the college building. We also called on Maria
Mitchell. For this we had to put on water proofs
etc. as the observatory where she lives with two
girls is in another building. She is a very interesting person, and showed us very interesting things.
Then came our early tea, and then we dressed for
the evening. At 7.30 I reported in Miss Terry's
parlor. I believe I told how she recognized Nelly
from her likeness to you. She is General Terry's
sister, and I guess very well fitted for her very difficult position. There met the Trustees and principal
people of the guests. Then they were taken to seats
and finally to solemn music there marched a procession arranged thus:

Miss Terry	Papa
Pres. Raymond	Miss Cushing, Marshal

into the chapel, which was already full. Observe
Miss Cushing is a Boston girl, the President of the
Students' Association, who was to introduce me,
and deliver the Commemoration Address.

"Then came a prayer of great length and much
logic on the education of women, and the need of
a larger endowment, offered by the President. Then
Miss Cushing made a very pretty speech, and then
I spoke my piece, doing on the whole sufficiently
well. Then to solemn music as before, we went to
the collation."

TO MRS. HALE

"BUFFALO, *Dec.* 17, 1874. I have your letter of
Tuesday, announcing Bellows's rather sudden change
of base. It makes very little difference, as I should

quite as lief preach at home as in New York. Whatever Clarke determines on therefore, is best, and I doubt if I shall even telegraph for instructions till I arrive at New York, where I shall be Friday morning at Bellows's house, and if you need you may telegraph me there, 232 W. 15 Street.

"I am at the last disappointed by ——'s letter.[1] They had a rumor about Yellow Springs that he was coming. There is this about it, however, if he cannot see that the opportunity is something much larger than the presiding over a boarding school of a hundred and fifty scholars, if he cannot see that it involves, in the best hands, the moral and spiritual direction of the public education of the state of Ohio, and for that matter of the neighboring states probably he would not make it do that.

"When we blame the man who makes through cowardice the great refusal we forget that only the man who is born to set the world right can set it right; and that for an apprentice, quite incompetent, to put his tool into the running of the watch, will most likely smash the whole.

"I had a very nice day yesterday, in its way a day of rest, though with its share of actualities. It is a pleasure, in itself, to be in a house so lovely with such charming people. I said to Mrs. Sprague yesterday something about my being a visitor, and she said, very heartily, 'Why you're not a visitor' — a *mot* which I think shows the manner of the woman. You laughed at my saying she reminded me of you,

[1] Declining the Presidency of Antioch College.

as she does constantly. This morning one of the girls came out with, 'Mamma, Mrs. Schermerhorn says that you look a little like Mrs. Hale.' She is just about your age, and has had seven children, of whom three are in heaven. She urges me to bring you and Nelly here in June on a visit, when we can all go to Niagara together, perhaps to Watkins Glen and to other of their New York scenery.

"Schermerhorn was only too eager and hospitable in showing me lions. But the thing easiest to tell of was a visit which Mrs. Sprague arranged when Miss Charlotte Mulligan lunched with us, the person who founded 'The Guard of Honor' among the working-men here. Your mother, or Maria Gilman, told us about her. The Guard of Honor was almost exactly like our Christian Unity, with the difference that it has a woman of sense at the head, instead of a man who is an amiable fool. I pumped and pumped, and got a great deal of curious detail out of her about the management of it. Of all which the English is that she is investing her whole life in the uplifting socially, religiously, and morally of some hundred and fifty men. A pure piece of apostleship. Of whom and of which I shall have much to tell you."

TO CHARLES

"*Dec.* 22, 1874. I got happily home last night, and the first news I got was the good news of your admission to the bar.[1] Of course I never had the

---

[1] Charles, on returning to Boston from Washington, had determined to practice law, the profession for which he had originally prepared himself.

slightest question or anxiety about it; I wish you could have had as little.

"I am sorry to say most of my business is in the criminal courts, where people of your dignity do not go, more's the pity. There I have a good deal of business, and am well fitted to be admitted myself. As my business never by any accident pays fee or honorarium, the loss of it is not so severe. I shall, however, promise you in advance all my business, and seriously I think you will be very glad to have a ποῦ στῶ.

"I have had a beautiful time as I believe I said before. I think I like a Pullman better than any place open to me in the world; no door-bell, no letters, no bores, enough to eat, to drink, and chance to sleep."

The following letter shows a mood that one should not overlook, though one should not take it too seriously. Such humorous grumbling helps us to appreciate the spirit that was able to override all such obstacles.

TO MRS. HALE

"*April* 13, 1875. The grounds of my being blue were these; see if I am not justified. In a fit of extra good-humor — sitting in George's parlour, drinking Annie's tea, and penitent because I had been there so little, I assented cordially to this plan, that we should all go to Wayland together — spend the night in the old house, and read 'In His Name.' Today is the day for the execution of the scheme thus easily formed. There are already three

inches of snow on the ground. George is not well
and will not go. I have therefore condemned myself
to sinking twenty hours of a world which needs to
be set forward, in going to Wayland, of all places
in the world (by the way I preached there the
second time I preached at all), and whispering soft
nothings in the ear of Mrs. Wayman, who is I fear
deaf. *Memorandum,* In these places where you
lecture for nothing, the tables are wholly turned
and they patronise you. They treat you as a deserving young man who ought to be encouraged. They
hope you understand that though they might have
staid at home, having, indeed bought no ticket for
the entertainment, yet by way of showing that
Wayland was interested in bringing forward young
debutants, they have come to the reading. They
are not wholly sure that you know that Dr. Hayward of the Revolutionary army made the home of
his family in Wayland while he was in service, and
that it is not every man who has the privilege of
reading a lecture in the meeting house of the town
where Dr. Hayward as above left his family under
such circumstances. Nay! did you perhaps know
that there was talk of naming Wayland by the name
of Hayward, but that Dr. Wayland gave the town a
library so they thought they would call it Wayland.

"Ah, me! what wickedness to write you this
gossip. Since I wrote it my foot got to sleep, and I
have walked up and down the room to cure it, and
Nelly is here, and the world does not seem to me so
utterly blank. Still I wish you to observe that I
am to sink the 20 hours between 3 Tuesday P.M.

and 10 Wednesday A.M. *Moral.* Never do another good natured thing as long as you live. I have been wondering what Salter, the minister of Wayland would say, if I wrote to him this note:

"'Dear Mr. Salter;

"'If you would give a day to writing us a careful and entertaining article of thirty pages for *Old & New* you would give pleasure to a great many people, and altho' we can make you no remuneration, and would like to have you pay your own expenses of all sorts, still I assure you, we shall be very much obliged to you'— If my mood of cussedness lasts, after I have written to Hetty to tell your news, why I shall write a blank for all invitations for Mary Edes, or the staff to copy; thus —

"'Dear Sir; —

"'I have your favor of the –th. I am truly sorry to say that I am so much in arrears in all my engagements in my parish that I am obliged to deny myself all such agreeable proposals as this you make to me.'

"Would not this be a good blank?

"Ah, me! and all this grumbling comes to you in the midst of real anxiety and sorrow. How can I be grateful enough that we are all perfectly well, and have nothing to growl about but such outsides as these.

"Give much love to Katy. We pray for her and hope for her.

"Ever yours,
"PAPA."

TO MRS. HALE

"*April* 16, 1875. I was awaked at 3.25 this morning from my first nap by a tap from Katy, who informed me, without any agitation, that the girls reported that the next house was on fire. I, of course, spoke with similar calmness, as if the next house was on fire every night; bade her wake the children up stairs and tell them to dress, and as soon as I could get my slippers and pantaloons on, I enforced my own order. The up stairs people dressed at once, I told Bridget to start her fire to make coffee for the firemen, I saw Katy under weigh with her boys, and then, for the first time, I reconnoitred. I am sorry for the romance of the story to have to confess that the fire, even then, was extinguished. But I could hear the steamer on Highland Avenue pumping away, a hose was laid through Mr. Shepherd's garden, and firemen were at work in the cellar and yard of the first brick house below Mr. Shepherd's, which was the house which had been on fire.

"The cellar had taken fire from the furnace. Mr. Macomber confessed to me that they had smelled the smoke as long ago as Wednesday night at ten o'clock; his sister, who had just returned from Varley's preaching having observed it then. Whether she had thought it something else of which Varley had told her, or whether such people expect to have a little smoke round them all the time, I do not know, but they left the fire smouldering for thirty hours, before it broke out. Our Ellen testifies to seeing it from out of the back cellar windows. This is more than I saw. I saw galore of steam and smoke, but no fire.

"After I had got all the children down in the parlor and dining-room with their boots on, item the basket of plate with the porcelain portraits of the little boys in it, I went round into Highland Avenue myself. There were four or five steamers with their retinue of hose, etc. The etiquette is to speak low, lest you disturb a sleeping neighborhood. All told, neighbors, police, engine-men, and the family burned out, I should not think there were a hundred people there. The engines were already limbering up to go home. The drivers bade each other good bye courteously, as gentlemen leaving an evening party might do. I offered the civilities of the occasion to Mr. Macomber. His parlor furniture and that of his dining room had all been moved into heaps in the middle of the room, and was all covered by the rubber cloths of the protection men. His aged mother and children were already at other neighbors, and as the firemen were all driving off, I returned and countermanded my orders for coffee. The children had had about enough of it by this time, I sent them all up stairs again, and by four o'clock they were all in bed and asleep. I think I am most amazed of all that an affair involving so much work should have been so quietly done. The inside of the cellar is a good deal burned. They cut through from the kitchen, so there was a hole through the floor, and they pulled down a good deal of lath and plaster looking for hidden fire which they did not find. The cellar of the house is running with water now.

"We had all your dresses out on the bed ready to pack. I directed my mighty mind to some studies as to what was valuable and what was not, and had your watch and mine both in my pockets. But, as it proved, we moved nothing but the pictures which caught my eye as I said, before I left our room."

TO MRS. HALE

"*April* 19, 1875. It is certainly reported that the cruel Red Coats have marched out of Boston,[1] and at this early hour I have summoned all your family who can bear arms to follow them to Concord. May God grant that we may all return safe home. I need not say that your four youngest children Phil, Berty, Harry, and Robby would be glad to join in the march. But I shall leave them under Katy and Mary Edes to defend the camp. Indeed they will press so far into town as to go to the Pantheon and the Panorama of Jerusalem. It is a very glorious morning as Sam Adams said, if it will only stay so. The vane looks to me vilain west, but the sky is cloudless and it is something not to have it vilain east, as it was yesterday. But if more patriots do not lay down their lives from eating collations in pavilions, hearing orations in them, and eke dancing in them at balls, it will be because Nemesis even sheathes her sword and joins in the rejoicing of a grateful country.

[1] The day, it will be remarked, was that of the centennial celebration of the Battle of Lexington.

"I forget if I told you that I was going to dine with the President [General Grant] at the Commercial Club. Mahlon Spaulding, whom you hardly know, but who is always very mindful of me invited me, and I had an excellent time. I sat between the Secretaries of War and the Navy most of the time, with Clifford and Judge Hoar on their right and left; not a bad quintette, as the President was on the left of Clifford. You see I group the world around myself, as people are apt to do. The speaking was not very good. I made rather a poor speech myself when my turn came. But the spirit was excellent, and it was very interesting to see these men.

"Grant looks the impersonation of bulldog obstinacy. He has that heavy neck, which makes you think of apoplexy, and there is something painful about the hardness of the lines of his lips; the difficulty with which he smiles. He looks anxiously on a person in whom he is interested something as you have seen a dog look, who would give his life to speak and cannot. Yet I am sure that his eyes filled with tears at a compliment to his father. He handed me a cigar which I have kept as a not uncharacteristic memorial. First he asked me very cordially after Charley, and sent his love to him. I do not know how late they kept it up, but I came home at eight, and had got in the spirit of the thing so much that I changed my line of battle, and preached a puritan sermon on the moral forces of the Revolution. I stole the text from Silver-tongued Sam's sermon at the inauguration of the constitution. It is so good you ought to look at it; Jeremiah 30. 21.

"So goodbye. Breakfast is here. But I thought we should get off no other dispatches today. Perhaps you do not understand that Nelly goes with Mrs. Hooper and the Centennial Committee on the train with me. Nelly will sleep at the Munroes at Lexington."

TO CHARLES

"*July* 18, 1875. Judge Potter thinks the act making the presidential election uniform is thirty years old, and connects it with the New Jersey difficulty. I do not. I think it is as late as the choice of Buchanan, say 1855.

"Thanksgiving is merely a custom. In the 18th century it was earlier than with us.

> "'Twas up to Uncle Tracy's
> The fifth of November,
> Last Thanksgiving night
> As I very well remember.'

"I have seen a letter from Gov. Lincoln to the Governor of Connecticut asking him what day he expected to proclaim *Fast*. Commencement was the fourth Wednesday in August in 1834. I think the change from a *later* period was not much before that time.

"I was very glad to get your letter. I am deep in my work, of which the time is 1803–1805 at New Orleans and Texas, including Aaron Burr. Can you give me any help in the way of memoirs of people? What do you know of Gov. Miranda or of Lafitte, the Pirate of the Gulf?"

TO CHARLES

"*July* 25, 1875. My letter of yesterday left my letterbox at one, and before one-thirty the parcel of books had arrived, also your Palmerston, and the poison, for all of which many thanks.

"I sat up an hour last night reading the Palmerston, and have taken another pull at it this morning. One of the first pieces of modern history which I remember is the creation of the Kingdom of Belgium, a transaction which has been much ridiculed, but which has proved more important, I think, than they then supposed. That France and Prussia could only get at each other through the narrow line between Belgium and Switzerland was no unimportant feature in the late war.

"The *Transcript*, which is the only paper I see except the *Globe* and *Advertiser*, was very learned in its protests about Bismarck's letters to the Belgian government, and lashed itself with indignant inquiry as to what we should say if he sent such letters to us. The difference was simply that the Prussian government (with its allies) created Belgium on the fixed condition that Belgium should always be neutral in their affairs. When Belgium made herself a fire-brand, Prussia had every right to remind her of the vows made for her in her baptism.

"I think I can arrange my fly-poison so as to do no harm to warm blooded vertebrates who seem to have rights in our ethical codes unknown to invertebrates or insects.

"One of my children's books has this piece of

moral. 'Naughty pup, to kill the pretty birds; puss should kill mice', a curious and delicate solution of the intricacies of the 6th commandment.

"The books Fred sent me would probably be more attractive to you (and me) than to any people living.

"Burr's trial, Blennerhassett's Life, Stoddard's Louisiana, Pike's Wilkinson's memoirs. This last contains all that I know of the original Philip Nolan.

"A shoal of black fish is reported on the shore, and they say the fishermen are bearing down upon them. I shall know more soon."

TO MRS. HALE

"NEW YORK, *Oct.* 31, 1875. I have just come from Uncle Henry's, and went there from Moody and Sankey, where I attended, a platform guest, by the magic of a note signed by Moody himself, of which I will tell you at another time, because now I want to write of the distinguished reception of the novel yesterday.[1]

"First of all, imagine my feelings, when yesterday morning I sorted out the precious *parts*, from February to June, having to deliver five, beside the one which they already had, imagine I say my feelings, when I found I had *over*-written and had one part nearly finished *more* than was needed. I had intended to finish it yesterday morning, but as you may suppose did not trouble it when I found it need not be delivered till next April! Then Miss

---

[1] "Philip Nolan's Friends," which was to be published in *Scribner's Magazine*.

Casey and I, — she was Katy's governess last year, — tied up the five parts of five parcels, and I started with them, as much pleased with my discovery of Part VII as if I had stumbled on a roll of $208.33 in greenbacks in the street, and learned by the envelope that they were my own.

"Dr. Holland is at the west, it proved. But Mr. Roswell Smith and Mr. Gilder and Mr. Johnson were all in, and received me with all the honors. They were, in fact, just examining a new drawing by Abbey, for the very beginning. It is really very good. You see the shipping at the levee at New Orleans, — while Silas Perry, well done in jack boots and small clothes, waved his handkerchief to the boat already in the distance.

"I sat down and Mr. Abbey was sent for. Mr. Roswell Smith told of his European voyage, most of which, strange to say, was spent with the Adams Ayers in Switzerland. Was not that funny, seeing that they were so closely *liée* with *Old & New*.

"He was very much interested in little scraps that I told him about the story and the contemporary history; made as if he knew something of the Adams and Jefferson politics, tho' alas, few people do. But I think he is still well pleased with his bargain, and hopes that his mermaid is alive.

"Mr. Abbey could not be found, and I am to see him tomorrow. But when I left, they said, 'They want to see you down stairs.' Which meant they want to pay $1250. So I went in. But alas, *they* had all gone. I am not able therefore to inclose you that little check, but expect to be tomorrow."

TO MRS. HALE

"N.Y.C.R.R. ON THE WAY TO ANN ARBOR.

"*Nov.* 17, 1875. I have been reading steadily on 'Madding Crowd.' It is a wonderfully powerful book. Such books as this and 'Middlemarch' make me ashamed of my novels, and make me think I will never write anything but sermons and short stories and newspaper articles. I should think women would hate it. Yet it is such a woman as George Eliot who has done most to introduce this picture of a woman, and one is almost surprised to know that a man has drawn this character.

"The book, strange to say, has reminded me a good deal of William Weeden's novel. I do not think that he has any such vigorous characterization, to take a bad word from the newspapers. But there is a good deal like it in his determined way to go right at the description of the rustic life of the surroundings of his people. And he also got hold, in his book, of what is, after all, passed by in some novels, the power almost absolute which a woman has over the man who loves her, to make him do just what she will, — I do not say what she chooses. People are so fond of making their heroes perfect, that they omit the thing which is, *au fond*, essential, — viz. that, perfect or imperfect, the woman of the story can draw them with a hair.

"I have to write at the stations. Between whiles I read. And I have absolutely put the book down at the moment, if you remember it, when the Christmas festivities at Boltwood House are beginning and

Susan Tall's husband tries to persuade himself that he can tell Mr. Boltwood that Troy has come back again.

"P.S. Well I have finished the book and at Buchanan I can finish my letter. But the circumstances are not favorable to profound criticism. Miss Taylor told me yesterday that the first half of the book was better than the last, and I should think most women would say so. Truth is that so soon as the author gets tangled up with the story, he can no longer handle his characters with that dainty affection with which poor Breck makes a salmon-fly out of a few feathers and hairs."

TO WILLIAM B. WEEDEN

"*Jan.* 31, 1876. The Examiner nights seem fated. I shall be away tomorrow night and shall not see you. All the same we shall be glad if you will take tent with us here.

"Here is your 'Blue Eyes' which I took to read on my journey. If you have not read this, and the other which is rather better, the 'Madding Crowd,' you ought to. Both of them remind one curiously of your novel. I am at a loss to know why; unless it is that they frankly acknowledge the power, physical if you please, which a woman has over a man, which he cannot explain, and which makes him do very inexplicable things.

"Women dislike the books and there is no wonder. For the women in the book abuse their power very badly. Whether that is or is not a habit of the sex is, of course, the question. I am afraid brother

Hardy, whoever he may be, has been very cruelly jilted in his day by some very pretty women. The two novels are one in the little incident that each heroine has, at the same moment, three men in love with her, and has indeed, given very direct encouragement to each of the three."

TO MRS. HALE

"LAKE SHORE ROAD

"*June* 19, 1876. I think I have never traveled over this road in the daytime in summer before. It is very beautiful. Almost everywhere the northern horizon is made by the lake, which has today a curious greeny blue which reminds you of Niagara, as it should of course, and of the Swiss lakes also, as of course also it should. And this journey, all the winter I have dreamed that you and I should take now for a holiday pleasure, ah me!

"What do you think? When the book boy came round he had a new novel by Hardy, 'Ethelberta's Hand.' I bought it, for you of course. But I thought you would not mind if I read it first. It is very good. Just like all his others for the woman has three lovers at once all along, but she is so unconscious that there is anything in it amiss, or rather she persuades herself so naïvely that she cannot help herself, that you would think it all right but for remembering in Hardy's other novels that it is all wrong. She is very handsome, as you know I like to have them."

"LAWRENCE, KANSAS, *Sept.* 12, 1879. We wrote from Atchison yesterday. The two names will be a contrast to you, and perhaps nothing to the children, so far does a quarter of a century rub out our little asperities. Gov. Robinson says that the Stringfellows, who are now 'good' Republicans, are to be at our meeting, in the capacity of Early Settlers. Judge Lecompte, for whom Lecompton was named, — which you will remember as the center of villanies, of which he perpetrated as many as he could, — is another sound Republican of today, who is to be present at these solemnities, and to whom I shall have to be decent. Time works wonders.

"Not yet at Gov. Robinson's house. We are in the Ludington House, which has changed its name from the old Eldridge House, which was built on the site of the Hotel which the Border Ruffians burned on the 22nd of May, 1856. Oh, how mad we were in Boston in those days! I made my first Faneuil Hall speech apropos of that business. The Eldridges kept the house for us. The first and only meal it ever served was for the guilty who burned it down, who, with a grim humor, ordered dinner, which they never paid for, and then, under order from the U.S. Marshall, destroyed it. We have a claim against the government for it unto this day. The silver, etc., is still marked Eldridge House. But the hotel sign is the Ludington House.

"For the boys' amusement I will cut out some

memoranda from the local papers. Save only the base ball matches, which are of national importance, no syllable of Eastern news is published here. That probably will tell who is to be Democratic candidate in New York but this also with profound indifference. What interests us much more is the downfall of the bridge over the Kaw River. A herd of cattle, in a panic, all ran on one span Tuesday, broke in, and 60 or 70 of the poor creatures were killed. This calamity cuts off the town from Bismarck Grove, where our celebration is to be held Monday. But a ferry and a new bridge are contemplated before that time, three days let us hope being sufficient to build a span of a hundred feet or more with the river rising. The same accident prevented our going to the Governor's house last night, and we have spent the night here. We now take a little walk, and shall then ride over there, crossing in a boat."

GENERAL ORDERS

"Post Pappoose Talk. *March* 9, 1880
"To the F.M.,
"Post Woodland, Hartford.

"I have the honor to submit to your Excellency the reports, as they shall come in, of the engagement of yesterday, an engagement, as your Excellency will perceive, almost without precedent as to the length of time involved, and the wide distances of the points of encounter. It is as yet too early to report full results. It is sufficient to say, that, at midnight, the enemy was no where visible, while your forces, of which in your absence I have the

honor to hold command, had retired upon this and
the other posts held by this detail, in good order.
Two of the junior officers having left me at eight
by a rapid flank movement, to take possession of
Posts Science and Literature, and the youngest of
all at eight-thirty for similar posts, I left this station
myself, unaccompanied even by my staff; and, having effected a junction with Mrs. General Andrews
at nine, we promptly attacked as instructed, in
the general plan of battle, the Unity Chapel. Here
we were completely repulsed, there being neither
key nor janitor, nor anybody who knew anything
of either or of any other subject. By a rapid flank
movement, retiring in good order, we sharply drove
in the doors of the Sailor's Chapel, North Bennet
Street, where I need not say we were wholly unex-
pected, and where the Enemy of Souls retired before
us. An engagement at once began along the whole
line, without precedent for noise and rapidity of
movement. At twelve I was obliged to part with
this valuable officer, who pursued her own line of
battle in directions which she will report, while by
column of fours I proceeded, still without my personal staff, to Mt. Auburn. From this extreme
westerly line of movement, returning at three, this
time accompanied by my personal staff, Gen. Nelly,
who reported promptly, we delivered battle at the
Sea Shore Home on Arlington Street, Gen. Nelly
making the necessary quorum. My next duty was
to assist at a grand council of war held at Gen.
Rufus Ellis's quarters, where all the heads of department met for consultation, tea, and oysters, and

I was by this time in condition to do justice to the latter, the supply trains having, in general, failed in the day's transactions. Leaving the council, which, so far as I observed, agreed in nothing, I reported in person at Mrs. Andrews' where the conspirators of the day had assembled, having put down their new dining room carpet, and sent in the India dinner set. Also ice cream galore which we then gobbled together. At ten-thirty I withdrew my contingent in good order, and at twelve M. the grateful bugle sang thrice. But, as above, the E. S. was nowhere visible. I have the honor to be your Ex's most obdt. servt.

"E. E. HALE, M. G. C."

TO MRS. HALE

"MATUNUCK, *Sept.* 8, 1880. I am made happy by another letter from you (to Nelly) assuring us that you begin to feel well.

"One of Rob's presents was 'Swiss Family Robinson' in the ten cent edition. They read it aloud evenings; and it has brought up the details of a plan in which they delight. As they are all a year too far advanced in their studies, they propose to spend the year here, living on the native productions. I have consented that, if they will study all day on the stormy days, there shall be no school on the pleasant days. It is also conceded that the Cyclopaedia and Nelly and the two aunts and you and I know all that is worth knowing, so that there need be no other instruction, though I think they yearn for Fred Almy a little. For food, they agree to have pork and beans once a week. The other dinners are to be

Sea perch, from Salt Pond
Pickerel, guaranteed by Berty from our pond.
Oysters, from Trustom's, or clams or mussels.
Blue fish or a Spanish mackerel.

(All this conversation was started by a peerless Bonita or Spanish mackerel, which some of us have just made a little hole in at tea.)

Chickens, for they consent to take care of the hens.
Ham and eggs.

I have agreed, if they keep up their supplies, to furnish sugar, flour, meal and rice.

"I think they are rather encouraged by bringing in today fifty pounds or more of ripe grapes, really not bad to eat, and, while the M. G. C. supplies sugar, very good in jelly. We still have huckleberries and our daily cake from them at breakfast. We also have six quarts of bayberries and shall make the mythical candle tomorrow.

"For you, we are afraid you will not like this plan, but will prefer to board at the Parker House, the Hoffman, Willard's or the Hotel Chatham. Perhaps you will come and see us sometimes.

"I see I have not put into the list the rabbits, woodchucks, yellow legs, plover, etc. which Edward promises when he kills them.

"Love to all from
"Papa."

CHAPTER THIRTY–ONE

EUROPE AGAIN

1882, 1883

THE great interest of the year 1882 was a journey to Spain. Spain was for Americans in those days, and for a long time had been, the country of romance. My father had kept in his heart since the days of Irving the charm of this country of the Alhambra and Seville. There was also, however, the historical interest: he wanted to see the country whence Columbus had sailed; he wanted to look in Spanish libraries for documents on Verrazano and Magellan. With him in this excursion were his daughter Ellen, who was at the time studying painting in Paris, and his sister Susan, who was traveling with Miss Mary Marquand. One or two of the earlier travel letters are of value, if only that we may see the different lines of his interest, as shown in letters to different members of the family.

TO EDWARD

"LONDON, *April* 28, 1882. I sent you this morning the *Daily News* with a report of Gladstone's Budget Speech, which I hope you will read. I have read the Budget speeches now for many years, and it is an admirable way of keeping *au fait*, not with

English politics only, but with the method of administration, — indeed, with what administration is.

"I write this at midnight, on my last night in London, after sitting five hours in the House of Commons, where by great good luck I heard Gladstone make a short but very characteristic speech. If I get up early enough tomorrow, I shall make a little note of it for the *Advertiser*. But I will say now to you, if the man who is talking to me will hold his tongue, that it was a great pleasure to hear him. It was as I have heard Bellows or some such man, — not to say myself, — called up at the end of a public meeting, and standing good-naturedly talking with all the people, assenting to this man, dissenting from that, encouraging both sides, cordially and courteously acknowledging his opponents' good points, but, all along, talking as if he liked to talk, and knowing that everybody else wanted to hear him.

"I waited, thro' a debate on *Slavery* of all subjects, to hear Sir Charles Dilke. Oddly enough, like master like man. And Sir Charles, probably without knowing it, lounged on the table and even in attitudes resembled his great chief. This debate I will send you too, — not so much the slavery one as that in which Gladstone spoke, which was on the question of the issue of one pound notes. Gladstone's doctrine was admirable, though it would be horrifying to the finance managers of the *Daily*, and frightened the old fogies here. The subject compelled him to go into all the mysteries of finance and to take some views quite bold and fresh, and which showed that if he were ten years younger, they would have to prepare for new adjustments of the whole currency.

"The man has talked steadily, is talking now, and probably will continue to, after I have left the room, when he has nothing to talk to but the candles. I will go, and let him try.

"Saturday morning, 7 o'clock. This much offending man is a man named Dening, a reporter of the *Evening Post*, with all the faults and, let me hope, all of the excellencies of his [calling]. These last, I am fain to say (he has been so busy talking) that I have not yet seen them. But I believe them to exist. He holds this parlor of Bowker's by a Box and Cox right, rising long after Bowker goes out and returning to the lodging long after Bowker goes to bed. This works very well. But I, coming home near midnight from the House of Commons, launched you see on a famished talker who had seen no American who could understand his language, for days, and so, when I wanted to write to you, he talked me to bed.

"Now about dear Nelly's picture.[1] I received *no* ticket. All people, even Lowell, shook their heads at the absolute impossibility of my getting in yesterday. It was *Private Day*, of which you have read, when no money is taken but only high swells of the highest kind go. The truth is that, on this day, they hope to sell their pictures. Each Academician therefore has five tickets to give away, and he gives them to people who buy pictures. 'If I had only

---

[1] At the Academy Exhibition.

known in time, I would have spoken to Leighton,'
Lowell said. Leighton, you know, is the President.
This Lowell said to me at 4 P.M. When I left him
I took a cab and bade the man drive me to Burlington
House. You go into a court, and my elegant cab
took its place among the carriages of Dukes and
Marquises. Flunkeys in every livery lined the
stairways, which were elegant with azaleas, and
laid, to the carriages, with red carpets — heavy
carpets at that. I sent in my card to the Secretary,
and in ten minutes more Papa was led personally
by a very swell attendant in a red gown like an
Oxford doctor's among the Lords and Ladies into
the exhibition. My child, as I went up the stairs
the first picture I saw plainly enough to make out
was Nelly's. It *carries* admirably, and at that distance I recognized the well known Annie Page.
Really, had I been on the hanging committee, I
could hardly have placed it better. You walk up
this grand staircase; you naturally walk through
the principal room. Opposite you are [here follows
a sketch showing the pictures]. You see, unless
you actually hung it on the line, you could not have
placed it better in the room.

"I did not happen to meet Northumberland or
Westminster or Devonshire or any other of my
peers, so I could not see how it struck them. But
I saw that it is better than many portraits there,
and I am sure it will hold its own. The exhibition
is like all exhibitions, good and bad.

"But I must pack for Paris. I shall see her
tonight!   God bless you all."

TO PHILIP

"PARIS, *May* 3, 1882. We went yesterday to the
Salon for the first time. The dogs had not accepted
Nelly's charcoals, so we had to buy tickets and go
with the public, for which we did not, however,
abandon the adventure. The place is the Salle
d'Industrie Palace, which was built for Napoleon
III's first exposition. The annexes, etc. were removed, but it left them a building of stone, somewhat larger than our new Mechanics' Hall, for
permanent uses for just such things. It was here
that they had the Electric Exhibition, and we saw
them removing the debris of a Horse Exhibition
they had just had in the court yard. It is built
around three sides (perhaps four) of a long beautiful garden, which is under glass. In this garden
they have the sculpture, each piece well parted from
the others by green sward. In the building around,
second floor, they have the pictures. There are
nearly 5000 pictures, some of them of immense
size, so you can see they need a good deal of space.
I do not know how many rooms there are; I should
think twenty, some very large, none smaller than
our large rooms at the Museum.

"In this collection (annual) are admitted without
criticism or question two works offered by persons
who have been two or three times 'crowned' as they
say here, — i.e. recognized as artists by tokens of
public favor. For the rest they have to pass the
ordeal which we see so much discussed in *L'Art*.
Pretty strict it must be, for, from the point of view

of technique, there are absolutely no bad pictures.
There are plenty of pictures you do not like, but
no one where you would say that the man did not
do well what he set out to do. The man himself
thought the thing well done. Nothing makes you
feel more than this, the point to which they have
carried art education. I am told twice as many
are rejected as are passed.

"We have discussed a good deal the question,
which picture of them all we would take for a present were it offered. I do not know, I am sure.
There is a great deal of admirable landscape, much
more, as I remember it, than I saw here nine years
since. There is almost nothing of what we should
call genre painting, clever little interiors and small
figures. There are a few elaborate fruit and flower
pieces such as people so like to exhibit with us, but
only a very few. There are a great many portraits,
some admirably good. There are a good many pictures cleverly executed for government works, ceil-
ings in imitation of fresco, and such, and an immense
number of large pictures painted simply for exhibition, too big to have in any house, and indeed to
have anywhere outside such a place.

"Of these the two spoken of as most certain to
be crowned are a very large painting to which the
motto 'Ludus pro Patria' is given, in imitation of
fresco, and in that half color a good deal affected
in such things, representing Gauls at their exercises.
It is almost as long and as varied as one of my
imagined frescoes, and admirably done. Three well
nigh naked men are engaged in throwing the javelin

and in other athletics in a way to delight you three
junior gentlemen, while the thing is varied by
groups of women and children and an agreeable
paysage. An old-fashioned paper on a large parlor,
such as I fear you never saw, would not have a
greater variety of groups or of characters. The
other most discussed picture is the Spanish dancer
whom you see figured in *Figaro*. By a clever trick
in the gilt frame the reflected light seems to be the
very light of the footlights before which the woman
dances, and she stands or moves quite out into the
room. These two pictures seem to receive most
suffrages for the highest prizes.

"I am finishing this the day after its date. I
may not have said that there are more than four
thousand, nearly five thousand pictures. They
arrange them in the ten rooms, nearly by the letters
of the painters, A B C and so on; so let no man
say that they have given to X or L a better place
than to F or G. As always, I suppose the pictures
of people of fame have a better chance on the line,
but none are badly placed.

"Comparing the show with what I saw here ten
years, or nine, ago, it is clear to me that the French
are more amiable than they were then. Everything
then was blood and thunder: — vengeance against
Prussia appeared at every turn. There is, alas, no
lack of blood now, but there is a great deal of pleasant subject, of pictures which savor of domestic
life. There is also rather an unpleasant suggestion
of mere technique. It recalls what I was saying to
you about an artist so ignorant that he has noth-

ing to say after he has learned to say it. The choice of subjects seems curiously jejune or crude, and you are fairly surprised that men who know so much of the details of art know so little of what art is for, or even of what it has attempted or achieved in other days.

"But I am conscious of hurrying over my last pages at the Salon, because I want to tell you of today, our lovely summer excursion to Barbizon and the forest of Fontainebleau. Mr. and Mrs. Gilman, of whom Nelly is so fond, are living there. They had been, however, at this house for two days, so as to be present at the opening of the Salon. We made a little party to go out with them and to picnic in the forest. Till today the weather has been very cold. Today proved itself one of those lovely spring days which are in fact perfect summer, and we have had a charming visit. The country is far in advance (I mean the season) of what I described in England, the apple blossoms just trying to open, oak leaves as big as a rabbit's largest foot, and the full shape of every forest tree perfectly defined in its fresh, light green. We were screaming all the time as we rode from Melun to Barbizon because we saw so many of Millet's subjects, — women leading cows, men at work in the fields. We found the gardener who cares for his place, and he took us through the modest little house (of three rooms) and let us draw in the atelier and bring home forget-me-nots from the garden. Then we had our picnic in the Forest, and then walked to the Brigand's Cave. It is a big hole in a great terminal moraine, which makes a pile of rocks some 200 feet high commanding a beautiful view over the great plain of Barbizon, — a perfect Esdrael of agricultural beauty. Then we resumed our fiacre, rode back to Melun, and so home.

"It has been a charming expedition. Understand that Melun is some forty miles away."

TO MRS. HALE

"MADRID, *May* 18, 1882. Here we are at last after a long night ride. By a stupid misunderstanding we did not get the famous *wagon-lits*, which are said to be the best in Europe. Burgos held out to the last the most queer and fascinating place conceivable. Look up, if you have not read it, Lathrop's bright description in the April *Harper*. The pictures were actually taken from convenient places right by our hotel. He calls our dear hotel dirty and smelly. This angers us, for the people were very good to us. There was the drollest mixture of the barbarous show in carpets and chimney ornaments, which you might expect of a gasping over-built hotel in Canada or Iowa, with the feeling that you were in a building some 500 years old. I do not believe there is a house in Burgos proper which has been built in the last 200 years.

"The Cathedral is perfect of the kind — I mean R. C. kind. That is to say, there has never been any lack of the sort of faith which reared it, and with what Mr. Ruskin would call loving care it has been maintained all along in the spirit which built it. Thus we saw a bodily procession of the high clergy of the region start with the Host to go in procession through the streets, with a band of music. In truth, we inspected the church in their absence, it being rather convenient for us, alas, that they were not there. . . .

"Here intervened the first breakfast (you know we have two a day in these countries) and Nelly and I by a visit to the bankers got a nice parcel of letters. I enclose a precise list. It was a week since we had heard, nearly a week since we met Susy, so you can imagine the pleasure they give us. Thank every one for prompt and full writing, and try to feel yourself, dear child, that you tell us exactly what we need to know. I hope the first rough storm of business has lulled permanently.

TO PHILIP

"We had left the two others at Seville, as the business in hand was rather historical than artistic. I ought however to say that Molly has a perfect historical passion, and that I think the shells I brought her back (for I write on the 28th) from Columbus's place of embarkation have given her as thorough pleasure as anything she could have had. Well, thus there began a charming excursion, quite varied, as you see, from anything we have done yet. When I say that I wrote the introduction to 'Stories of Discovery' in Columbus's own room, with ink from his own inkstand, while Nelly, on a lovely corridor without, was making a careful drawing of what must have been his pet ocean line, — you get the key-note to a day of very great pleasure.

"It seems that Huelva also, on the west side of the bay or river, was a port not inconsiderable in Columbus's time. But the flow of the Tinto River since, while it has not injured Huelva on the west, has piled up silt or sand against poor Palos on the east, so that Palos is now a mile and a half from the sea, a poor little hamlet of 150 houses without foreign trade, or any trade, of course. But, just outside of Palos, on a beautiful bold headland overlooking the bay was the 'convent dedicated to St. Mary,' where Columbus 'asked of the porter a little bread and water for his child.' Now he went there, not in attitude of a beggar, but because the Prior, Brother Diego de Marchena was a learned and far-sighted man. This Prior became his backer in the whole enterprise, and it was his introduction to Isabella which interested her and gave to it its success. The Spanish nation, therefore, with great propriety, makes the convent now the national monument of Columbus, as it was the moral centre of the enterprise. Naturally, while the expedition was fitting out, Columbus would have stayed with the Prior, and the traditions of the chamber and his inkstand are in all probability true.

"What is better for tourists, and recalls the anecdote of Aeneas's grave, the monks, as I said, chose a lovely spot to live in as they were wont, and a spot accessible, by boat only, from Huelva. So in a large lateen sailed boat, as if it were Jerry's, we proceeded to it in the lovely early morning of what promised to be elsewhere a hot day, but which to us was tempered by a delicious Atlantic breeze all day

long. It is a good climb from the salt-marsh up to
the convent. There the view is magnificent. The
convent is perfectly habitable, and I could wish
that the government would make you and me cus-
todians, for visitors very seldom come. Like everything else it is built around two or three pretty
patios, and like all patios, except those very squalid,
these blaze either with fruits of several sorts or
with geraniums, roses, etc., or with both, — the
whole very neatly kept. The rendezvous place of
the day was in the shade of the corridor around the
largest patio. Here the mother dressed her baby,
the children washed their faces, while in other
parts Juan (the guide) took his nap and Nelly and
I our lunch. The patio serves the general purposes
of an English hall.

"With the ejection of the monks their rooms upstairs are not occupied. There is a pretty chapel
neatly decorated and kept up by the Duke de Mont-
pensier, who is a sort of general patron here. I
said my prayers for you there, but there is no
regular worship. The Columbus room is finished,
and has several modern pictures devoted to him
and his patrons and the great history. And a little
outside, as I said, is the corridor from which Nelly
took her ocean picture, of the stone palms below
and the mysterious horizon lines above. Some
resemblances to Matunuck — in the sand-hills, bars,
breakers, and vegetable growth of the middle distance — made the place all the more interesting to
these tourists. For my part I drew the picturesque
gate-way, which has staggered all the artists, where

the little boy (thirsty, like all boys) had his water, and I shall be able to show you the outlines of the whole building. Then, as above, I wrote for Jack's book the introduction, which I shall show him in a few days.

"Afterwards we took a long sail to a good beach for the shells I spoke of. Palos itself is practically inaccessible from the sea."

TO MRS. HALE

"GRANADA, *June* 9, 1882. This is our last day here. I hope you are not tired of our enthusiasms. But I know the *Summer in Spain* people had inoculated you with it, you inoculated me, and you will not be sorry to know that we have had so pleasant a stay here. Today we are to make several last visits to places which we think we must see again, and to one place, the Carthuja, which is, I hope, mentioned by Mrs. Ramsay and her friend, but which we have put off from day to day. Susy and Nelly have been very successful in drawing and painting, and will be able to give you some very good impressions of the Alhambra. But there are enough points to occupy people for years. You know that Fortuny and Regnault really made their homes here. The inn opposite has signs in front, one to say that Fortuny lived there, and another to say the same of Regnault. I need not say that Nelly's enthusiasm about Regnault gives another interest to the place for her. Dear child, she is down stairs in the garden now drawing 'the Gypsy.' The Gypsy is a swashbuckler-looking fellow who dresses up in what is supposed to be gypsy costume, and stands round the hotel to pose for artists. Nelly has had relations with him from the beginning, but has told him she was not ready for him. Today she has covenanted with him for two hours, which she and he are to take in the gaps of other exercises. The chance was so good that I was tempted to go down myself to try my hand, in what would be a variety in my sketch-book. But this temptation, as you see, I have resisted. If Lothrop will engrave any of Susy's things the 'Horners in Spain' will have some elements which most books of travel lack. The day we went down town to see the Festa, Susy and Nelly both drew bravely in the plaza, and we were surrounded by a crowd of delighted Andalusians, never better pleased than when they recognized their own faces. These little things give great life to the sketch-books of the ladies. I am sure my two books will amuse you. I have one always at hand, and of course, in such artistic surroundings, I am always drawing. In the other, when there is half an hour's leisure, I immortalize in color the sketches which I think most worthy. I need not say that the pencil-book is by far the more satisfactory of the two. But, in a land of color, one is always tempted. The saying is that green, red and blue are the colors of Granada, green for the trees, red for the rocks, and blue for the sky. Susy and Nelly are both in despair because it is so hard to get color enough into their pictures. Add to this that, excepting one day, there has not been a cloud as big as a man's hand on this blue sky, which is a defiance to the deepest ultramarine. For all which blue sky in June, we are so high that the air is even bracing. I am still in my flannels. The thermometer as I write is 66, and there has been no hot day since we were here. As we came home from the exquisite Generalife gardens yesterday, Nelly said, 'Think of it, we are listening to nightingales singing in June and looking on the snow of the Sierra Nevada.'

"Have I dilated on nightingales? You know I never heard any before. I have veered to and fro in my views about them. At one time I said that if a single frog, neither of the shrill chirping kind of the spring or the deep bass Onderdonk kind of the autumn, could be set at his lonely tunk-tunk-tunk at midnight, he might be mistaken for a nightingale. But since that, I have had better luck. I think I was fairly waked by one one night, in the very dead of night. The *n* of the '*tunk*' ameliorated itself almost to *l*, so liquid was it. The tone is so deep as to suggest that the bird sings contralto and not soprano, and the tout-ensemble is a sort of richness which certainly few notes have. Sometimes a mocking bird gives you the same sound. This midnight song is more interesting, though more monotonous, than the twitter of the same bird at sunset. Do you know that the song is the conjugal duty of the husband? He sings to his mate (not to the rose) while she sits on the eggs. If he fail to sing she dies! Susy says it is as if he were reading his wife to sleep with the *Transcript*. Poor fellow, what do you suppose his rights to be if she should lapse for half an hour? And this reminds me, that in the admirable arrangements of our partie-carrée Susy really likes to *read aloud.* So when our long table d'hôte dinner is over, I lie down on my bed, which is in our large salón, and Susy reads or recites Irving's *Conquest of Grenada* to us. We are wholly convinced of the truth of Lucretia's theory of schools, that history should be studied in the countries where it belongs."

TO MRS. HALE

"LONDON, *July* 11, 1882. Last night we went, all of us, to see the original *Patience.* It is capitally well done, with a luxuriance of effect of which our little Museum stage is quite incapable. The theatre (the Savoy) is the prettiest I ever saw and not too large. The second scene, — a 'glade,' the bill calls it, — is the prettiest I ever saw. Real tree trunks stand on the stage, with leaves on which the electric sun casts cross shadows 'as in Castile.' The cast is so full that 'the twenty lovesick maidens' are really twenty-nine, and everything else lavish in proportion. I think Lady Jane must have been written for the woman that does it. She is well nigh six feet high, overtops Bunthorne by six or eight inches, and could crush him like a shell if she chose. Then they have done it so much (more than 400 times) that they sing, dance and so on in perfect accord. The dances are much more of an affair than in our rendering.

"In the advertisements they give the *temperature* of the house. They have the Edison light, and this has the great advantage of not heating it up, so that

on a summer night the house is at 71 degrees. But
we have known no summer nights. I was glad to
sit by a fire in the studio yesterday. And I need
not say that it virtually rains all the time. . . .

"Thursday morning. The dinner party at the
Reform Club was very pleasant. Mr. Clayden took
me in a cab, so that we arrived at eight sharp. The
building is very large and very handsome, I think
the largest club house in London. The host was
Robinson, the Walter of the *Daily News*. Queerly
enough, he used to eke out his honest living by writing letters for the Chicago *Tribune* and for the
Daily Advertiser. I sat at a square table, at his left,
the others as I write them.

Clayden	Parkinson
Payne	Pigot
Laing	Butler
E. E. H.	Robinson

The most interesting man by far was Col. Butler,
at his right, the Military Governor of Plymouth.
He knows America thoroughly, having *walked* from
Hudson's Bay to Nootka Sound on snow-shoes.
Payne is the novelist Payne, an amusing, not very
profound, talkative man. Laing is a younger man
than I, a little elegant, who writes a good deal in
Scribner and such, and does the funny articles in
the *News*. Pigot is the examiner of plays, under
the Lord Chancellor; and Parkinson, former leader-
writer of the *News*, who has married a rich wife and
does not have to dilate in public now. It made a
very amusing and entertaining set.

"James Payne told a funny story about dining

with the Archibshop of Canterbury. He said, first
of all, the cabman could not find the entrance to
Lambeth Palace. At last they drove in, but all
seemed very desolate. However, looking from the
window, he saw Matthew Arnold following him, so
he felt sure all was right; but when he and Arnold
came into the drawing room they were the only
guests. Payne could hardly believe that the Archbishop had made a dinner party only for him and
Arnold, and so it proved. In a minute more they
were summoned to *evening prayers*, and he and
Arnold had to sit through the whole evening service
of the day. *When it was over*, dinner was served;
the party proved to be forty-two persons, but all
the other guests, knowing that an Archbishop's
dinner party began with Evening Prayers, had
come an hour late, in time for the dinner, but not
in time for this somewhat prolonged grace!"

TO MRS. HALE

"Monday morning. Nelly has just left me to
take Alice to the studio to pose. I am writing at
Mr. Clayden's, but it is our last day here. I hardly
remember any so long visit which I have ever made
anywhere. But we like each other very much, and
it has been very pleasant. Yesterday I preached
at his church, as planned above. The congregation
is sympathetic and I enjoyed the service. They use
Martineau's ten services, and I am quite reconciled
to them. Clayden, whose pulpit bearing and manner are faultless, read the service, and I preached a
sermon which in my last volume is called, I believe,

'Not less but more.' They sing, as perhaps I said last week, á ravir. The whole congregation joins with great spirit in the long chants of their service, and Clayden, who has a fancy for hymns with movement and go, keeps them up to a very spirited singing of the hymns.

"In the afternoon I made quite a pilgrimage to see and hear the *Salvation Army*, and I found them. I need not say that, having been organized for street preaching, they are trying, like all other successful Bedouins, to have a fenced city of their own, and are moving heaven and earth to buy the Eagle Tavern, of which a part is the Grecian Theatre, which they will change into a sort of Tabernacle. To the front of the Grecian Theatre, accordingly, I repaired, — as if I had gone to a trivium at South Boston. I found a red silk banner, borne by a proud boy, a Mrs. Leonard speaking simply and prettily (an American), perhaps twenty of the Army scattered in the crowd, and about 200 other people, some drunk and some not drunk, but all listening respectfully and with interest. The woman spoke five minutes, and then they sang, admirably. Then a handsome, eager boy of twenty spoke, well enough, and they sang again. Then the leader offered prayer, and they sang again. He made a benediction, and they started home to their chapel singing. The whole was like a spirited temperance meeting, but that the appeals were to abandon sin and seek a Saviour, instead of to abandon drink and take the Pledge. Clearly it did no harm and one could not but think it must do some good. These 200 people would certainly have gone nowhere to hear the speakers, but when the speakers came to them they listened. Lucky for the poorer English of London that the R. C. church did not start the same thing first, as they do everywhere else. And stupid indeed in the Establishment if they do not in every way encourage and befriend these people."

My father saw Europe again much sooner than he had expected and under bad auspices. When he came back, my sister remained in Paris to continue her work in painting. On April twenty-sixth of the next year, 1883, a cable was suddenly received saying that she had typhoid fever and advising my father to come to her. My father and mother both sailed on the twenty-eighth in great anxiety; fortunately when they reached her in Paris, in the middle of May, they found that she had passed the crisis of the fever and was growing better. On May sixteenth he wrote home, "Nelly's bulletin continues good. She sleeps well, eats with good appetite, and is able to bear more effort. But she does not for a moment leave her bed, which she took four weeks ago. I visit her twice a day, and we talk of everything. But the threat of nervous fever is held over us if we talk too much, and she is very patient and good and so (I need not say) am I." They planned to go, as soon as she could be moved, to some quiet place in France and thence to England.

TO BERTY

"Paris, *May* 17, 1883. . . . I have not told about
her picture.[1] First, it is admirably hung, about as
well as a picture could be. There are thirty odd
large rooms in the Salon, and of course in the middle
of each wall there is some large or important com-
position. Naturally the sight seer goes first to this.
The corners are cut off, so as to make the room
octagonal, with very, very short lines at the corner.
And in one of these corners hangs Nelly's Beppo —
le garçon qui rit, as I called him. He is a long picture,
about as big, not quite, as her portrait of Robby in
the dining room.

"I say it is not in vain that her brothers have
posed to her so often. This Beppo was a little
Italian model whom Margaret fell in with one day,
and whom the girls liked. He has galore of hair
— Rob not more — rather roughly hanging over his
face. The charm of the picture, which is very charming, is the perfect naturalness of the boy's attitude,
and his good-natured, not specially smiling expression. He has on an immense neck tie of a sort of
dingy orange woolen, which has a good effect of
color, his thumb is in his pocket on one side, both
his hands show. His long vest is a dingy red, his
long jacket of a dingy blue, and the worsted leggins
come up far enough to be seen. All these various
stuffs are well wrought out, but do not force themselves upon you. The balance of color, indeed, is
very satisfactory."

[1] Ellen's picture was hung in the Salon.

As their anxiety for my sister died away, my father and mother settled into a quiet and pleasant life in Paris. There were a number of friends in town, and my father found excellent opportunity for the studies on the Pacific Ocean which have been already mentioned,[1] and also for his general interests in politics, not only in following the debates in the Chambre des Deputes but by going to whatever political meetings he could find. The first of June he wrote, "The Doctor made his farewell visit this morning. A fine fellow, more like a rugged country doctor, with large knowledge of men as well as of science, than your ideal professor followed by fifty admiring pupils in the Hotel Dieu. He made a distinct farewell speech to Nelly, and told her that she was well." Early in June they moved out to Saint Germaine. "I announced when we got here that I was going to rest, and I have dropped letter-writing with my other occupations." He did write a little, and the following shows the characteristic way in which he settled down even in a French country town.

TO SUSAN

"St. Germains, *June* 10, 1883. You know something of these lovely old played-out French towns. I amuse myself by comparing this with some town of as great population at home, Newton Centre, Westborough, or Meriden. Their dear old palace, in which Louis XIV in his younger days flirted and generally misbehaved, is their one love, as the mills at Lowell or the Falls at Niagara. Louis gave it

[1] See II, p. 259.

to poor James II, who went to mass every morning and to sermon every afternoon till he died. Absolutely of the Pretender, James III so called, there is not one syllable in the elaborate guide books (which rake up every scrap of history they can find) except the date of his death. Of Charles Edward I have found one anecdote new to me. Well, when they died, the palace ran down and became a cavalry school, I believe, then an army penitentiary. The old salons were divided by stories run across half way up the walls, and cut up into cells. Then Napoleon made it a sort of West Point for cavalry officers; then it was some other sort of barracks.

"But the new Napoleon had all these improvements cleared out and set a M. Niellet to restoring it to the architecture of Francis I. What was much more to the point, he put into it all the prehistoric things which that Mr. Perthes has discovered at Abbeville, — stone age and all that. Also all the things he had had dug up in writing his Julius Caesar from Gallic and Roman entrenchments, so that it is now a great museum of human progress from the dawn to the tenth century in France. Then there is a lovely little departmental Public Library, a sort of mitigated Fellowes Athenaeum, from which I have taken out Mad. de Sévigné's Letters, as abridged and selected for the use of schools.

"The next day.

. . . "We took quite a walk just now, because it is quite too cold to ride. We went first to the Gallo-Roman Museum, to find that on this particular day it does not open till 11.30. We therefore diverged into our dear Park and Terrace, and were in time to see the mountebanks and giants packing up their properties to carry the fair to Neuilly. As you may imagine, I love them all. Clearly theirs is the life for which you and I were predestined, had it by good chance existed in our beloved land. I am more eager than ever to import a whole fair, than to go into any other business. It is just what our people would enjoy. Nothing can be more suggestive or dramatic than the sight of a box of Aunt Sallies, just waiting to be nailed up and carried to Neuilly, there to appear at another fête. I was able to gratify a secret passion today, and buy a box of *nonnettes*. *Savez-vous?* Much love to all. There is great good in being lazy."

On June seventeenth they left St. Germains, spent a day or two in Paris, and crossed to England. There they spent a while at Tunbridge Wells and by the end of the month had sailed for home.

CHAPTER THIRTY-TWO

EVERY-DAY LIFE

1882–1892

ON April 3, 1882, my father was sixty years old. In his diary he notes the fact without comment; he mentions the birthday presents from the family and the "pleasant and large parish party" in the evening. Probably he did not feel much older than he had felt in 1872. At this particular time he was full of pleasant anticipations of his journey to Spain, and the cares of daily life lay lightly on him. In the course of the journey it occurred to him now and then that there was no good reason why he should not make this relief from routine work more permanent. Speaking of the winter's work he wrote from Spain, July 3, 1882, "Not that I mean to work again as I have in bygone times. Let the younger men pull stroke and I will tell them how." Really he still continued to work as much as most busy men; his church work was undiminished, his day-books are as full of engagements as ever, his literary work rather increased. But he felt that he was changing the kind of work, that he was giving up the active direction and leadership, for which in some of its developments he had never felt himself especially competent, and taking advantage of his store of experience to help others do the things

312

he had been doing so long. In the church the question of a colleague began to be talked of, though it was not till 1887 that that position was filled by Reverend Edward Hale, already a valued friend. In the broader field he began about this time to act as Councillor of the Chautauqua Literary and Scientific Circle, and also to be one of the Preachers to the University at Harvard. In literature he ceased almost entirely to write stories and devoted himself mostly to historical and literary studies and reminiscences, and to the comment and advice on public affairs which were the natural result of so long work in the service of the public. The first of the letters that follow shows the breaking of one of the connections with the older life of labor and work. His brother Charles had for some years been failing. He was much younger than my father, but as has been seen (and far more than could be exhibited in this book), the two had been most closely allied in the direction of family affairs. That alliance had for some time been unnecessary, but this final event must have seemed the definitive breaking of an old tie.

TO WILLIAM EVERETT

"*Mar.* 2, 1882. Our poor dear Charley died last night. I was with him almost all day, — but he knew nothing and nobody, and died without any struggle. It is the last of the series of paralytic attacks, of which the first came in July, 1876.

"We have fixed the funeral for 3.30 P.M. Saturday. Come if you like, but you know I am careless of the etiquettes, and I am perfectly sure of your love and sympathy."

The following letters indicate some side lights on personal or family life.

TO MRS. HALE

"*Mar.* 24, 1882. I have asked the Zuñi chiefs to lunch here with Mr. Cushing at one. Mary Perkins, Mary Edes, and Lucretia do the honors. We give them prairie hens which they ought to like, and oysters and frozen pudding and cake.

"I have asked two or three people to come and meet them afterwards, but most of these have said that they cannot come; Mrs. Howe, the Governor, and Phillips Brooks, that is to say. We are charmed with them. There is nothing of the North American Indian about them, but the gentleness and high-breeding of Mexicans.

"After which we are to go to Prang's and then if they will to Mrs. Howe who had invited them before she heard from me. It is edifying to me to see how all the world is excited about them now, when I found it hard to make people contribute two hundred dollars to pay their expenses hither."

TO MRS. HALE

"*Mar.* 25, 1882. The boys' letters will give you some idea of our party, which was very successful. The guests came an hour late by accident, which horrified Ellen. But I suppose their home cuisine may often give them cold provant. They are perfect gentlemen, have none of the surliness or *mau-vaise honte* of Englishmen or of Indians. Their Aztec gentleness is observable all the way through. Cushing is the most remarkable part of the exhibition, modest, intelligent, full of emotion and sympathy. I hope you may come home in time to see him.

"Dear Longfellow is dead. I am glad, of course, that he dies with his powers unbroken; but I remember Aeschylus and Dandolo, and thought his life was so well balanced we should keep him long."

TO EDWIN BOOTH

"*Nov.* 20, 1883. I cannot say or do anything else, till I have written to thank you for the great pleasure we all had in 'Hamlet' last evening; I say 'we' for at my age a man enjoys most what he enjoys with his children, and all my troop are eager in expressing their pleasure at what is really a new sensation to most of them.

"I had some hard experiences with Shakespeare when I was young, and have avoided the stage rendering ever since. Unconsciously I have kept my boys and my daughter from it. I had seen your Iago, with Salvini, and one or two other of your parts, but I had always taken pains that the younger people should see the modern plays, and get their Shakespeare on the side of literature. So I can hardly make you understand how like a person new-born, I entered into the whole performance last night, and how much you have added to my reverence for the play. Indeed I suppose I am the only man who can read in America, who has lived to be sixty, without seeing 'Hamlet' acted before.

"Mrs. Hale and the young people wish me to express their thanks to you as well as my own."

TO PHILIP

"WASHINGTON, *Dec.* 18, 1883. This is a letter to all, but you can explain to the younger ones that I do not put the names of all on the outside, lest it should make the Postmaster laugh. Such was the message my mother sent to me, when I was the youngest of the four of us, and she and my father were shooting ducks with Mr. Webster and Judge Story at Sandwich on the Cape. It must have been in 1825, for in 1826 we all accompanied them in the discharge of this annual duty. . . .

"I had a thoroughly characteristic Washington day after writing to Nelly, Miss Devereux, Mrs. Andrews and half a dozen people. I read Franklin for two hours in the Department where Dwight showed me a new drawing, just received for the 'great seal.' Oddly enough the two which have been used since the United States was, have not conformed absolutely to the Law. Dwight found this out, and was empowered to make a new one. He actually consulted Gray about olive branches, had a genuine eagle sent to the designer, and a bunch of thirteen Iroquois arrows. For the eagle should hold thirteen arrows in one claw and an olive branch in the other. Hitherto he has had only six arrows. Now the olive branch has thirteen leaves and thirteen berries. They wanted to give the eagle thirteen tail feathers but they found no authority in nature. Tiffany's men had made a beautiful drawing from these *entrefaites*, as we say in diplomacy.

"At twelve I had to leave my diplomacy, where you see Fine Art saunters in, for Mrs. Dall's at Georgetown. Mrs. Senator Pomeroy called after lunch, and brought me back with her to make some calls I had to make on Mrs. Woodhull and other old friends. I took my nap and at five called on Matthew Arnold with Dr. Loring. We afterwards went to Club where I saw Gov. Lyman and your cousin Mr. Hopkins. He is your cousin by marrying a Wise, whose mother was my own cousin.[1] The object of the call on Arnold was to fit him out with letters for Richmond whither he goes today.

"At six, by appointment of course, to dine with Mr. Bancroft, tête-à-tête, and a charming time it was. I wished for the stenographer of Charles Grandison, behind a screen. He got talking about Shakespeare and begged me to hold him up to writing Shakespeare's biography from what we really know. He says there are three points to be dwelt on.

"1. That very early he knew his own genius and was determined to be the great poet that he was. That this is shown in the introduction to Lucrece or one of the other poems, and that he went to school steadily, learned at once whatever he had to learn, 'like Milton or like Edward Everett,' said Bancroft.

"2. That he married very early, and set to work

[1] Charlott Everett; see II, p. 80.

like fury to support his wife and family. His father had been a lazy, worthless fellow, and warned by that example Shakespeare set out as an industrious workman, and says very early that he is so engaged with the work he has laid out that he can do nothing more.

"3. That on these plans, and sticking steadily to his business he comes out on 'Macbeth', 'Hamlet', and 'Lear', and Bancroft almost screamed as he brought him to this climax.

"After this I broke away really, having promised to go to Arnold's lecture where we saw him again. I have promised to take Jack to Mr. Bancroft.

"Was not that a good day?"

In November, 1884, my father resigned his position as President of the National Council of Unitarian Churches. To his own congregation he spoke of his work on this Council as follows:

"In presenting the report of the National Council to the National Conference, and in bidding their members farewell when they adjourned, I discharged my last duties as president of the Council, and thus withdrew from a close connection with our National Missionary affairs which had begun in December, 1864, when I was appointed one of the Committee of which Dr. Bellows was Chairman, which formed the plans for our National organization as a Church. That connection has directed the employment of much of the best part of twenty years of my life. A selfish parish, which existed only for its own prosperity, or for such advantage as its members might directly receive from their minister, would have complained at seeing him give so much time and effort to duties of which the success affected the Utes in Colorado, the Hungarians in Pesth, or others farther removed. And such a parish would have been right from a selfish point of view. I ought then, to say here, what it is a pleasure to say, that this church has, from first to last upheld all such effort for a larger Christianity for mankind, and, so far as I am concerned, has encouraged me and helped me in carrying it on. I have had the satisfaction of knowing that the South Congregational Church exists not as a club of well-to-do Christians, who have associated for their own profit or pleasure, but as a working force in the world, of men and women who want to bring in God's Kingdom. If their minister thought he saw his way clear to any work in that service, this church, all its members and in all its organizations, have at all times and in all ways seemed eager to advance those purposes with him.

"None the less am I glad, now that my constitutional term of office as a member of the National Council has ended, to leave such larger work to younger men and more skilful hands, and to give what is left of life to the special business of our own work here at home, the creation of the Possible Boston in the coming of the Kingdom of God at our own Doors."

The first of the following letters was written to one of the several young men whom he thought of as a colleague; the others will explain themselves, and give a slight idea of the different occupations and interests of these years.

"*Oct.* 27, 1884.

"My dear Mr. ——:

"You must have known that I wanted you to preach in my pulpit, because I wanted you for my colleague.

"I am glad to find that the most trustworthy of my people share this wish, and I write frankly to tell you that it exists, and to ask you if it is possible that you can come here to work with me. I know that young men have a dislike to such positions. But I should insist on an absolute equality for you, in all rights, dignities, and privileges from the very first. I am a very hard person to quarrel with, and I am quite sure that we should like each other. My idea would be that we should preach alternately Sunday mornings, that we should divide the other services equally, by whatever seemed most convenient to both.

"My salary is $6000. I should propose to divide that also. After the first year I should propose that your share of it should gradually enlarge and mine should gradually diminish, with the understanding that you would take more and more of the active duty.

"The church is large, strong, prosperous. I see that it needs the sort of work that I could (and did) give at your age, the work that interests young people and calls into it young families. Of such we have an ample constituency right around us, and if I were thirty years younger than I am, I would ask no better or more interesting field. (I ask no better now, but I wrote that to put myself in your place.)

"You will observe that half your Sundays will be at your own disposal under this plan, and there is so much relief from incessant sermon-writing, and so much opportunity for giving 'supplies' outside.

"I would come and see you to talk of all this, but that I fancy that if I went to Hopedale, it might start a little unnecessary gossip. If you are in Boston any day, could you not let me know that I may call on you? And could you not fix a Sunday, near at hand, when you can preach for us again?"

TO MRS. HALE

"NEAR BRIDGEPORT, *April* 14, 1885. This is certainly a way of life that does me much good. I suppose I could go into the Red Parlor at ten, sit on the sofa and look at the pictures half an hour, talk to you an hour, sleep an hour, and then take you out to lunch, go back to my sofa and read a novel, talk twenty minutes with a visitor, and so on till four, not changing my seat and not doing a stroke of work. I might do so but I never do.

"The twenty minutes talk, last mentioned, has been with Mrs. Robert Collyer, who proves to be on board. She took the train at Providence, but we only discovered each other just now. She says Phil called at the house last week with Oliver Herford. She did not see them, but her daughter did.

"Yes, I am delighted with the 'Fellah.' But you know it is my way to read with manifold drop-curtains and entre-acts. I wonder if it comes from retailing the Divine Truth in bits of thirty minutes in length, no more and no less.

"Here we are at Bridgeport and the rest of my note shall be more legible. Only I am sorry to say I brought no pens with me. I asked Mr. Smith to fill them, and neglected to take them when they were filled. I hope you may have this by the first delivery."

The following letters written from Chautauqua rather need as introduction a part of an earlier letter, written when he went there first:

"The place is simply marvellous. It is a large camp meeting where people live in nice cottages, several hundred, and instead of occupying themselves with emotional religion, occupy themselves in well-organized summer studies. . . . There are regular religious services at fixed hours. But these are not even the principal part of the thing. It is a great college for the middle classes. How many people attend it I do not know. But at the three Sunday Schools Sunday there were 1800 men, 400 young persons and 300 children, people of the population who chose to go to Sunday School. They say I spoke to 6000 people this afternoon. Certainly there were 4000. But you pass by cottages in walking where people are living as quietly as if they were at Tucker's, and perhaps have as little to do with the meetings."

"*Aug.* 17, 1885. My father's birthday. I write before taking the boat for Chautauqua, which I had in sight when I spent all day yesterday, three miles down the lake. But people are not permitted to land there Sunday, and I had a quiet day at this very pretty house. Mayville itself is a lovely village on the hill above us. Tourgee lives there, the editor of the unfortunate Continental. I called on him but found no one at home.

"The sail over this lake reminds one of Lago Maggiore, as I may have said when I went over it before. You know how high we are, higher than Tom Crawford's house in the Notch above the sea. At both these hotels, that at the other end of the lake and this, they had fires yesterday morning. I breakfasted at Jamestown, but when I found that by our excursion boat I could meet my first appointment at Chautauqua I was glad to take it. The sail was simply lovely as I say. Five miles of it is through a winding river where the maples I am sorry to say, begin to show thoughts of autumn and where unnumbered cardinals filled up the foreground."

"Chautauqua. *Aug.* 18, 1885. I sent you this morning a newspaper which will tell you more of me than I could write in many letters. I have already in thirty-six hours delivered two addresses, and, in a little more time, I have written the greater part of a third. I have made a good many acquaintances, the more interesting of them among women whose names I cannot remember. The deficiency of the place, as of most watering places, is that the men whom it attracts seem to be quite inferior to the women. I sat half an hour this morning in a Hebrew class of very dull-looking young men. But afterwards I spent another half hour among a dozen or twenty very intelligent and fine-looking women, who were taking their first Latin. At the end of three weeks they understand the Latin questions of the teacher, and replied, of course to simple questions, in the same way. But there are three weeks of three recitations a day, of eager study, mostly in the class room, with the teacher. She is a very fine woman, a Miss Townsend, niece of our Mr. Albert Tolman. I had met her before. Now I am to write a telegram in which you will read the account of my Commencement Speech, probably before you read this letter.

TO MRS. HALE

"New York, *Sep.* 24, 1885. This is the last day. I am so sorry they had the rough weather of yesterday. But if the Genesta stood it I think the C. of C. could. I have just read the account of the two yachts. They passed Matunuck after dark going and coming.

"I did not write yesterday, because I was at Plainfield, in a crowded day, till too late for any practicable mail. I had an extremely satisfactory conference there with Dr. Hurlbut, Miss Lathbury, and one or two other people, which will I think relieve me of no end of responsibility while it really ought to advance the King's Work. With all these shoals of letters about Wadsworth Clubs, Look-up Legions and the other 10 × 1 things, there has been no central office to send out circulars, badges, mottoes, and all that: — and it has pretty much ended by the thing being done by me, Mr. Smith, Hatty Freeman, or some other girl of the church, or more probably not at all. Now I knew that Hurlbut, who is at the head of the Methodist Sunday School interests, and an admirable fellow, was immensely interested in the whole thing. He has also that genuine tact for effective organization, which seems essentially a part of the Methodist make-up. We had with us Kate Kimball who with her sixteen girl clubs conducts a correspondence with the 100,000 Chautauqua readers. We made a simple plan, with their lights, which will, I think, work well, by which at 3 Hamilton Place, the office of *Good-Cheer* and *Lend a Hand*, our Mrs. Davis will make and keep the lists, issue the various circulars, give instructions about the half-dozen badges and so on. Dear Miss Lathbury seemed ready to sing her *Nunc Dimittis*. She had had the same feeling of annoyance that I have had, only ten times worse. It is very interesting to see the courage with which the Methodists attack such things, and the accuracy with which they attend to the least detail."

One should add here a bit of a letter to Miss Lathbury, though it was written after this time (January 8, 1893), for it gives an idea of the deep pleasure he received from the work that resulted from the organization here set on foot.

"It gives me exquisite pleasure to feel in this interchange of life and love among those widely parted in space, the real thrill of brotherhood which makes one of the race, that we do bear one another's burdens whether we have known it or not. You get something of the same feeling in one of the great central offices of the telegraph or telephone; where you really see the physical wire which acts as a thread for the message to run on, and where you are taught how each of these wires can be connected with each of a thousand others. The Unity of the Spirit is more perfect, and needs no visible or tangible threads."

TO MRS. HALE

"*Saturday morning.* The event of yesterday was the boatrace, and very exciting it was. I appeared first at the fence on Beacon Street, a little too early. To me came Bob. To us came Nelly. To us came George Clarke. As we had made no provision or appointment for meeting, we thought this rendezvous among five thousand people showed that the divs were dispossessed and the demiurgos in good force. Well we had a jolly time gossiping and joking, till off the river mouth three smokes of the tugs appeared scattered like this [the letter is illustrated with hasty but excellent pictures], and soon tiny specks between us and them, like those I have made above. Soon the specks showed oars, but still this mysterious distance to the left of one set. Then

it was announced that this was Berty's boat, and
that having won the toss they had elected to row
here as the best line. Gradually but very quickly
they looked more like boats with their guardian
tugs behind. Then they were wholly boats, and
swept down like eagles on us, the whole people
cheering. Berty's boat actually passed so close to
us that one could have thrown him a cracker easily.
I varied the cheering by howling 'Bert, Bert, Bert,'
but he says he did not hear me.

"My dear, my feeling afterwards was that for
once I had seen one thing perfectly done. They did
not look right nor left. They did not seem excited.
They simply did their work and made the thing
fly. Observe, the four lines were now concentrating,
and Berty's boat dashed in, a boatlength ahead of
the others. I told him I was glad to have my boy
ahead of all the others. He said, Yes, he was the
first of thirty-six.[1] Then all howled and the boats
blew their whistles, and the boys put on their jerseys
and rowed home again!"

TO MRS. HALE

"ALBANY, *May* 28, 1887. I consecrate and bap-
tize the new inkstand by a most interesting interview. Observe the place, breakfast room of the
New York Central. — Waiter girl places me at a
table I do not select. Et voila, my next neighbor is
Howells, just returning from a farewell visit to his
father in Ohio! Howells on his own road. He had
two hours and a half, — I had one and a quarter.

---

[1] Rowing bow of the winning boat.

"My dear, we have talked of everything! He was just from the natural gas country. They had lighted their wells for him, made him a public dinner and wanted to serenade him and then we came round to the most serious subjects man can talk to man about. You know how deep he is in Tolstoi. Tolstoi has really troubled him, because he does not know but he ought to be ploughing and reaping. But he is as sweet and good and eager to do right as he can be. I dare not begin to write down what he said and I, I went nearer the depths than perhaps I have ever done to any one but you. Then when we had sat at table so long as to astonish the waiter girls — I showed him the way to the Hunt pictures and left him. So queer that he of all people should never have been in the streets of Albany before. Really, if I did what was wise I should spend this morning in writing in short hand in my note book, all he said and all I said, about Tolstoi's theories and the Saviour's wishes. Howells is a loyal Christian, and hates to have anybody say that Jesus made plans or demanded things that are impossible. Now, as you know, he found the right customer there, in me; — for I think the Saviour was among other things the most practical political adviser the world has had. Let Nelly hunt, first on the small oval table, and next in the pamphlet files behind the extensor chair for Savage's two sermons on Tolstoi. They had troubled Howells. The train begins to move and if I write more you cannot read it. Is it not a good anfang?"

TO MRS. HALE

"Chautauqua. *Aug.* 18, 1886. . . . It is as interesting as ever here, but I am quite conscious that I should enjoy it more if you were here, that I might show you what is no longer new to me. I am pretty busy, having my second lecture to finish, which I deliver tomorrow. My favorite Miss Lathbury, our nice cousin Kate Kimball and others of the elect are here. Kate Kimball, I am sorry to say is not well. She is worked too hard, which every one says and no one helps. We are all awaiting at this moment the great solemnity of the year. 'Recognition Day' means that the readers on the ground, near 1000 in number, 'march through the arches' and receive their diplomas. Dr. Carlisle the Southern Trustee makes the Commencement Address. I delivered it last year. Then Vincent, Carlisle, and I, the three Councillors present, deliver the diplomas personally with a word of congratulation to each graduate. So far as I can see there is to be no Levee and no handshaking. If there is any I shall make and wear a sling, and say my right arm is lame."

TO WILLIAM EVERETT

"*Feb.* 8, 1888. I had accepted the invitation, a little unwillingly, from pure loyalty to Abe Lincoln. I had not observed that Ingersoll was to be there or was asked. I think if I had noticed it, it would have decided me not to go. But I do not think I could make it a matter of principle. There might be a Jewish Rabbi there, or an absolutely profane adulterer, or my friend Ben Butler, or many men worse than Ingersoll, and I should go. I do not think we go to meet him. We go to commemorate Abe Lincoln.

TO MRS. HALE

"Weirs, *July* 24, 1889. It is just before breakfast. I did not go to the morning chapel, because I disapproved of the leader yesterday, and I thought the service as far as I was concerned led to spiritual pride. Last night I went with Abbott of Lawrence, to a hotel in a magnificent situation on the hill to call on old James E. Murdoch the elocutionist. He is ten years older than I am, has acted with Fannie Kemble in the old Howard Athenaeum. Oddly enough, he mixed me up with Nathan, whom he knew quite well, being one of the habitués in Hillard and Sumner's office, when Nathan and James Lowell and William and Charles Story had their offices in the same entry. There was more literature and general discussion of fundamental politics going on there than there was law. He told a great many curious stories, of which strange to say at this moment, I remember only one, and that cannot be written down, I mean it needs emphasis."

In 1890 he had an interesting experience of which one would gladly know something more than remains in the record; he was named one of the Board of Visitors to West Point, and delivered the address to the graduating class. The only letter which I find written while he was there is a short note to his publishers, asking for five copies of "The Man without a Country." Doubtless there are few places where the lesson of the story is less needed, but he probably liked to look back to the days of its writing, and the later days of the war when he had seen a little of military service and of young men trained to arms.

CHAPTER THIRTY-THREE

JOURNEY TO CALIFORNIA[1]

1891

MY father's journey to California in 1891 took him once more through New Orleans and Texas, and showed him still more of the southwest. I was again his companion, and shared his enjoyment of the beauty and romance of the country. We were very happy; and yet in looking over his letters, I miss something of the youthful light-heartedness which a man is lucky to keep, as he did, till he is fifty-four, and seldom retains till he is sixty-nine. My father retained more of it than most people, however, and California and the Pacific were all and more than all that a lifetime of study and expectation had prepared him to find. "The Pacific Ocean and its Shores," to describe which had been one of the dreams of his life, were no less fascinating seen than unseen.

He had a series of lectures to deliver in California, and I suppose would have gone there in any case; but as my health was delicate then, he had an added motive for going, and for taking me with him. His first stop was at Marietta, Georgia, where he picked me up.

[1] This chapter is by my sister Ellen, who was with my father on this journey.

TO MRS. HALE

"Marietta, Georgia,
"*Feb.* 5, 1891.

"My dear Child:

"It is not yet, you see, forty-eight hours since we said good-bye. If you were here, I believe we would give up California and spend the spring here. Nelly met me at the cars, well and happy. . . . It is a cold day, but not raw, an inspiriting day, thermometer outdoors 42. The violets are in bloom under this window, and such early things as jasmines, Christmas honeysuckles, and maple buds as they would be with us in April. Send to this house any one who wants to escape winter. It is large, well furnished, and warm. They know that people come here to be warm.

"The ride yesterday was perfect. It is a historical country, and a pretty country, with the Blue Ridge for a background. We were but ten or twelve passengers all told, beside three babies, in a Vestibule train and three elegant new cars. Library, writing desks, observation and dining cars, to make us comfortable."

At New Orleans we joined the Raymond Excursion, with which we were to go to California by the Southern Pacific Railroad. We passed Mardi Gras in New Orleans, and renewed our intercourse with our cousin, Sister Rose Genevieve, of the Sisters of Mercy, whom we had visited there fifteen years before. This lady, who had been, in the world, Rosamond Everett, was my father's first cousin, and it was singular and touching to see the well-known Everett face, resembling my grandmother's, under the Sister's white cornette, and to hear her and my father, remembering their distant youth, calling each other by the old names of Edward and Rosy.

We had a fine sight of the Mardi Gras procession, and the general enthusiasm impressed me as far greater than what I had seen on that day in Paris. But it was a cold winter day, and I do not think we were at all sorry to return to our train, and establish ourselves in our comfortable sections there. We met pleasant people in the Raymond party, spent much time with them, and according to my father's constant yearly custom, wrote valentines to the young ladies on the thirteenth of February.

We rode through Louisiana, west of the Mississippi, with very affectionate recollections of our former days in the Têche country and on the Côte des Acadiens; we entered our much-loved Texas again, and ran down to Galveston on February twelfth.

TO MRS. HALE

"ABOVE GALVESTON,
"*Feb.* 12, 1891.

"We are on our return from an amusing, but very fatiguing excursion to Galveston. That city, which is, within a few years, to excite the envy of New York, is cultivating a boom this week. I think I wrote to you that our Mr. Sam. Little and his son were there to represent Roxbury.

"Do you think, as we alighted, Mr. Little stepped forward among the gentlemen on the dock, and presented me to the Mayor. I presented him in turn to Nelly, and so on, with the different dignitaries, who, in some cases had their wives with them. The Mayor addressed the company and said that the city invited them all to take a trip in the harbour and see the jetties, which, accordingly, we did, and were for two hours on the boat, seeing pelicans and light houses and talking on the greatness of Galveston. Then we returned and rode to Mr. H.'s pretty house. Well, they had the loveliest lunch you ever saw. The most perfect roast oysters, served by the attentive husband and wife, on an open verandah. How is that for February 12th? Even Trustom Bay pales before such oysters, and even Matunuck does not in February embower you in tall geraniums, Marshal Niel Roses and Oleanders. The Oleanders and Pomegranates are not in flower. But they are not evergreen. The others I have named are. And in front of me is a great basket full of Roses, with a bunch of Nasturtiums which different admirers have presented to Nelly."

Once more we found ourselves at San Antonio, no longer arriving there in our ambulance, but in a Pullman car. We loved it still, for no amount of civilization can change its glorious situation or, I may add, the charming spirit of the place.

TO MRS. HALE.

"SAN ANTONIO, TEXAS,
Feb. 13, 1891.

"We breakfasted rather early. Nelly and I were both here May 2 and 3, 1876, and were eager to renew our explorations.

"The Southern Pacific, where our train lies, is half a mile from the Alamo and Post-Office. This last is a fine new building, built by Uncle Sam. Like almost all the new buildings, it has a suggestion of Spanish taste: indeed, most of the improvements since we were here, are not injuries.

"The river ramps through the town, wild and deep blue green. Of course in February there is not the brilliancy of the vegetation we saw in May, but spring has fairly begun. Someone told me that they never expect a frost after Feb. 22; the same man said that one winter the thermometer noted 90° in his office, that a norther came and within a day, ice formed in Galveston Harbor.

"We found our dear old market place occupied by an elegant new City Hall, and we trudged round vainly, searching for Mexican women who would sell us tortillas. But on a pretty verandah, overlooking the river, we established ourselves, with the kind and cordial assent of Mlle. Emilie Huth. Afterwards we saw her father, an old man of 79, I think. He said he brought over the first German colony, six months before the Prince de Salm's.

"In the afternoon we drove to the Concepcion Mission, quite a large party. The place has been refitted, but has not lost its outside picturesqueness. Thence we crossed the city to the wonderful San Pedro spring. I here saw a menagerie of native animals, some alive and some dead. Thence by the Government Hill, and the Military Station, home. Dinner and Valentines."

We passed our Sunday at El Paso, and made two

excursions into Mexico by the International Bridge. My father has not mentioned, in his following description of our church-going in Juarez, that the only place where we were treated with anything like unkindness or incivility, on this long journey, was in the gallery of that church. Perhaps the old woman who was cross to us had had disagreeable experience of the Gringos. The poor people we met outside were kind and civil enough. How little we foresaw of the excursions and alarums which were to make El Paso, Juarez, and the International Bridge, household words all over the country.

TO MRS. HALE

"EL PASO,
"*Feb.* 15, 1891.

"We arrived at El Paso about sunrise or a little later, and as soon as breakfast was done, Nelly, Allen [the Reverend Joseph Allen] and I started for Mexico. The joke is to say that it is the only foreign country one can visit in a horse-car.

"Five minutes from the station there was a car waiting for us, and we crossed the river. A customhouse officer passed through the car, and bowed as I opened my carpet bag. The Mexican government has a handsome custom-house and neat-looking officials. We were one square from the church and went there at once. Perhaps there were a hundred people there already, but there was no service, but a woman dusting the altars and ornaments, and after waiting half an hour we went off to draw. The people all live in adobe houses, but there seemed to be a good deal of brick-making proper. The people were mostly in Mexican costume, with more than one could wish, however, of ready-made clothing.

"In three-quarters of an hour perhaps, the bell rang again for Mass, and we found the church crowded. However, there was some room in the gallery, where I knelt by a Yang-yang melodeon, which had doubtless come from my own home. There must have been a thousand people in the church.

"The priest was in full rig, and I thought he was addressing a smart remonstrance, perhaps excommunication, to four young men in the chancel. I tried to make out whether their air and faces were defiant or penitent. But it proved that these were the regular altar assistants. I suppose there were not robes enough to go round. One was clearly in his shirt-sleeves and the others in unmistakable ready-made clothing.

"In the afternoon we went over there again. Nelly made a good pastel study of an old cottonwood on the irrigation dam, with the distant hills. We palabra'd a little with some good-natured people in an adobe hut."

TO MRS. HALE

"*Feb.* 16. We are in Arizona, thus far, all day. At Tucson the train waited an hour and a little while at Casa Grande. This station is, however, 12 miles from the Casa itself, which we did not see.

"The mountains, for there are such, approach the road, sometimes quite close, and sometimes perhaps five miles away. The country we pass seems nearly level, almost without trees, but with a slight growth of mesquite or such, sometimes with nothing but dwarf palms and cactus. These last are very curious, and take on curious forms. Some of the chandelier ones are 12 feet or more high. We see no snow on the hills. We had been promised dust but there was no trouble. At C. G. there appeared a group of picturesque Indians. I bought a cup and saucer, but we tried vainly to make a child pose to be drawn.

"We struck the Gila, on one of its head waters, where it is a stream you would not like to jump across. And, of course, to see water flowing into the Pacific, makes you feel what the journey is. It is idle to say that there is no American desert left. There is plenty of desert, but all interesting to a person who does not want to plant it. Everywhere, I think, we saw signs of ranch-men and their work. The state of Texas rents its cattle lands. In Arizona I hardly know how the titles are given. We came to Yuma late, greatly to the grief of the natives, who had planned an excursion for us on the Colorado. 'It is the Nile of America,' said a Major Allen to me. To the sea it is 160 miles, and above them it is navigable for 500. But their place is a mere frontier post waiting for Uncle Sam to irrigate them. I fancy that here is the secret of the California 'Nationalism.' We saw the lights of the Indian school, and a few of the scholars were permitted to come to the station."

We agreed in our admiration of the Arizona landscape. There were few, in those days, to rave about the severe beauty of its "mountains cut in cameo," as Mr. Izsley has called them, violet, pink and blue as they withdraw across the desert. But I must say we were glad enough to wake up one morning in the full glory of California spring, at Riverside, with groves thick set with oranges on either side of our train. We had enough of the tenderfoot about us still to think they were planted there to impress Easterners like us; but a few hours of Riverside changed our view.

TO MRS. HALE

"COLTON, RIVERSIDE,
"*Feb.* 17, 1891.

"At 8 we were at Riverside. It was a fine morning, and we walked gleefully up to the town. The streets are wide and fine, with good sidewalks, well shaded with large palms. Eucalyptus, pepper, which is a beautiful ornamental tree, and cypress. The irrigation is carried to every house and garden. There are almost no fences, no cattle at large, and the whole place is kept in neat order.

"So it is perfectly lovely, to our desert-tired eyes. . . .

"Thence west, and then south, and at three-thirty or thereabouts by a sudden curve we struck the Pacific."

"PACIFIC OCEAN,
Feb. 17, 1891.

"'Silent upon a peak in Darien.' You could not ask for a better introduction than we had. The sun was shielded by bright clouds. The water below was bright. We were high above the beach on a bluff, and on this rode for two hours, in sight of the sea with these magnificent breakers below us. The brooks from the shore cut out deep chines like what they describe at the Isle of Wight, which the Railroad bridges. We needed nothing to do but to watch our old friend till it was dark. Then we packed for the final parting from the train.

"I write at the Coronado, where we arrived at 8.30, an enormous caravanserai, amusing in the rush of people and in its lavish size after our constrained small quarters."

TO MRS. HALE

"HOTEL CORONADO, SAN DIEGO,
"Feb. 18th.

"You will be glad to think of us as at our journey's farthest bound. Without looking at your map, imagine the farthest corner of the United States and we are there, that is, this hotel is but thirteen miles from the 'corner stone.' Unless we go to the city of 'Aunt Jane' (Tia Juana) as I am tempted to do from family pride, we shall be no nearer that point, nor was I ever, I think, so far from you in my life. That is, I think on the globe the distance is as great as to Europe, possibly not so far as when I was in Rome.

"The week, from New Orleans, seems curiously short to us looking back on it, much shorter I think than a week of home life. But it is curiously entertaining. It has exactly what a sea-voyage has not, and what you long for, a constant variety. The great American desert itself, which is by no means abolished, is all the same as interesting as Beacon

Street or the Mohawk Valley, not to say more so. A group of Indians, a yucca palm in seed, the stray cactuses, gophers and their houses, irrigation canals, snowy mountains, Mexican and other ranchmen, all such things are new, at least to the decorous Bostonian sated with home. Whether the desert be a desert or no, makes no difference in the interest.

"This road has a great advantage in the approach to the Pacific. We swept out on it suddenly about half past three, and rode on the bluff above it for more than two hours. 'Silent upon a peak in Darien.' I can hardly tell you how intense one's feeling is, all that there has been and all that there will be in that ocean."

We stayed a week at the Coronado Hotel, and learned a good deal about California there. We made friends, chief among them the family of Mr. Charles Nordhoff, who then lived near the hotel. My father had known Mr. Nordhoff before, they were most kind to us, and we laid the foundations of an intimacy which became one of our closest. We saw, with our old friend Mr. Kimball, the opening of the wonderful Sweet Water Dam, at National City, and saw what amazing things can be done in "three years from sage brush," as my father says, on fruit farms of ten acres.

TO MRS. HALE

"San Diego, Pasadena,
Feb. 21, 1891.

"Up early, breakfast 7. Train left station at 8.30. We were in Los Angeles at 1.30, at Pasadena at 2. Lunched at the Green Hotel and go to Mrs. Dexter's boarding house, Dr. Channing's, Orange Grove Avenue where I write.

"The ride to Oceanside is the same which we took southward on Tuesday. The Pacific, as before was very grand. It is interesting that one does not see a sail or a boat. Apparently, there is no fishing, no coasting trade, and the foreign commerce is too far away.

"Every inch of the journey is interesting. You have all the satisfaction of Europe, in that it is all new, and a curious feeling of home-ishness; that you are in your own country. I have but just made out, that I am more in the midst of Americans than I have been for forty years. In these three or four days at San Diego, I have seen one Chinaman, one negro, and one Irishman; all the rest apparently, of pure Yankee blood and manners. The charm is inexpressible. You have all the pleasure of foreign traveling, and you are all the time at home; as if some one brought you in your parlour stereoscopes from Europe.

"The flora is absolutely new. Even when I thought I saw peach trees they were apricots. I had never seen orchards of English walnuts. We saw one enormous ranch which was in Indian corn last year, and but one. That is hardly an exception, in novelty, the stalks are so high. Olives, oranges, lemons, limes, guavas, apricots. Walnuts, eucalyptus, cypress, agave occasionally, not in bloom but in fruit, thirty feet high; palms of four or five varieties, Norfolk Island pines, — take that for a rapid catalogue.

"As for fauna, horses, oxen, cats, dogs are cosmopolitan. We had also rabbits, gulls curiously tame, herons, cranes, mocking birds, what they called morning larks, gophers and burros.

"Mem: The cats, or some of them, hunt the gophers, and are very useful in that capacity.

"It rained hard at the Los Angeles Station. But everyone was friendly and the transfer easy. It rained hard here, but the hotel is almost a part of the station."

At Pasadena we lived in a house belonging to my father's old college friend, Doctor W. F. Channing, which was carried on as a boarding-house by Mrs. Dexter of Providence. It was an agreeable house, in charming grounds, and the company in it was excellent. This was fortunate, for the California rainy season had begun, and we were kept much indoors. Communication with the East, and with most of the rest of the world, was cut off by the floods which followed. My father wrote away on his "Life of Columbus," and made excursions in the beautiful hours between the storms.

TO MRS. HALE

"PASADENA, *Feb.* 25, 1891.

My dear Child:

I find myself constantly tempted to write April. There is a certain absurdity about larks, and oranges, and roses in February, while in April in literature at least one gets some notion of spring.

"Nelly and I are writing as we wait for breakfast. The rain is over for the present and the sky absolutely clear. The day is cool enough for us to be glad to sit at a good coal fire. They have the best of cannel coal, hauled here from New Mexico. They say there is good coal on this coast, but not yet developed. We went in to breakfast. At each plate was a large fresh rose, a slip of myrtle, and a slip of diosma. One of the nice things is that so many green-house plants are everywhere at hand in profusion. I have always had a sentiment about laurestinus. You will find that Lucretia has. My mother had a poor struggling plant in 1830, and it is my first idea of indoor gardening. Of course I regarded it as the noblest and most important plant in the world. Well, here it grows in all lawns, in full blossom, as high as is convenient, quite as an Althea might, or a privet bush, and this month of February happens to be the month when it is in blossom."

When, as my father says, the blockade was broken, and the rains which had been imprisoning us, were over, we went to Los Angeles and passed a few days crowded with hospitalities, largely those of our friends of the Unitarian Church. Already the town was immensely large in ground-plan, and we were both struck with the great beauty of its situation. No one had ever told us of the snowy mountains which we saw in the distance, about as far off as one sees the Alps in Venice.

We went from Los Angeles to Santa Monica on the coast, to the delightful house of Senator Jones of Nevada. Senator Hoar had given my father a letter to Mrs. Jones, introducing, as he said, the most agreeable man east of the Mississippi to the most agreeable woman west of it. I thought his epithets well applied. In any case our visit was one more revelation of what the seaside can be in California. Hedges of La France roses, the roar of the breakers beyond, far more terrible than I have ever heard on any other coast, and within doors charm and comfort, with the tone only a cosmopolitan Californian like Mrs. Jones could give.

We went next to Santa Barbara, where we stayed with Mr. Philip Thacher, the Unitarian minister, and spent much time with our old friends, Mr. and Mrs. Rowland Hazard, in their house on Mission Hill, close to the Franciscan Monastery, which gives it its name. This was one more delightful California home. My father's affection for staying in private houses was well justified in this journey of ours. We had but little to do with hotels after the Coronado. Three pictures of our dwelling-places stand out, bright and strong, in my memory. I see once again the dazzling flowers and sunshine above the wild sea of Santa Monica, the heavenly views from Mission Hill, with the Monastery to the southward and the wide Pacific with its mountain islands beyond, and the glorious mountains of the Ojai Valley, where my dear father left me at the ranch of our cousin, Sherman Thacher. Of this place he says to my mother:

"If you do not see me on the 18th of April come to look for me here, as you look for boys at the monkey-tent of a Zoological Garden. Simply the place is perfect. This place is lovely beyond words, and to sit on this piazza and look off on the valley, which is like the Vega from the Alhambra, is delightful. Of all the places we have seen, the Ojai is the most attractive to people like you and me, and I feel very happy in leaving Nelly there."

My cousin, Mr. Thacher, had already established his school at the Casa Piedra ranch, and my father was charmed with the way of life there, and with the outdoor as well as indoor education the boys were getting. Our hostess, Mr. Thacher's mother, was my mother's near relation, and the warm welcome she gave us was full of family kindness, as well as of her own vigorous and brilliant individuality. That individuality lasted, in full force, for many years, and it is only a few months since she died, in full mental vigor, the queen of her mountain valley.

My father made an interesting stay in San Francisco, at the house of Doctor Stebbins of the First Unitarian Church. That city is one of the most fascinating places in the country, and for him it was full of memories of his intimate friend, Thomas Starr King, Doctor Stebbins's predecessor, who had been an apostle of patriotism in the dark days of the Civil War. My father gave lectures in the city and at Berkeley; he preached in the Unitarian Churches, he made many friends and enjoyed much. But he was glad to leave the engrossing life of a city for his comfortable section in the Raymond train, where he could enjoy the amazing spectacle of a journey through the Sierras and the Rocky Mountains.

"CARLIN, 584 miles east of San
Francisco, 24 hours from there.

"DEAR E:

"I took this train at Sacramento, where I was surrounded with kind friends. I am in the Berkshire, with my nice friends the Sargents, who were with us in the Lenox, coming out. They have the two staterooms. I have section 5, right in the middle.

"In crossing the Sierra Nevada, they were true to their name, and we had a heavy snow fall of moist snow. The effect on the evergreens of the gorges was magnificent. There is a large pine, I know not what, whose needles are six inches long. To see the masses of these, like a great giant's hand, held down by the weight of snow, and so the great branches bent down, was, as my dear Columbus keeps saying in his diary, wonderful.

"From any chances of delay from such snow-falls the traveller is protected by forty miles of snow-sheds, on exposed points, and after dark, if you looked out, the chances were even, until bed time, that you passed one of these.

"Almost in the middle of the train, just in the middle of the car, my berth was, I believe, the cosiest I have ever had. I did not even wake, as I generally do, at the wood-up stations. I had a queer vision, which I could make into a poem, had I one atom more of imaginative faculty, of a presiding guardian genius all night. Look in your own diary, and see if you are conscious of having been far away from 39 Highland Street, assigned on duty or pleasure in the Rockies. This, perhaps, should have been written in Latin.

"I pulled my curtain at 5.30 to that grey desert look which Nelly once preserved in a Colorado sketch which we have somewhere. Snow peaked mountains in the distance, and a cup of olive green, or salt marsh green 'Sage-bush' struggling with white yellow sand. It is the fashion to speak of the ride across as tedious. But I never tire of it, and am quite careless about reading. My chattering seven companions were shrieking to each other, all at one time, I looking out in wonder at what we were passing, when the guide who 'personally conducts' us came through the car, to announce in his cicerone way, 'You are now viewing the Palisades.' God forgive him, for I was the only person in the car viewing them. But the rest rushed to the windows, to see the wonderful sight, which else they would have neglected. This sort of thing, you know [here follows a capital sketch], like Rhenish castles, mile after mile on both sides of the railway and the 'Creek.' It is my first dose of winter since the 3rd of February, when I left you. And yet this is what I do not understand. Except the days in Pasadena, and the Ojai, I think I have worn my heavy coat every day. And I should have been lost without my thickest flannels."

He preached at Denver, sketched once again at Niagara, "after all is said," he writes, "the wonders of the world put together do not impress you as Niagara does alone," and on April seventeenth my brother Robert met him at Ayer Junction and they came home together. "The crocuses were in bloom," says my father; "it was the warmest day I had known since I left California, and everything seemed like spring."

This journey had one result which was far more important than any one supposed at the time. My father stepped off a verandah in the sudden darkness of a California evening, and injured himself severely. He thought little of it at the time, and kept up his usual habits of activity, but he was always lame after that, and became more and more so. How great a trial this was to him, and how bravely borne, no one can know but we, who were constantly with him.

CHAPTER THIRTY–FOUR

DAY TO DAY MATTERS

1892–1900

APRIL 3, 1892, was my father's seventieth birthday: it was a beautiful day, and he noted that the
thermometer was 70 when he got up. The day was
full of calls from friends, with congratulations,
flowers, and presents. It was a Sunday and he
preached on the Victory of Love, and, as he notes
in his diary, walked most of the way out to the
house. The next evening there was a party at the
church with crowds of friends and more presenta-
tions. He wrote to Ellen, "I said to Mamma the
next day that there was not a functional moment
about it all; the whole thing was pure affection
from one end to the other." On the eighteenth of
the month there was arranged by his friends a
dinner to commemorate his seventieth birthday. In
the afternoon there had been a reception in which
as he wrote "all sorts and conditions of men came
to pay their respects. It was a little pathetic that
the first person who came was the black minister
of the South End Church. From him the people
ranged round to governors, not to say generals. . . .
The best part of it was the very large attendance of
Kings' Daughters and Lend a Hand Clubs. They
would come in squads with their crosses on." After

the dinner there was speaking and the different topics called attention to the many interests of his long life.   Doctor Lyman Abbott spoke on "Our Guest and the Church Universal," his old friend William H. McElroy of the New York *Tribune* on "Our Guest and Journalism," Doctor A. P. Peabody on "Our Guest and Literature," representative men spoke on his relation to the nation, to the Commonwealth of Massachusetts, and to his native city; others spoke of his connection with organized charity, philanthropy, education, politics; others still on his relation to his brother ministers and to his personal friends.   And as one looks down the long list of topics, each illustrated by some pertinent quotation from his writings, one feels that it is no formal enumeration, but that each topic represented a real and a large interest in a life that had been long and was still active.   Journalism, literature, philanthropy, the state, the church, — for each he had done enough almost for the life work of a man. And, though he had already passed the period which his boyish imagination had set for his life,[1] he was still ready and able to continue to work further in each direction, if not as an active administrator, yet with the riper wisdom for direction that came from the experience of many years and much work.

This he felt himself, had felt for some time as has been seen;[2] and there are many expressions of the idea of which the following are among the more intimate.

[1] He had thought of sixty-eight years as a probable age; see I, p. 149.
[2] See letter of July 3d, 1882, II, p. 312.

TO WILLIAM B. WEEDEN

"*Dec.* 13, 1902

"DEAR WILLIAM: —

"I am pefectly delighted by your note. It is a perfect illustration of what I long ago laid down as a wish but not as an expectation.

"That the best men should give the last twenty years of life to the public service, definitely, intentionally; giving up lesser interests for the larger, — this is what one wishes for.

"A perfect illustration is Bryant's giving up the management of a daily newspaper to translate Homer, while he was strong and well, for the benefit of mankind. Another instance is a certain person named John Milton who gave up translating foreign documents into Latin for the English office, to write 'Paradise Lost.'

"I am glad they show you what you want at the State House. I hope you will command me there if in any way I can help you forward.

"Truly yours,

"EDW. E. HALE."

The following lines come somewhat later; the original is inscribed "Written in the Smoking car, South Shore R. R., Feb. 25, 1899. Emancipation Day."

"SCHOOL'S DONE!

"Sixty full years, if next September come
Since I was sitting in my attic room,
I knew six weeks of holiday were done
I knew the work of manhood was begun.

"For sixty years to live at some one's cry
  'Go there, my Figaro! — Come here, my boy!'
  'Sleep on your arms to march at some alarm
List! — if the Red-Coats land at Phipps's Farm.'

"For sixty years! — And now the trumpets cease,
  Was not my last appeal the cry for *Peace?*
  Life's bondage over — See the silent sign
Quiet for you, my boy, — along the line!—"

He did an immense amount of work in these years — it would be impossible to give more than a very general account of it — but he did it not as a young worker but as an older guide. His mind, indeed, went back more than ever to the past years and their meaning. The next year he had an interesting talk with Mr. Herbert D. Ward, of which an account was published in *McClure's Magazine*, then just established.

"I have written twenty-five books but I'm not an author; I'm a parish minister. I don't care a snap for the difference between Balzac and Daudet. That isn't important in life. I do care about the difference between the classes of men who migrate to this country.

"Here I [Mr. Ward] interrupted him.

"'Is it better to do twenty things than one?'

"'Not best for every one; but for a man who writes forty sermons a year, it is better not to get into one rut. To write those sermons well he must come into touch with forty things or forty men. As a man of letters I say the same thing. An author must be an all-around man and take a many-sided view of life. My friends think it harms one. I say it does not.'"

I wish I could give his own feeling concerning all the interests that occupied him during this time. First in his mind always was his church. His colleague, Edward Hale, took much of the parish work off his hands, but he himself also did much. His daybooks are full of his parish work and engagements, his sermons and his calls, his classes and his other church occupations. The South Friendly Society and the Standing Committee were his right and left hands in continuing and carrying on the traditions of fifty years. In 1887 the church united with Hollis Street Church and the united body moved to the present church building on Exeter and Newbury Streets. This removal followed the wide changes in population which had so scattered the congregation that the church at Union Park Street was no longer in any way central. He had also at this time been one of the preachers to the University and his connection with young men both at Cambridge and at the church had led to the formation of the Tolstoi Club, an association for social work, which in time established Hale House for settlement work. He was much interested during these years by the ideas of the Nationalist Movement which had lately grown out of Edward Bellamy's "Looking Backward." He had also interests connected with the growing Peace Movement, but these took so much of a place in his interests that they must have an especial consideration to themselves. He wrote constantly, much for the *Commonwealth* which for some years was his especial interest, and afterward for the *Christian Register*, which had for many years been the especial organ of the Unitarian denomination, and now under the editorship of Samuel J. Barrows had reached and was maintaining a high position of real value, aside from its denominational interests. This, however, he would perhaps have set down as journalistic writing; he also continued his historical studies and added to them some biographical writing in which he began to gather the reminiscences of his life already so full of interesting people and things. Beside "A New England Boyhood" he wrote "James Russell Lowell and his Friends," in which his lifelong friendship supplied him with a store of material and a point of view that few others could have had.

He lived in the now old house at 39 Highland Street during these years; in 1892 he and my mother made a last trip to Europe with his old friend, George R. Carpenter; in 1896 he made with Ellen a trip to California, as has been told. His summers were passed chiefly at Matunuck, where the nucleus made by Mr. Weeden's house and his was now gradually extending into a summer colony. Often he went for a time to Folly Cove on Cape Ann, where Ellen spent much of the time in the summer, and where my mother was rather more apt to go than to Matunuck. He also went in the summer to Intervale, New Hampshire, where he would stay with Miss H. E. Freeman, who had long been one

The South Congregational Church
Exeter Street

of his earnest assistants in all sorts of work. Here
he enjoyed the mountain country immensely, and
felt entirely at home. Here it was, chiefly in later
years, that Miss Freeman was led to note down,
often from his dictation, the details as to his life
and interests which have often been cited in these
pages.

In these years he looked back over his own life
a good deal and one finds among his papers a good
deal of memory and reminiscence. He wrote during these years "A New England Boyhood," — an
autobiography which carried the story of his life
down to the end of his college course. It is a very
entertaining book not only on his own childhood
but on Old Boston. At this time also he tried for
a while an experiment which was rather in his line,
as he would have said. He found a blank book
and wrote in it "I am not sure if this be a book
which Frederic Greenleaf bought and gave to me,
when we proposed to go to the Holy Land together.[1]
It is like it, and if not that book it was bought because like it. I take it today, Oct. 7, 1893, to try
an experiment in writing down every night, one of
the most interesting things of the day."

This, I say, was rather in his own line; that was
the kind of thing that he thought one wanted to
know of a man. He sometimes said that the way
to write a biography of any one was for a hundred
friends to put down one incident each of the man.
That, to his mind, would give a better notion of
anyone than all manner of studies of influence and

[1] See I, p. 127.

358 EDWARD EVERETT HALE

environment; that would give a real idea of the way a man appeared to his own time. So these daily notes, — there are quite a number of them, — give a personal idea that is otherwise hard to get.

"Alas!¹ *Oct.* 21. We have been to Worcester — to the 401st anniversary.

"Hoar was betrayed into telling me a pretty story of his visit to George Herbert's parsonage. He has a passion for Herbert, — and last year he and Ruth went there together. By good luck they fell in with Mrs. Vaugh, the wife of Canon Vaugh of Salisbury, who is Herbert's successor. She did the honors very prettily, and took an hour or more to show them the old records and what memorials they had of Herbert.

"When they went away Hoar asked her to take a five-pound note and use it for one of her protégés and say it was 'for love of George Herbert.'

"So she did — and two months after came a pretty note telling how a girl with danger of permanent deafness had been taken to London to a great aurist, and he had operated 'for the love of George Herbert' — and the operation had succeeded, and the girl could go on with her musical training or whatever. And within a day or two a nice letter has come from the child herself, thanking [him], and in a postscript she says, 'I have not been deaf one minute since I came from London.'"

"*Oct.* 29 — *Sunday*. It has been cold today. I think there will be a frost tonight. Thus closes the

¹ Because the previous entry had been October 10.

most remarkable autumn, in regard to cold, or the lack of it, which I remember, and I think since I was born. For there has been no frost here (in Roxbury) until now, and none except in very low lands in Eastern Massachusetts. It was said, in 1861, the summer when the Rebellion began, that we could have ripened our own cotton, had we planted it. Certainly that could have been done here this year. We have been cutting autumn flowers, — salvias, geraniums, cosmos, (or cosmea) marigolds, nasturtiums, fuchsias, steadily in the open air until now. I cut a long stem of perfect chicory on the Back Bay today — and the tall asters in the Charles Fen gardens are lovely. I notice that our morning glories ran through their time of blossom, — and we have none. They are generally cut off by frost.

"But we have a large handsome squash blossom on the grass by the grape house."

"*Nov.* 21. We have been reading Mrs. Claflin's pleasant anecdotes about Whittier. It is a book written in the pure Plutarch way. A selection of stories about him, with no effort at chronology, and hardly any of moralizing.

"I met him first on an April evening in 1846 in a stage-coach riding from the Fitchburg R. R. to Lancaster. I did not remember the interview but he did, to my advantage. Many years after, — before sunrise one winter morning, I took my seat in the train at Newbury Port for Boston. I was sleepy and promised myself a good nap, — when some one approached me and called me by name. I was inwardly furious, that I could not sleep in my own car, but had just conscience enough to restrain the expression of my rage, — and asked him, with a manner more civil than my heart justified, to sit by me. In a moment it proved that it was Whittier, and I was left to thank God that I had not shown my indignation. We had a pleasant talk all the way to Boston.

"And I learned pretty thoroughly the lesson of behaving decently to strangers. Afterward we saw each other a good deal."

"*April* 30, 1894. I try, every year, to take my staff, or those who want to go, to the State House to see the way their country is governed.

"We went today, the chaplain, Mr. Waldron saw us, and came and asked me to offer the opening prayer, which I was glad to do. I did this in Washington, one of the war years when Channing was chaplain, but I have never done it here.

"Mr. Meyer is the speaker, I believe a very good fellow. They say he is the youngest speaker they ever had, except Charles.

"They continued the debate on the destruction of this State House. I came away before the result, but will put it on this page.

"It is fifty-five years since I broke into life here, as reporter for the 'Advertiser.' We had the Northwest Reporters' Gallery, and I have the keys now, though the doorway has been long since built up, and those four galleries, little 'boxes' they were — are disused. The northern and southern galleries have been introduced since then. We had more than 600 members, and many of them sat in what are now the men's and women's galleries. But the general aspect of the house is not changed.

"R. C. Winthrop was speaker. In that year and in a later year, perhaps 1843, when I was reporter again, Wilson, Thomas, Stevenson, Hillard, I think, were members."

"*July* 22, 1894. I have been reading at Sunday service some of my stories about Emerson to the young people. William Weeden said that when E. came to Providence, 'we were all crazy about the Union for Christian work,' and so he took the twins over to the evening meeting of that society, that they might see what was going on. He thought Emerson would think this crazy and foolish. But no. Emerson said the next day — 'That was a good thought of yours to take those boys to the meeting, — to put them in touch with their own people in their own time.' The two, — William and E, were riding to Boston together. 'He was the shyest of men, unless he chose to speak out.' But this time he chose to and he said — 'What I am for — and what I am doing is this: — I am speaking what New England has always said, and will always have to say.' This is quite true, 'The chief end of man is to live to the glory of God and to enjoy him forever.' That is what New England has said, and has to say."

"*Oct.* 8, 1895. How little I thought what I was next to write here. I am waiting for the hour of

362 EDWARD EVERETT HALE

our dear Rob's funeral. His mother is upstairs, where she has lain for four weeks and so weak that they dare not tell her of his death.

"He is the purest, noblest and most faultless human being in the shape of a man whom I have ever seen. As my sister Sarah seemed to me in the shape of a woman.

"George Clarke said last night he cannot think of a man as resembling Christ so closely as he.

"His fight with fever at the last was so terrible that I was not going to look upon his face again, so sad was the expression, almost of agony, when he was dying. But Phil told me I should see nothing of this, and it was true. As Phil said, it was just the look of interest in a new problem before him, and there was the dear smile on his face which belonged to his determination to solve that problem. I changed my order for the church, — I had said the coffin should not be opened there, — and told Frank Smith to leave it open for any one to see his face who wanted.

"Dear Phil said 'You knew I confided everything to him, and I would take his advice about very little things. Whatever I asked about, however trifling, he would not answer without this little pause in which he should make a decision, and with just this expression which he has now of a new experience before him.'

"Several of the boys were here last night, who are the pall-bearers of today. They have but one thing to say, and that is of his force of character and of his intense love for everybody.

"Nelly says that not long before she went away he said 'Why, Nelly, my heart is so full of love for everybody that sometimes it really frightens me!' This was not the real conclusion of the sentence, but it roughly expresses the feeling, almost perplexity, which this weight of love gave him.

"For myself, I am only so glad now that I have never thwarted what seemed his vague plans for study and for life. Low down in them, I am sure, was his wish to take care of me and his mother until we died.

"I am amazed when I think of it and when I look round, to think of the force of character which has made this boy absolutely a power in this community. In the neighborhood here, in all the circles of society, of which he was really fond, as in his college class for instance, — everybody respected him, while everybody loved him.

"He was popular in school, quick and strong, admirably formed, and so went to college. He went to college resolved neither to drink nor smoke, and to save me expense he took one of the meanest rooms in College·House. He thought that merely from these causes he should throw up what boys call 'popularity in college,' which they prize so highly. And with his eyes open, he threw it to the winds.

"Of which the consequence was, that so many people came to see him that he had to go to Hugh Tallant's room to do his studying.

"I think that perhaps every one of his brothers has more of the literary knack than he, more for

one instance of what I call the 'lyric swing.' But
he had an absolute purpose in choosing the literary
career, and such weight of character that he would
have compelled words to serve him, and people to
obey him. This people were beginning to find out.
And before he died, I think he had the satisfaction
of knowing that he had passed the crest line, and
that success was before him.

"It occurred to me only this morning that Bob
was the first person to share with me what came to be
eventually my chief success in letters. He is the first
person who ever heard my story of 'In His Name.'

"I had taken all the boys and Nelly on a sleigh-
ride with the children. We had a little feast at the
church after it was over. Then, as it proved, we
had to walk home. For it was too late for the cars.
This was pretty hard measure for a little fellow of
four years old. To keep him awake, and to entertain
him, I told him the story of 'In His Name.' I had
written out the beginning of it, and finished it next
morning, in the first draught, in which the story is
sketched in fifteen pages."

"*Jan.* 14, 1897. We were at work at the church.
The last letters I dictated were to tell Mrs. Stanard
that the Froebel lesson was on Work and Play —
giving the pages — I should try to be with her, etc.

"I took a cab, made a sick call — came home
and told the man to come again after my lunch and
nap at 3:15. He did so.

"I took the cab, attended to three necessary
errands, and then — not half an hour from home,

— was absolutely bound to come home. It was in vain to say that the cab was under me, that this was cowardice and shirking duty. I ordered him to come home. I bribed myself by saying that I would finish the Defoe and Robinson Crusoe article for the *Outlook* — that it was nearly done, had been promised, etc. And I came home. But I knew this was because I wanted to finish the article. So I said — by way of self punishment, I will take and sort out the scraps Lucretia sent me in November, — a mass of relics running from 1862 to 1888 which she had tumbled together and wanted me to sort out.

"So as soon as I dismissed the cab, I took the box — and lighted up. The first paper was a note from Elizabeth Peabody, written to repeat a long anecdote of Susan Tyng's about my mother's views on *Work and Play* told at length, and exactly applicable in their Froebel conversation.

"The second was an old envelope of McElroy's addressed to me of which the contents were newspaper scraps. The first, three columns long — was a long, original study, which pretends to have new material on the relation between Robinson Crusoe, Defoe, and Selkirk — fitting on in exactly the place where I laid down Wright's chapter on the same subject, when I went to bed last night and on which I was to begin this afternoon.

"The rest of the box was curious enough — but these two papers, one in MS. and one in print — belonged exactly in the current of my day.

"How she got McElroy's letter — who knows?"

TO WILLIAM EVERETT

April 27, 1893. Let me congratulate you on your plucky and spirited canvass and on your success. Besides the ordinary pleasure in such success you have the satisfaction of knowing that you have won it against very heavy odds. You ought to be glad also that you have broken up the absurd superstition that a man must live in his district. That lesson alone will greatly improve our delegations in Congress.

"You will remember that several of the towns in this district were in your father's district. I am old enough to remember his house on Winter Hill.

"I have some new lore on genealogy — but you will be too busy with gold and silver to think of such things. There is no doubt that Mercy Brown is Mercy. They have her grave stone — Mercy Everett at Dedham.

"Susy will be here on the eighth from California."

TO LUCRETIA

"*April* 14, 1893. I dictated a lot of messages to you, — but this is my personal note to thank you for the what-not. I think this must be its name.

"It is delightful, as all your presents are. They fall in exactly with my habits: — and are in more constant use than you have any idea of.

"I think you will be amused to know that the table cloth charged with paper-cutters — which lies on the end of this table — is still full of the original cutters. Not one of them is lost, for there was no son of perdition there. They flow to the other end of the table, and when there are seven there Miss Adams takes them back again.

"Your work box, your pen and ink tray, and your miniature bureau are all in use on one table or another here — and take back one's memory for a five years at least.

"I am keeping holiday at home and editing my own poems."

TO MRS. HALE [1]

"*Sept.* 27, 1894. We had a really sublime ending to all our doubts and difficulties, — a real uprising of the people and answer to prayer. You would never forget the closing moment. After the different leaders of any faction had said a word counseling the new formula one unanimous *Aye* went up from the crowded house. Hoar put the noes and all was still as death. He declared it unanimously voted — and people rose and cheered and Frank Peabody led in the doxology and I gave the benediction. The eternal words always come in place —

"'May the *peace* of God which *passeth* all *understanding*' is exactly what would come on a logic-splitting crowd, and had compelled them to *pass* their intellectual processes to a spiritual plane."

TO MRS. HALE

"*March* 3, 1895. I am just waiting at 8 A.M. for the carriage which is to take me to breakfast with George Hoar and Ruth. I saw him yesterday — and this Sunday breakfast has come to be rather a custom when I am here. I had an interesting day

---

[1] This letter was written at the conference of Unitarian churches at Saratoga.

yesterday. McElroy, strange to say, had never been in the Capitol. It is a curious illustration of his interest in men, rather than places. For he has, of course, often been here before. He stayed at the White House I think in the days of Arthur's dominion.

"There — in the Library — we copied Anacreon in Heaven. It was written by Ralph Tomlinson whom he met. Perhaps some of you will look in my Lempriére's Biography.

"At lunch we had Mr. Brown, Mr. McElroy, and Gen. Vazie and Langley. After lunch Langley and I called on Kipling — who was very pleasant. Unfortunately Spring Rice of the Legation, grandson of Spring Rice of the Reform Bill, came in and we came away.

"I made several calls afterward — but almost everybody was out.

"Shippen has retained Miss Sewall of the congress to preach for him — so I am free. I am going with these people to their church.

"I really want you to know Mrs. Hubbard. She has had her cataract operation performed — with success since I was here."

Throughout these years he had certain elements in life which can hardly be regretted, for they were such a natural, almost necessary result of his way of thinking and acting. He had some time before formed an organization called J. Stillman Smith and Company, chiefly for the publication in popular editions of his own books. He had also become connected with the *Commonwealth*, a weekly newspaper in which he had a good deal of financial responsibility. In both of these enterprises were to be seen the same motives, — a desire to help people and enterprises of which he approved and a confidence in the value of his own work and energy. But without comment on his own feelings, it must be said that neither of these sentiments was of sufficient value in the business world to carry the enterprise. He had, at no time of his life, been a thorough business man, and he was less so than ever at seventy.

In the mass of letters of these years there are not a few on these business matters which are hard reading. Even among these, however, one occasionally comes across something very characteristic, like the following.

TO J. STILLMAN SMITH

"*Jan.* 21, 1895.

"MY POOR DEAR OLD BOY:

"I thought to have seen you today.   But it is so wet and I am so tired that I will come Tuesday, instead.

"Take your ease and rest. We are all right and things go nicely. I sold a thousand of 'Jesus in Boston' today. You are to fix the price. I have 200 from Lend a Hand, — from which I paid Mrs. Whitman $35.00. I have 200 for *Commonwealth* from which I paid myself $75.00. So I have enough for Wilcox's acceptance, and we can easily manage Lovell.

"They took 149 dollars at the *Commonwealth* last week — and have something in their till today.

"But I will not bother you about business."

His friends regretted this drain on his powers, but it was probably one of the necessities of his temper and character. I do not even mention any of the details, except to say that in 1896 his friends succeeded in relieving him of any responsibility with either organization. His constant feeling for journalism led him to ally himself to the *Christian Register*, where he was able to write without being responsible for business arrangements which he could not really control.

This last decade of the century was in some respects the happiest of his life. He was still in active work but he had already done so much of it that his function was more that of encouragement and advice. He was still able to enjoy to the full travel and leisure, and he got in one way or another plenty of travel and leisure to enjoy. He had a large and full recognition of what he was and what he was trying to do. His family life was happy; he lived with his wife, his daughter, and his youngest son in the house which years ago he had chosen as the family center. His four other sons were either married and settled or well on the way to be; and he began to have the pleasure of seeing his grandchildren. If (as was the case) the boys lived at different places out of immediate reach, yet at one time or another he could stop and see them in some of his journeys here or there, and they were very apt to be at Matunuck some time during the summer.

He began, however, to feel more and more strongly that he had done the regular and definite work that he had been called upon to do. We have seen his feeling in the verses "School's Done." It was not long after that he wrote the following letter to Mr. W. P. Fowler, the Chairman of the Standing Committee of the South Congregational Church.

"*May* 15, 1899.

"Dear Mr. Fowler,

"When I placed my resignation in your hands a year ago, you asked me to withhold it, and I did so, though with grave doubts, as you will remember. I am now sure that you must present it at the meeting to-morrow evening.

"I say this with great sorrow as you know. It is forty-three years since I accepted this charge. I feel sure of the regard of every one in the congregation, now that I lay it down. For all these years our relations have been as tender as they have been intimate. And now that I leave the pulpit, I am still as truly as ever a member of the dear old South Congregational.

"But I have known, — oh, for a long time, that the church needs a minister as well as a preacher. And nothing but the kindness of every member of the congregation has justified me in remaining so long in a charge where I have left so many of a minister's duties unfulfilled. My conscience has been relieved by the watchfulness of yourself and the other members of the committee, of all the members of the church, of the South Friendly, of the Alliance, and all our workers of every name. But all the same, the church ought to have a young and active minister.

"I am not young and I am not active. Will you then say to the meeting that I resign the duty and privilege to which they invited me by their vote of June 4, 1856? I should like to have this resignation take affect on the first day of October next.

"The years which have passed in your service have been happy years to me. I have seen the children of those who called me, and their children's children, grow up to manhood and womanhood. And in all the relations between me and those whom I love to call my people there has never been an unkind word or jar.

"Do not encourage any suggestion that I may recall this resignation. We *ought* to place this duty in other hands. And of course *ought* is final.

"With love to each and all,
        "Yours truly and always,
                "EDWARD E. HALE,"
"Minister of the South Congregational Church."

On December 31, 1900, he took part in a ceremony which aroused the deepest interest in his mind. The Twentieth Century Club arranged a welcome to the New Century in front of the State House, Boston. The services were simple: First, trumpets from the State House balcony; then, a hymn sung by the assembly; then, selections from the Ninetieth Psalm read by my father; then a hymn which had been said or sung on the observance in Boston of the dawn of the eighteenth century;[1] then the Lord's Prayer, said by all the people, and "America" sung by them; and a closing flourish.

My father writes of it: "At quarter past eleven we went to the State House. Our little personal party went at once to the Governor's room. He was very gracious, and we waited there until it was time to go to the balcony. Here was the whole chorus of the Handel and Haydn, and ready to sing 'Old Hundred' and Sewall's hymn and to lead 'America.' The spectacle was magnificent, — a sea of upturned faces below in the State House yard and extending out in every direction as far as you can see, the lights of the carriages on both sides of the street, stretching off into the dark horizon. At quarter of twelve precisely our trumpets gave the blow. Just before the turning of the year I read verses from the Ninetieth Psalm,[2] and when the bell of King's Chapel began to strike twelve, our trumpeters began to blow their twelve blasts. Personally I heard nothing but the blasts of the trumpets; I should not even have known that the chorus was singing, but they were singing, 150 voices of them. . . . The whole service was very satisfactory and I am writing under the influence of its solemnity."

[1] I suppose this earlier observance was the suggestion of the later. We read of it in the diary of Samuel Sewall. "Jan. 1, 1701. Entrance of the 18th century. Just about Break a day, Jacob Amsden and three other Trumpeters gave a Blast with the Trumpets, on the common, near Mr. Alfred's. Then went to the Green Chamber, and sounded there till about sunrise. Bellman said these verses (my verses upon New Century) which I printed and gave them."

[2] Beginning "Lord, thou hast been our dwelling place in all generations. Before the mountains were brought forth, or even thou hadst formed the earth and the world, even from everlasting to everlasting, thou are God."

CHAPTER THIRTY-FIVE

PEACE

1885-1907

WHEN my father began his work as a minister, his mind turned chiefly to the question as to the duty of a follower of Christ and a preacher of the Gospel among the people within immediate reach of his church resources, within the hearing of his own church bells. When he came to Boston his ideas broadened as his opportunities broadened; he found more to do in a large city than in a small one, but he still held to the idea, harder to carry out in a large city than a small one, that each church was to a large degree responsible for the Christian life of its own neighborhood. With the War, as he often said himself, he found larger opportunities and felt that he ought to grasp them, but he did not neglect the nearer duties. He strove to manage matters so that the South Congregational Church could see to the charities and the Christian opportunities of the region between Dover Street and Boston Neck, while its minister, not estranging himself from that interest, undertook also to help those who were at work pressing the New Civilization in the South and the West. The organization of the Ten Times One Clubs, which spread out all over the country, and his own travels in this or that piece of business, led him to be interested in the way things went, not

only in the parish of the South Congregational
Church nor in Boston only, but all over the country, to be interested and to feel that he had something to do in that progress. He had never confined
his life to one place; in the years before he had
settled in Worcester he had traveled much about
the country on business and on pleasure; while at
Worcester his work for Kansas and Nebraska in the
Emigrant Aid Society had accustomed him to the idea
of common interests throughout the whole country.

At what time his interests turned particularly to
the question of international arbitration as a means
of general peace I cannot say. It was natural that
he should have begun to think seriously on such
things; having extended his ideas of the function
of the Christian Church from the affairs of a parish
to the affairs of a nation, it was hardly probable
that he would have withheld himself from the further extensions which passed from the relation of
individuals within the nation to the relation of
nations in the whole world.

It may have seemed to some that his earnest
championing of arbitration and peace was a new
step, though perhaps one natural enough for a man
of Christian principles and philanthropic activities,
but it was really not so very new. He had always
been interested in foreign nations and had known
a great deal about them. It was but natural that
he should have extended his ideas on Christian
civilization to the stage of the world.

I do not know, however, at what time he began
to interest himself particularly in this question, nor

have I sufficient knowledge of the matter to trace the general progress of public thought on the subject. It is, however, well known that from the early years of the nineteenth century there was in men's minds the conception of some congress or confederation of nations, formed with a view to universal peace. On March 9, 1838, there is mention in my father's college diary of his writing a forensic "on the practicability of a Congress of Nations." He took the negative on the subject.[1]

Among the papers belonging to his college days is the forensic itself. It will be of interest to transcribe a few lines:

"Those well meaning visionaries, who hope by one stroke to do away with the worst evils of society, propose as a means of establishing universal peace, a Congress, to which every nation in the world shall send deputies; which shall be empowered to arbitrate in all disputes which may arise, and make a final decision thereon. They hope that the decisions of this Congress will be acquiesced in by all the powers represented, and thus will put an end to dissensions which would otherwise result in war between the parties. The scheme is a plausible one, but there are too many difficulties attached to the execution of it to allow us to hope that it can be put in practice."

Thus early at the age of sixteen did he have in mind the idea of a congress of nations [2] as a means

[1] See I. p. 38.

[2] He afterward called it a High Court, but even in this college forensic the duties of the congress are judicial rather than legislative; it renders decisions in disputes that arise rather than passes laws to regulate future cases, — it arbitrates rather than legislates.

of establishing universal peace. It is true he con-
demns the plan as the idea of a visionary, but the
difficulties which he foresees are chiefly those of execution. Difficulties would arise at the very beginning concerning the choice of a place of meeting, the
language and rules to be adopted in deliberations,
the rule by which the number of delegates should
be allotted to each country, what nation should
supply officers to preside over the meetings. Further, as the congress would not be in session all the
time, it would take half a year in any given case
before it could be settled, during which time the dis-
puting countries would be at the greatest enmity.
Were these difficulties surmounted, however, the
debates of an international congress "would tend
but little to the promotion of peace among its
members." Nor would all nations readily acquiesce
in the decisions of such a congress. And if they did
acquiesce, there would still be difficulties in the way
of universal tranquillity. In this last point it must
be admitted that the writer who has hitherto gone
rather triumphantly along finds difficulties of which
he seems conscious and ends rather ineffectively.
He believes that with the reduction of the regular
establishments of armies and navies there would
be such an increase in the number of outlaws and
desperadoes as would be a serious menace to the
tranquillity of the world. All these arguments, however, are really only objections, difficulties to be
overcome, or perhaps more accurately, points which
a bright collegian intent on making out his case
would readily be able to think up.

This early argument with its objections, which practical history shows to be so easily overcome, except in the crucial matter of acquiescence in the decision of such a congress, is of value to us simply in showing that the idea of a high court of nations which should arbitrate the disputes of the world was no new idea, belonging to the end of the century. It had been in other minds; it had been in his own mind fifty years before he began to advocate it. It was an idea widely current before Tennyson wrote "Locksley Hall"; was one of the generous projects of the idealistic youth of the day. But I do not think it held an important place in my father's mind until the latter part of his life. It seemed visionary, not because he could think up half a dozen objections to it, but because it actually seemed rather a vision of the future than a plan for the amelioration of present conditions. The mind absorbed in the difficulties of Irish emigration, the settlement of Kansas, city charities, homes for workingmen, Southern schools, and Western colleges, not to mention the administration of the South Congregational Church or the closer organization of the Unitarian churches, would be likely to put on one side plans which seemed to deal with no actual necessities of the time.

It may be that the Civil War turned his attention to the subject. Certainly it gave him a first-hand idea of the horrible character of war; certainly, too, it led him to deal with larger questions than those he had so far felt to be his province. The Alabama Case, ending in the Geneva Arbitration of 1872,

undoubtedly set him thinking of the possibility of
extending the principle of arbitration. I find among
his letters the following invitation, which he sent
to Charles:

"BOSTON, *March* 12, 1874.

"Dear Sir:

"The undersigned respectfully invite you to be
present at a conference of a few gentlemen on the
subject of the Codification of International Law as
a basis of Arbitration in cases of dispute between
nations, which will be held in the parlors of Judge
Warren, No. 16 Marlboro' Street, on Monday Evening, 16th inst. at 7½ o'clock.

"Hon. Charles Francis Adams, Hon. Robert C.
Winthrop, Professor Peabody, and others will par-
ticipate in the conference."

He wrote on this to Charles:

"I think you will like to come to this. Adams is
to speak. I have committed *Old & New* to him for
senator."

He wrote to Charles a day or two later: "I went
to the International Code meeting last night and
heard curious and interesting addresses from Winthrop and Charles Adams." But Charles was at
this time living in Boston, and they, therefore,
expressed their ideas in talk rather than by letter.
Nor does it otherwise appear that he often thought
of the subject. It was not, in the seventies, a matter
much in the public mind, either in America or elsewhere. The Geneva Arbitration, of course, gave
rise to many hopes that a new means had been found
for settling international disputes. But such hopes

were still "visionary." Practical observers failed to
see in arbitration an adequate means for securing
international peace.[1]

My father in those days, was strongly opposed to
standing armies, and I have often heard him express
his views on the subject. I do not, however, remember ever hearing him speak (till a much later date)
of arbitration or of a permanent tribunal as a means
of gaining general peace.

It was in the early eighties that his mind began
to turn over the subject with some care. He was
a good deal of an admirer of James G. Blaine, who
was Secretary of State under Garfield. He must
have considered with interest Mr. Blaine's proposal
of a congress of the American powers for the purpose
of considering the better establishment of peace,
and must have regretted the withdrawal of that
proposal. However it was — and I can say little
of his view of the matter, save that he was often in
Washington in these years (1880–1884) and always
saw and talked with Mr. Blaine — by the end of
Arthur's administration he had come to feel that
the question was one of deep importance. "For
myself," he wrote a good deal later,[2] "I paid my
respects to the end of the century as early as 1885.
I was then in the City of Washington, and I was to
preach on the Sunday before Mr. Cleveland's inauguration. I foresaw many of the evils which that

[1] Thus the *Nation*, June 18, 1874, says at the end of an article, "Let us
cherish war a little longer, and cultivate the military virtues until we see real
signs of something better to take their place. They are perhaps barbarous,
but they are wholesome."

[2] "Memories of a Hundred Years," II. 285

administration brought upon the country. In that
sermon I laid down as the three initial necessities
most urgent for the work of the new century with
us: First, the uplift of the school system so that it
should educate men and boys, and not be satisfied
with their instruction. Second, the systematic and
intelligent transfer, from the crowded regions of the
world, of men and women who should live in regions
not crowded. Third, and necessary for everything
else, the institution of a Permanent Tribunal for the
nations of the world."

Such is his own account. It is very possible, however, that he was at this time confusing two addresses.[1] The utterance concerning an International
Court that is commonly quoted as a prophesy of a
permanent tribunal occurs in a sermon preached at
Washington four years afterward, just before the
celebration of the Centennial of the inauguration of
Washington. The sermon was entitled "The Twentieth Century" and in it he said: "The Twentieth
Century will apply the word of the Prince of Peace
to international life. The wisdom of statesmen will
devise the solution which soldiers and people will
accept with thankfulness. The beginning will not
be made at the end of a war, but in some time of
peace. The suggestion will come from one of the
six great powers. It will come from a nation which
has no large permanent military establishment;
that is to say, it will probably come from the United

[1] He was in Washington at the time he mentions, but I find few letters
written there and none which speak of the subject. Unfortunately, although
I was also there at the time and probably heard the sermon in question, I have
no recollection of it.

States. This nation in the most friendly way will propose to the other great powers to name each one a jurist of world-wide fame, who with the other five shall form a permanent tribunal of the highest dignity. Everything will be done to give this tribunal the honor and respect of the world. As an international court it will be organized without reference to any special case under discussion. Then it will exist. Its members may prepare themselves as they choose for its great duty. Timidly, at first, and with a certain curiosity, two nations will refer to it some international question, not of large importance, which has perplexed their negotiations. The tribunal will hear counsel and will decide. Their decision will be the first in a series which will mark the great victory of the twentieth century."

These general thoughts and suggestions were not widely noticed at the time, but when in the spring of 1896, an Arbitration Conference met at Washington my father was present at the conference and in writing to my mother he made this remark:

"Well, we finished our Convention yesterday — conference they call it. I am afraid it will go where other conventions go, but it has left a Permanent Committee even if it do not create a Permanent Tribunal."

From this time on the questions of peace, international arbitration, a permanent tribunal, were often in his mind, and he was constantly writing or speaking about them. He was not one of those who could take the practical steps which should carry out his ideas; such functions perhaps belong to

Czars of Russia or Presidents of the United States. We know, in fact, that he did not consider that his especial power lay in organization, arrangement, systematic business. He always felt, and now more than ever, that it was for him to advise and guide, consult and encourage. Such was his work for ten years. He was almost always at Lake Mohonk at the Arbitration Conferences, he was always finding opportunity to explain and to press the ideas of which he was so convinced. When he was more in Washington in the winter, he was especially able to see and talk to men who were actively at work in the matter. His letters and day-books are full of mention which shows how large a place this interest had in his life. The few letters that can be given will serve to offer a personal view rather than a summary of his thinking on the subject.

TO MRS. HALE

"LAKE MOHONK, Saturday morning.

"MY DEAR CHILD,

"The Conference proper wound up in a blaze of glory last night. But I have determined to stay over Sunday. They have asked me to preach, and it is a charming place, where I write more in a day than I do in three in Boston.

"I think you have seen the photographs. They give you some idea of the beauty of the Lake itself, and of the admirable location of the house. But nothing can make you comprehend the region till you see it. There are these very high mountains, more sheer and sharp than Holyoke, covered, where trees will stand, with a growth of hemlock, chestnut, birch, sassafras and the rest, all in the glory of autumn now. Up and down these ridges, like Andernach and its neighbourhood in Switzerland, Albert Smiley has been cutting zig-zag roads, so that with easy driving you command the very summits. These summits control views almost infinite. They tell you coolly that you see one hundred and fifty miles in one direc48on or seventy-five in another, and I do not know how much more.

"Here comes breakfast, and ever since we have been bidding Goodbye. I propose to leave Monday morning, work my way across the mountains eastward as I can, stop at the Dawes's at Pittsfield, perhaps, and see you Monday night or at breakfast Tuesday."

TO MRS. HALE

"LAKE MOHONK, *June* 4, 1896.

"Here is the old familiar scene you see. And I open on my second day. I am at a table with Mr. and Mrs. George Hale and Martha Adams and Mr. Mead and Mr. Dole, and Mr. Logan whom you will hear me speak of a good deal. I picked him out long ago as a New York lawyer who was urging a *Permanent Tribunal*, and I wrote to him. It proves that he is, I should think, rather a distinguished patent lawyer. He has to defend the right of mining companies in Arizona and Sonora, so that he knows our dear semi-tropics better than we do. I brought him to our table and he is regarded as a real acquisition. I have had some very good talks with him.

"I made at length one of the opening speeches.
Pas mal, — and it is much commended by the
people who want to flatter me. It has, any way
struck the key-note of the meeting, for almost all
of them have to agree with Mr. Hale or to disagree.
Last night for the field speaking we had Mowry
whom you never heard, a Providence school master,
a Judge Shiner of the Supreme Court of Rhode
Island, and Ruen Thomas. The light and life of all
is Mr. Edmunds who presides, tells stories, smooths
roughnesses, and knows more about it all than all
of us put together. My private opinion is that Lord
Salisbury and Mr. Olney have something on foot
which will make us all cheer our throats out with
enthusiasm!"

TO PRESIDENT ROOSEVELT
"*Nov.* 14, 1901.

"DEAR MR. ROOSEVELT: I guess from the Press
dispatches that there are people at Mexico who want
to make a brand new separate American Tribunal,
to show that we can do as well as the people did at
the Hague. Pray do not let them. We made the
Hague Treaty. It is American from end to end,
and a great victory for our diplomacy, according to
my notion. To make another is to appear to distrust what we did with great success and to our
great credit.

"All which I know you know. But those of us
who count the Hague a real step upward and forward, hate to see a fifth wheel put on the coach,
which really destroys the work of the fourth wheel

which the coach needed badly. Could this be said in the message perhaps.

"Compulsory arbitration, which one of the Mexican plans proposes, is absurd almost in name, when you come to states. You cannot make a man sue his neighbor if he does not want to. Their plan for a sixpenny board of claims seems impracticable, for that reason alone, that it says the nations *shall* do this or that.

"Pardon my writing this, and do not be afraid that you will often hear from me. But this happens to be the subject to which I have given more study and time in the last three years than to any other.

"Always yours,

"EDWARD E. HALE."

"You see, if a question arose between us and Brazil now, we should appoint our (American) judges, they would appoint theirs, and the four or six appoint one more. The Monroe Doctrine has been completely asserted and conceded at the Hague.

"Let me give you a good epigram. They want you to make a new Secretary. Call him a Secretary of Peace, as we already have a Secretary of War."

TO OSCAR STRAUS

"*July* 24th, 1904.

"MY DEAR MR. STRAUS:—

"Would it not be possible to find some authority which could call together now at the Hague five or seven or nine of the Hague Judges, who might be there to sit at once on any case like this of the Malacca, — and define the Law at once?

"International Law is changed, more or less by the Hague votes of 1899. If we had our court really in session, no matter who called it, either nation might refer to it, (I should think) with much more dignity than if it had to wait for the progress of an old fashioned Admiralty suit, in some Admiralty Court.

"I have no right to address you, but that you know more of the Court than any one, — and really believe in it, — as some of us, at least, do. How we miss our dear friend Frederic Holls in such a crisis.

"Mr. Roosevelt would do whatever you suggested."

TO MRS. HALE

"LAKE MOHONK, May 22, 1907.

"You remember much how Life passes here. At our table we have Sim[1] at my left, — next to him Mrs. Charles Eliot — at my right Nelly, and at hers Mr. C. W. Eliot. Then come Lyman Abbott and his wife, — and the Rev. Mr. North and his wife opposite me. We sat a good while at breakfast. At a quarter of ten all met in the great common room, — a new room which I believe you have not seen — Mr. Smiley read the 33rd. Psalm — I offered prayer and we began with the reports. Our real successes were Chandler's opening speech, and a very good speech in English by a German Publicist named Baith, who is, I think, probably the most im-

_____
[1] Governor Baldwin of Connecticut.

portant person here. He is the Editor of the *Nation* which is a great liberal organ, I believe, at Hamburg.

"This afternoon Nelly waived the invitation to drive and went out in one of the boats and now we are in that great writing room where everybody talks to you awaiting supper and the mail."

CHAPTER THIRTY-SIX

LAST YEARS

1900–1909

WITH the new century my father's activities rather changed in character; he still preached, he still gave lectures and addresses; he still wrote. But he began about this time the habit of passing a part of the winter in Washington, where in 1904 he received an official position. Before that, however, he found the mild climate not only delightful but almost necessary to his health. He had always had good health and for many years had suffered only from slight ailments. Nor was his health really impaired. But he was near eighty now and suffered somewhat from sciatica, somewhat from a lameness which he had got from a fall, and somewhat from asthma, so that though he was still able to go about much as usual, he saw the necessity of taking care of himself.

The characteristic element of these years is his life in Washington. He was generally at 39 Highland Street in the spring and fall, at Matunuck, at Folly Cove, at Intervale in the summer. But his winter home for these years was in Washington. He lived at first in apartments at one place or another, but in 1905 established himself in the house at 1745 N Street, which his daughter had purchased as a winter home. Here he and my mother lived the remaining years of life very happily. They had with them their daughter and Miss Abigail W. Clark, my father's secretary, who was both able and devoted. He had often by him his eldest son Arthur, who during these years had generally a house in Washington, although his railroad business took him all over the country. He also had a large and growing circle of friends. Some of these went back even to the early years when he had been settled for the winter at Washington as a clergyman, while others were among the many public men with whom he came frequently in contact. In Washington he was able to continue his interest in the schools at Hampton, which had ever since the war been very near his heart, and almost every year he would go down there for a while with my mother or my sister. In the summer in like manner, he generally went for some days to Lake Mohonk, as has been seen.

Of his literary work much was still done for newspapers or magazines, especially for the *Christian Register*, the *Outlook*, the *Woman's Home Companion*, and for a year or two for the Hearst newspapers. He liked these opportunities to speak to a large audience, — he knew he had something worth saying, and he wanted to say it to as many people as he could. For the *Outlook* he wrote his "Memories of a Hundred Years" which was exactly the kind of writing that he liked. It was a history of the United States in the nineteenth century from a personal standpoint. Not that he remembered back for one hundred years, but that in the papers of his father and his uncle Edward he had the personal view of history that he wished to give. To these articles, which were republished, he gave a great deal of time and study, so that in spite of the personal form, the book is a definite statement of his opinions.

At this time also he collected a Standard Edition of his writings. Such an edition could not include everything that he had written; he could not himself have made a list of everything that he had written, even had he wished to. His early lists, such as that mentioned,[1] are never complete, nor do I imagine that later lists are.[2] But though he made no pretense at completeness — indeed, many of his writings had been for temporary purposes and he had no desire to preserve them — he had a chance here to preserve what he thought for one reason or another really worth preservation. The collected edition in ten volumes was completed in 1900.

His daybooks during these years present a better view of his way of life and thought than do his letters, and from them will most of our final extracts be taken.

On the twenty-fifth of June, 1902, he went to Commencement. The occasion was of especial interest on account of the presence of President Roosevelt. It had been arranged by the Harvard Chapter of Alpha Delta Phi, to which he had belonged while in college and with which he had always kept up

[1] I, p. 353.

[2] A bibliography of my father's writings is now being compiled by Nathaniel T. Kidder, the son of his old and dear friend, Henry P. Kidder, with the invaluable help of Miss Abigail W. Clark.

392 EDWARD EVERETT HALE

his relation, to present him with a gold medal in recognition of his eighty years. President Roosevelt was to make the presentation. My father wrote as follows in his account of the day:

"The Commencement fête was very successful. I took Emily and Fred Nazro out, leaving here at nine o'clock. As we passed through Massachusetts Ave., the crowd had already gathered to see the President, who was breakfasting at the Somerset. The regulation exercises were very good and the enthusiasm magnificent when Roosevelt received his LL.D. Afterward I took Nazro to the Union which entertained the graduates of more than fifty years' standing. Here we met Hoar and some other of the older men. I voted, looked in at the Marshal's party, and then we went to Sanders. Governor Long was a little anxious about his party. He was presiding. But he warmed up and the audience warmed up. It is but a cold audience of its nature. But Roosevelt spoke magnificently, giving his whole time and energy to an enthusiastic eulogy of his three great lieutenants, Wood, Root, and Taft. I said afterwards at Alpha Delta that I remembered no such thing in literature. Hay made a very re-markable speech, very remarkable. While he was speaking, Long came down to me, to ask if I meant to speak. But I said I had better go with the President to Alpha Delta. And as soon as Hay was down, Long asked Gordon to ask the benediction. This was an improvement on the old habit of petering out. We all went over to Alpha Delta and the *Advertiser* report of that is really very good.

All three of the boys were there, Arthur, Edward, and Berty. This to me was the best part of the function. Phil is still at Niagara."

In these later summers he generally spent some time in the White Mountains, where he stayed with Miss Harriet E. Freeman at her house at Intervale. Here his love of the mountains and his interest in conservation led to his taking part in the movement to give the United Statest the control of the mountain forests.

TO JOHN HAY

"*August* 30th, 1902.

DEAR MR. SECRETARY:

"We have a public meeting here next Thursday for the preservation of the forests on the Presidential range. I really think we can do something. We want all the mountaineers and their neighbours.

"If you could and would come up on the morning train, it would give the meeting a distinguished success. Pray do if you can.

"We shall have Edmunds, who knows all about it, to speak, and one of Mr. Pinchot's gentlemen. I want to make a National Park of all the higher mountains.

"I like to think that the mountains do you as much good as they do me.

"Give my regards to the ladies and
          "Believe me
                    "Always truly yours
                              "EDWARD E. HALE."

On February 18, 1903 he wrote in his daybook:
"Very successful day. The Duke of Northumberland could do no better." "When you are the Duke
of Northumberland," he used to like to say, "you do
anything you choose and none of the things you
don't choose, and there is time to tell stories and
have a good time." There are a good many refer-
ences to the Duke in the succeeding years, and they
are a pleasant evidence of his enjoying himself.

In December, 1903, he was elected Chaplain of
the Senate. His old friend, George Frisbie Hoar,
who for years had been Senator from Massachusetts,
had some time before spoken to him of the matter.
My father had said that if the choice could be made
without controversy, he should regard it as a command. If, however, any sort of feeling were aroused,
he said that Mr. Hoar and Mr. Lodge must decline
on his account. On December 14, however, he
heard from Senator Hoar that the Republican cau-
cus had named him for the position, and later in the
afternoon the Senate had unanimously elected him.
"Election gives great satisfaction to both sides of
the Senate," telegraphed Mr. Hoar. "To tell the
truth," wrote my father in his daybook, "this
pleases me very much and I persuade myself already
that I can be of use."

On January 4, 1904, my father wrote in his diary:
"First day of service. Mr. Lodge introduced me to
Mr. Frye in the Vice-President's room. I entered
the Senate with the Secretary, and took the Vice-
President's seat. Mr. Frye who is acting President
of the Senate came a minute after. He tapped with

the gavel. I rose and the Senate rose. I read 'Wherefore we say Abba, Father,' and then repeated the Lord's Prayer."

This is the record of the beginning of my father's last large public service. It was a service very appropriate to his years and his public position, and one in which he was able to join in a manner in the government. Forty years before, more or less, he had offered prayer in the Senate, and he wrote then to my mother, as may be read on an earlier page (II, 81) that "You have a feeling that it is not your fault at least if that day they do not let the Holy Spirit guide them." This was no idle word then, — a man to whom the religious life was so real would not have felt that such a service was, on his part at least, a mere form. Nor could he have felt so later.

As Chaplain of the Senate, he felt, I am sure, that he was doing something well worth doing. He had long felt that he could no longer be one of the active leaders of the world. Even twenty years before he had begun to think that his province was rather to advise than to do. As time had gone on, he had more and more withdrawn from regular or active pursuits, from the administration work which had so long occupied him, and had turned more especially to the helping by counsel those who, as he put it, still labored at the oar. Now he held a public position wherein he stood — in a figurative way — as the representative man of God in the council of national legislators. He appreciated his position and enjoyed using his powers in this very appropriate way.

On April 13, 1904, my father made a number of
calls, one of them upon Count Cassini, the Russian
Ambassador. In his daybook he notes: "He says
that Kapnist is now their Minister at Vienna. If
this prove true I shall write to him." I believe he
had not seen Count Kapnist for almost forty years.
After the war they had met in Washington and
indeed had traveled together. "Was it not good,"
he wrote my mother, April 15, 1866, "to make Kapnist come? I hate to be alone." The thought of
his old friend remained in his mind for a long time,
and he finally wrote to him.

"ROXBURY, MASS., *Sept.* 10, 1904.
"MY DEAR FRIEND:
"As we pass the limits of four-score, we like to
recall the old friends, and to make them say they
have not forgotten us.

"Since I knew that you were at Vienna, I have
wondered whether I should not, — some day, —
send up my card to the Russian embassy there, —
to call in person, or whether I must write to you,
four thousand miles away, to ask if you are well.

"Just now, I have been looking at the kind face
of the Baron de Staël, who presided at the Hague,
five years ago. I asked myself if he were still alive.
And then I said, 'our good friend Kapnist is very
much alive, — and yet we never have a line from
him, because we never write to him.'

"Your Count Cassini told me of your health, the
last time I saw him in Washington.

"For I also am an officer of the United States now,

I am *Chaplain of the Senate*. This calls me to Washington every winter. And Washington is no longer the Virginia mud-hole which you remember. It is really a beautiful city, with many of the conveniences and luxuries of civilised life.

"At the moment I write we are in the dust and smoke of the beginning of a Presidential canvass. Believe me, — and on the 9th of November you will hear that we have chosen Mr. Roosevelt again, — a good man, resolute, 'strenuous,' but a man of Peace.

"We Peace men are distressed because our Japanese neighbors forced you into war. But we trust the Great Pacificator and we still hope to make the century, The Century of Peace. We have called the Peace Congress here for this October.

"How I wish that you could come with good tidings.

"Believe me dear Count Kapnist,

"Your old friend of a generation ago

"EDWARD E. HALE."

I think it must have been in January, 1904, that my father first met Mr. Andrew Carnegie. On the twelfth of that month he was present at a mass meeting in favor of Peace and International Arbitration. He mentions Cardinal Gibbons, General Miles, himself, Doctor Silberman who spoke "and Carnegie better than any one." In the evening was a reception in which he speaks of his conversation with "Carnegie who is a noted Peace man." It was some time after this that he read Carnegie's book on James Watt and was moved to write to him.

"My dear Mr. Carnegie:

"I have no right to take so much pleasure as your life of Watt has given me, without thanking you at once. It is admirably done, — and is most interesting. It bears the severest test, — which is reading aloud. My wife has been reading it to me, and she will want me to include her thanks with mine.

"I wish you would look again at Sir Walter Scott's account of Watt, — in the preface to the 'Monastery,' and see if you cannot guess for us at least as to some of the people whom Scott met *at one time* with Watt. 'Half a Score of our Northern Lights' — it must have been at some dinner party at Edinburgh — perhaps Christmas of 1818.

"I looked eagerly in Lockhart to see if he did not tell of that particular party — But no! I suppose Jeffrey was 'the critic.'

"I undertook to construct a dinner table — where some of my favorites could have met. Then I meant to make my son paint a picture, — like Rubens's portraits of the Dutch gentlemen at dinner.

"But it did not pan out very well. I had Watt at one end of the table, Scott at the other, Gladstone on one side and William Rathbone of Liverpool on the other. But alas in 1819 Gladstone had to be a (rather bumptious) schoolboy of ten years, — and William Rathbone a baby of six months!

"I am not strong in your Scotch geography. I wonder how far you are from Tay and Tay Mouth. I wrote to the Marquis of Breadalbane a month ago to ask about the American Bisons which they had there in 1844, when my uncle visited Breadalbane.

"Alas! the herd has all been killed. They thought them dangerous. Here, on the other hand, Corbin's herd numbers nearly one hundred.

"Will you give my regards to Mrs. Carnegie.

"And believe me

"Hers and yours truly,

"EDWARD E. HALE."

"*Oct.* 3rd. To Worcester [1] with Nelly and went at once to the house. Shippen took the service at the house and then I rode with him to the Church. The day was very impressive, — all Worcester and half Worcester county were in the streets. In short it is just what Hoar himself would have liked. The printed slip here is what I said to the press, and it answered well enough for what I said in fact. I was home at six o'clock dead beat, but I had a good nap afterwards though I didn't sleep any too well." The following is an extract from his address.

"He had all his life sat at the feet of his very near friend and distinguished townsman, the prophet Emerson, who gave to the little town of Concord a new fame. That sense of the real presence of Almighty God which gives light and life to every word of that prophet revealed itself in the daily walk of our dear friend. I do not say simply when he read the hymns or joined in the service of this church. I do not say simply when he had on him the care and responsibilities of a great lawyer at the bar, I do not say it of the great statesman speaking the word which might mean peace or war, might mean

[1] To the funeral of Senator Hoar.

prosperity or wretchedness; I say it of the daily life which was the same for child or man. And this inspiration made him so tolerant of the opinions of other men, tolerant of what was said, tolerant of what was done already, if only he were sure that the man was following the leading of the Holy Spirit, that a man was doing what he thought right or saying what he thought was true — that was enough for him."

"*Jan.* 5th, 1905 — The event of the day was Roosevelt's Forestry Address at the theatre. I wanted to hear it. But I was booked for Baltimore. The address is an admirable summing up of the whole thing. Nellie and I took the 4 o'clock train for Baltimore. We met Arthur and Berty at the station. We went at once to Gilman's house, and then Camilla and Arthur came round to see us. The occasion was an exhibition meeting, organized by Foster and the faithful here to quicken the Senate in confirmation of the Treaties. We had St. George Tucker and Page to speak, Judge Morris to move the resolution, and nice old Finlay to second them, and me."

"*March* 4th, 1905. In the face of all portents a beautiful day. At the Capitol there was a howling N. W. Wind, but even this died away afterwards. The Sergeant at arms sent his own carriage for us at half past eight, so we were at the capitol at nine. The Senate met at ten, and they let the ladies into the galleries, so they were able to see the whole ceremonial. It began with the last threads of business. The Senate sent its formal messages to the House, and the President and Allison made, as it

seems is the custom, a final statement as to the
appropriations as to the New Year. On paper this
is 600 and odd millions dollars. Then we had, in
the fit order of the program, the various invited
guests, officers of the Army and Navy, Ambassadors
and Ministers, the Supreme Court, the Cabinet,
and at last the President elect, and the Vice-President elect. The farewell resolutions of thanks had
been moved and passed unanimously. Our dear
Chief, Mr. Frye, made his farewell address which
was admirable. Then he swore in the new Vice-
President. It is thus that the continuity of the
government is maintained. The Senate is the one
permanent body which can continue itself. The
two-thirds who remain can swear in the new comers,
and so soon as Fairbanks had made a little address,
he swore in the new Senators who were waiting, who
were generally brought up the steps by his colleague.
In our case I think there are twelve new Senators.
So soon as this was done, all parties Senate and
galleries [sic]. I walked most of the way with Condon,
the Chaplain of the House. In passing out of the
bronze door to the portico I was separated from
him and it ended after a little in my finding myself
seated on the steps of the little octagon platform
from which the President spoke. The Chief Justice
was administering the oath, speaking very loud and
Roosevelt even louder. He made a short address
which was capital, walking, so to speak, from corner
to corner, sometimes so near me that I could touch
him. As soon as this was over, we really hurried
into the building again, it was so cold. A. joined

me at once and we all rendezvoused in the Commerce
Committee room. The parade was already forming
and a procession of soldiers and of people formed
in company front, began to march at quick time
through the avenue. We waited till nearly three,
then E. and I came home. The young people followed their various devices successfully. In the
evening they went to the ball which they found very
brilliant. I went up to our highest story to see
the fireworks. I do not hear of any misadventure
and the ceremony seems to have been thoroughly
successful. I spoke to the President who seems well
and in great spirits."

"*April* 3d., 1905. Waked at quarter of six.
Arrived [1] about 6:30 and landed. Scoville was all
ready with his carriage, and we came out to the
Treasurer's building in all the glory of Spring and
sunshine and my birthday. Aprilis indeed! I have
put the birthday presents at the end of the book.
We had breakfast with the old line, excepting
Frissell, who is away alas, with the funeral party.
Mr. Purves died on Friday. I count him as one of
the great men, and his loss as a national loss. Our
room was fragrant and bright with roses and car-
nations, and all day long people were bringing in
more flowers. At dinner the ladies had lighted the
table with 83 candles and in the evening with a
great deal of fun, Nelly and Elsie Nordhoff brought
in another birthday cake with 84 candles. There
could not have been a better birthday celebration.

[1] At Hampton, Virginia.

The mail waiting for me was of nine affectionate letters without a word of dust or smoke or other Philistindom. And all day long more of the sort kept coming in which I will try to add to the broken list at the end of this book. In the afternoon A. and I went over to the Institute store to select a present which the Thursday girls were to give me. And then we introduced ourselves at the new library, which I had not seen. I forgot to look up the portrait of Huntington for whom it is named. It used to be said that he and I looked like each other. After dinner we went to evening Chapel with the boys and girls. That service always makes me cry a little. Allah is great but Satan is strong. Beautiful serenade in the evening from the Quartette Club."

"*April* 8, 1905. Another happy day. It seems impossible that it is the sixth day since our arrival. I went over to what they call Science, and read a part of Phil Nolan to a quarter part of 2nd division, of the 8th grade of the undergraduate department or something else. Whatever it was — a nice set of thirty or more bright Indian and Negro boys. Then Mr. Frissell came round with a good three-seated wagon, and we had a drive half way to Newport News. I had hoped to see them draw shad, but we were too late. All the afternoon at home. We walked down to Frissell's on our way to dinner. We went to prayers afterwards which were conducted by Dr. Brown of the Union Theological School. Carla and Mary Williams came in in the evening. A very nice throw of the dice box."

"*June* 28th, 1905. Commencement Day. We made a real Duke of Northumberland day of it. Nelly and I and Arthur went out to Cambridge together at nine. Arthur left us at the Union. I took Nelly to Sanders. I joined the procession at Sanders as they marched in. As I came up the steps in Sanders which go up to the platform, Roosevelt saw me and ran forward and gave me his hand and arm. It was a very pretty attention rendered in a most unaffected way. The Commencement Exercises were all curious, not to say interesting. I took Taft under my arm until the policeman separated us, because he was of the President's party, and I was not. I walked across the yard and saw half the world, — Collar, Judge Lowell, Sanborn, Will Everett, Dr. Webster, and indeed I do not know who not. Charles Parker was there, I think the oldest graduate present. I sat an hour in the Brooks reception which the class of 1855 gave to the older classes. Then I went to the Marshal's luncheon [1] and so at two o'clock — with Arthur to Sanders. We had very good speaking at Sanders, and I did not get home till after seven o'clock with Arthur.

TO MRS. HALE

"MATUNUCK, *July* 18, 1908.

"This will be my last letter of this series: — and, Sagen treu, life is so monotonous here, that the three weeks have passed very quietly. Indeed you might

---

[1] The Chief Marshal this year was Robert Bacon of the class of 1880, which was holding its twenty-fifth anniversary.

put my twenty letters on each other as they did the Forbes Signatures on each other and throw them up on a screen, and each one should prove to be identical with the other.

"'Washed my doll's clothes,' etc., etc., etc.

"Look out for us as 1 : 30 approaches.

"Rose and her three arrived yesterday P.M., to afternoon lunch. The boys had their pieces of cake, and went to the Boat House and caught a good perch. Rose told us on the Piazza (East) the success of Hollyhocks. Edward went to Newport on Wednesday, — and in going like another Evangeline, crossed John Diman who was coming to the Hazard Wedding. However, by Thursday they were together, E. a good deal amused, I think, to find himself discussing Modernism, alas, with John and some one else in the great Dining Hall of the School."

TO MRS. HALE

"INTERVALE, *Aug.* 12, 1908.

"We were cheered and pleased to receive your nice note of Sunday: — and to know that all still worked well. The Tale of the Tomato reminded me of the time when I broiled the beef-steak in the Worcester kitchen.

"We are going to-day after our regular drive to a reception at the Merriams. Alas, there are no nice Bryces there!

"Think; it is seven days since we left you, and the time has passed very rapidly. Our customs are very regular. We drive in the morning, I am apt to take a short nap before dinner; a longer nap follows dinner and then two hours or more on the piazza. There are a few callers. I believe that I told you that Sarah Jewett called one day. She has now gone back to M. where she knows the Youngs. Alice Richards has asked us to drive there to-morrow. Her home, quite finished now, is charming.

"We do very little at regular reading. Nellie and Ethel take their cantos of Dante; we are reading a volume of Taft's speeches aloud. But that advances slowly. In the evening there is almost always music and I am in bed by nine o'clock. You must not be anxious about me. I sleep well, eat well, and wonder to think that seven days are gone since I saw you."

In the thousands of pages of diary, letters, speeches, articles which record the doings of these years, hardly one can be found that has not something characteristic. In the summer of 1907 occurred in Boston a celebration of Old Home Week. He presided "technically," he says, over a great meeting at Symphony Hall. "All of us who go to other parts of the country," he said, "are welcomed with kindness and hospitality because people remember the place from which we came. I am as much at home in Santa Barbara or Chicago as I am here, and it is because the people there have a great cordiality for Boston. If I should go to the North Pole and meet Commander Peary there, he would give me a welcome, not because I am Edward Everett Hale, but because I come from Boston." In pre-

MEMORIAL TABLET IN THE SOUTH CONGREGATIONAL CHURCH